Witness

THE LITERARY CLUB OF CINCINNATI

2024

FIRST EDITION

Published by Praus Press

CONTENTS

INTRODUCTION

For 175 years, members of The Literary Club have been writing papers that fulfill the club motto, *"Luciat Lux Vestra ewq Let Your Light Shine."* You are holding a book of selected works from a collection of today's members carrying on this tradition, letting their lights shine in papers written for an organization that is the oldest of its kind in America. Their labors of creativity are gleaned from a ritual that seldom varies. Each Monday evening, promptly at eight o'clock, one of the club's one hundred members mounts the podium in the historic clubhouse facing Lytle Park to read a paper he has authored on a subject of his choosing. Emblazoned on the wall behind, and above, him is a line from Shakespeare that reminds his audience, *"Here Comes One with a Paper."*

This volume, the latest in a series, features written pieces that underscore the many talents and interests of those who come with their papers. It's a rich menu of both fiction and non-fiction, in poetry and prose. You will read about a memorable mobster from Old Chicago and an unforgettable Sicilian immigrant named "Hatchet Face" who found a home in America. There are first-person accounts from a South Africa struggling to embrace democracy and of a Vietnam father spiriting his family in a perilous ocean escape to freedom. Local scenes from Cincinnati get their due — the riotous tale of a flock of sheep grazing in Fountain Square, a prayerful visit to a downtown chapel housing an art treasure, a quiet neighborhood disrupted by gunfire. There are gripping personal tales of a battle with alcoholism, of a young man struggling for independence from a domineering father, and of an Army officer confronting the stresses of jungle warfare. And what would a book with subjects both serious and rib-tickling be without stories about animals — yes, about spying cats and mad cows and historic horses.

Finally, the editors of this book are honored to include a touching paper from our recently deceased beloved member, Professor Bill Pratt, on his personal encounter with two of the 20th Century's leading literary lights.

All in all, we believe the collection speaks eloquently of a tradition that is carefully nurtured and that is uniquely Cincinnati.

– William Burleigh, *Editor*

1 Only in Cincinnati

C. FRANCIS BARRETT

CINCINNATI has long enjoyed its reputation of being a quiet, peaceful, conservative city in the Midwest of the United States and in the heart of America. Considering its rich tradition, its population base, and its many revered institutions, it is quite understandable that Cincinnati would be so regarded.

Our city, with its first settlements of Columbia and Losantiville in the late 1700s as a part of the Ohio Territory within the Northwest Territory under the protection of respected Generals Arthur St. Clair and Anthony Wayne, had a foundation grounded in the virtues of peace and civility. Cincinnati's conservative reputation was formed to a great extent by its original settlers and inhabitants. How could our city be anything but a place of culture, refined behavior, and a model for respectful urban living?

People frequently recall the famous quote of Mark Twain made many years ago: "When the end of the world comes, I want to be in Cincinnati because it is always twenty years behind the times." This quote is still given credence by those who continue to argue that Cincinnati is a conservative place.

Upon closer examination, however, circumstances dramatically changed. What may have been true prior to World War II that caused Cincinnati to be a quiet, reserved, and polite city was no longer the case. For whatever reason, and due to whatever forces, something happened. After the war, Cincinnati produced a collection of extreme and unusual personalities, and a list of high-profile individuals, all of whom had a profound impact on both our city and our nation. These colorful characters seemed to be inexplicably inter-related, enigmatically connected, and unique to Cincinnati. Somehow Cincinnati became the unofficial controversy capital of America. How did this happen? Let us see if we can find out.

Cincinnati was able to capitalize on its reputation as a highly moral, conservative, pro-family values municipality throughout the late 1940s and 1950s. As such, Cincinnati attracted many small conventions to the downtown hotels where businessmen travelling away from their families purportedly did not face the temptations that attracted conventions in the larger cities where there was nightlife, vice, sinful activities, and a host of other conditions that caused wives to worry when their husbands went on so-called business trips. With this reputation, Cincinnati provided the perfect cover, as across the river in Newport, Kentucky, there was Las Vegas-type entertainment with nude girls, gambling, burlesque acts, drinking and carousing. The Beverly Hills Supper Club in Southgate, Campbell County, provided the same type of entertainment one might enjoy in Las Vegas or Atlantic City. Most notably there was Monmouth Street in downtown Newport with a variety of strip clubs and drinking establishments.

Such excesses in Newport led to corruption in government, uncontrolled vice, scandalous activities, and the prominence of criminals. The most notorious of all was a gentleman by the name of Tito Carinci, the owner and operator of the Tropicana Club and the adjacent Glenn Hotel. Mr. Carinci had been an outstanding high school football player in Steubenville, Ohio, and was awarded a varsity scholarship to Xavier University where he distinguished himself on the gridiron and was inducted into the Legion of Honor, conferred on only the best of the best. Mr. Carinci had been steered to Xavier by one of his relatives, a high-ranking member of the clergy, who wanted his nephew to receive a Jesuit education. Mr. Carinci certainly received a liberal education, but it was not liberal in academic parlance.

The vice and corruption in Newport had become so pervasive that many of the civic and religious leaders of Campbell County formed the "Committee of 500" to elect a reform candidate for sheriff in 1961. They recruited and supported George Ratterman as their candidate. Mr. Ratterman was born of German Irish parents, came from a large Catholic family, lived in Fort Thomas, and his brother, the Reverend Patrick Ratterman, had long been dean of men at Xavier University. George had been well known as an outstanding athlete, a star quarterback in football, and he played for both the University of Notre Dame, under famed Coach Frank Leahy, and the Cleveland Browns, under the legendary Coach Paul Brown, who years later founded the Cincinnati Bengals. As such, Mr. Ratterman was popular and considered the favorite in the race for sheriff.

There were those in Newport who felt threatened by reform and thus took exception to Mr. Ratterman's candidacy. Hence, when he was having dinner one evening in April of 1961 at the Terrace Plaza Hotel in downtown Cincinnati, Mr. Carinci allegedly caused a "Mickey" to be slipped into Mr. Ratterman's drinking glass, thereby drugging him and allowing him to be transported against his will in a taxicab to the Tropicana Club in Newport. Because of his condition of being in a drug-induced stupor, Mr. Carinci had Mr. Ratterman taken to a bedroom in his adjacent Glenn Hotel where he arranged for one of his performers at the Tropicana Club, a striptease artist by the name of April Flowers, to join him in bed where Mr. Carinci would proceed to have Mr. Ratterman photographed and then forced to withdraw as a candidate.

Not part of the plan, a detective from the Newport Police Department happened to be at the Tropicana Club and saw Mr. Ratterman be-

Clockwise from top: Tito Carinci (and friend), George Ratterman, George Ratterman outside the Tropicana, Jerry Springer and Socko Wiethe

Clockwise from top: Jerry Rubin, Charles Manson, Marge Schott, Stanley Chesley, Pete Rose, Marvin Warner and Charles Keating

ing taken upstairs in the Glenn Hotel. Not knowing that Mr. Ratterman was about to be blackmailed, but rather thinking that Mr. Ratterman was there for illicit purposes and could be arrested and have his candidacy derailed, the detective had the Newport police arrive and arrest Mr. Ratterman on a morals charge. When the matter became public, Mr. Carinci became the focus of media attention. Mr. Carinci had the appearance of a person of his profession right out of central casting. Long before Marlon Brando won the Academy Award for Best Actor as Don Vito Corleone in The Godfather, Mr. Carinci swore on the grave of his mother that he had no knowledge or involvement in the matter. However, his appearance and friendships indicated otherwise. He had a Julius Caeser haircut, wore black turtleneck sweaters, carried a pearl handle pistol tucked into his waistband under the sweater, and his pockets were bulging with $100 bills, as he did all of his business in cold cash. One of his best friends was Albert Anastasia, Jr., whose father Albert Anastasia, Sr., was known for operating "Murder Incorporated" in New York City as a member of the Gambino crime family. Senior was infamously riddled with bullets while getting a haircut and shave in a Manhattan barbershop.

The efforts of Mr. Carinci to blackmail Mr. Ratterman failed miserably and publicly. Mr. Ratterman went on to be elected sheriff, defeating well known Newport personality, Johnny "TV" Peluso. Needless to say, Mr. Carinci's conduct drew national attention, causing the Justice Department under new Attorney General Robert F. Kennedy to launch a massive crackdown on organized crime. Mr. Carinci, as they say in the vernacular, went on to do a couple of stints in the big house. Where in America could such a bizarre scandal have originated? Only in Cincinnati.

During the 1950s and 1960s, a frequent visitor to Newport and a part owner of a couple of joints in Newport, even when he ran for prosecutor of Hamilton County, was none other than John Anthony "Socko" Wiethe. The story of controversy in Cincinnati cannot be told without reference to Mr. Wiethe. Mr. Wiethe was a legendary sports hero, a high-profile attorney, longtime chairman of the Hamilton County Democratic Party, and always the subject of media attention. He was the only person to be elected to the athletic halls of fame of both Xavier University, where he starred in football and basketball, and the University of Cincinnati, which he coached to national prominence in basketball. He was the captain of the original Cincinnati Bengals professional football team in the 1930s and later an all-pro linebacker with the Detroit Lions in the National Football League. His roommate on the Detroit Lions was Whizzer White, one of the all-time great running backs in college and professional football, who later became the Honorable Byron White, Associate Justice of the Supreme Court of the United States. Mr. Wiethe served as Mr. White's protector on the Lions, which Justice White never forgot and showed later in life that he knew how to return a favor, much to Mr. Wiethe's benefit.

Mr. Wiethe was known for his numerous and highly intense political battles, including multiple conflicts within his own party. He had highly publicized fights with such Democratic stalwarts as Jack Gilligan, Vincent Beckman, and Ted Berry. He also was under the scrutiny of famed newscaster Al Schottelkotte, who once remarked that Mr. Wiethe's reputation could not be damaged by adverse publicity.

Perhaps, the one episode which best encapsulates the saga of Mr. Wiethe would be the events related to his historic trial in Hamilton County in the 1970s when he was charged with reckless driving and driving under the influence. Although his driving had long been the subject of media attention and allegations of political favoritism, he was now facing charges in the courtroom for the first time.

On the eve of his trial, the Cincinnati chapter of the National Football Foundation and College Football Hall of Fame held a large banquet at which Mr. Wiethe was one of the honorees. The Cincinnati chapter was known as the Dolly Cohen Chapter. Dolly Cohen was the widow of Mr. A.B. Cohen, who had been the president of the U.S. Shoe Corporation, and her philanthropy funded many causes, including the National Football Foundation. As with everything that Mr. Wiethe did, there were vocal supporters and vocal detractors. At this banquet, a number of prominent political figures including congressmen, judges, and members of City Council heaped praise on Mr. Wiethe. Others took exception. Some of his former teammates who were present at the banquet had been worried that Mr. Wiethe might be sent to jail if convicted. In good humor, they baked a cake with a saw in it and had a former prosecutor present it to him in case he had to saw his way out of jail.

When his case was scheduled for trial, Mr. Wiethe demanded a trial by jury, stating that he had been targeted by the establishment because of his protection of the little guy and for his efforts in helping the downtrodden and less fortunate. None of the local judges wanted to preside over this trial because of the intense media scrutiny, political overtones, and potential impact on their ability to be re-elected. Mysteriously, on the eve of trial, the case was re-assigned to a visiting judge from another part of the state. Mr. Wiethe expressed renewed confidence in the system, stating that he now thought he could have a fair trial before an impartial judge, and waived the jury. At the trial, the judge threw out all the charges, finding insufficient evidence to sustain any one of them. Mr. Wiethe praised the legal system for working, while Mr. Schottelkotte and other members of the media expressed outrage. Where could such a performance make such a mockery of the legal system? Only in Cincinnati.

Mr. Wiethe had also been known for helping the career of many a politician, including being the first person to urge retired astronaut John Glenn to run for the U. S. Senate from Ohio. When a young Cincinnati Council member by the name of Jerry Springer had the misfortune of paying a prostitute in Northern Kentucky by a check that bounced and was forced to resign from the City Council, it was Mr. Wiethe who helped guide him to resurrect his career and return to the council.

Mr. Springer had been active in the 1968 Presidential campaign of his idol, Robert F. Kennedy, until Senator Kenndy's untimely assassination in June of that year. Mr. Springer was thereafter recruited to Cincinnati by the prestigious law firm of Frost & Jacobs, now known as Frost Brown Todd, where he excelled as an associate lawyer but was more interested in a political career. Mr. Springer had been part of the anti-war movement of the 1960s and became highly visible in Cincinnati in the early 1970s as a part of the "You cannot trust anyone over 30 years of age" generation. He caught the attention of many younger people, especially high school and college students, and his high-profile popularity drew the attention of powerful Democrats such as Mr. Wiethe and Marvin L. Warner, one of the wealthiest, most powerful, best connected, and influential people, not only in Cincinnati but also nationally. When Mr. Springer's career faltered after being exposed for paying a lady of the night with the check that bounced, many felt his political career had ended. But those people did not understand Cincinnati. Mr. Springer regrouped, won his seat back on City Council, and later was elected Mayor. He actually capitalized, in a humorous way, on his reputation. When he became the anchor newsman at WLWT Channel 5, he served as master of ceremonies at the annual dinner of the Chamber of Commerce. In looking out at the audience, he identified prominent politicians in the crowd. Pointing to Bob Taft he said, "There is Bob Taft with his wife Hope. With me, people say that's Jerry Springer and we hope it's his wife."

Exploiting his misdeeds, his humor, and popularity, Mr. Springer went on to become a nationally syndicated television personality in Chicago where his show featured persons engaged in unorthodox relationships, including but not limited to incestuous conduct and forms of sexual perversion. He became a national star and a multimillionaire. Where could such a career have commenced? Only in Cincinnati.

While Mr. Springer built his reputation by being opposed to the war in Vietnam, to social injustice, and to racial prejudice, he was never a part of the violence that became commonplace in the 1960s. But others were.

In terms of radical appearance, speech, and agenda, no one was more extreme than an individual by the name of Jerry Rubin. Mr. Rubin had reached the pinnacle of radicalism by co-founding the Youth International Party, known as Y.I.P., or "YIP", and referred to as the Yippie Movement. Mr. Rubin and his followers took to the streets of Chicago during the Democratic National Convention in August of 1968. He was arrested for conspiracy to incite violence and was tried in federal court as a member of the infamous "Chicago Eight" which later became the "Chicago Seven" after Black Panther leader Bobbie Seale was removed from court for disruptive behavior. Mr. Rubin provoked Judge Julius Hoffman to such an extent that he was held in contempt of court on numerous counts. In what city did Mr. Rubin have his roots? Only in Cincinnati. He was born in the Avondale neighborhood, went to Samuel Ach Junior High School at Rockdale and Reading, and then to Walnut Hills High School. Is it a mere coincidence that he came from Cincinnati, or is there something in the drinking water?

There was, of course, severe and extreme violence associated with the protest movements of the 1960s. The most gruesome and most horrific acts of violence were attributed to the Helter Skelter movement in California under the demonic control of Charles Manson whom California authorities deemed the devil incarnate. Through evil mind control, Mr. Manson was able to program such later convicted murderers as Tex Watson, Susan Atkins, Leslie Van Houten, and Patricia Krenwinkel to perform unspeakable acts of homicide. The bloody crime scenes at the home of the La Bianca family in the Los Angeles hills area and the estate house of actress Sharon Tate were grisly beyond belief. Another Manson girl, Lynette "Squeaky" Fromme, attempted to assassinate President Gerald Ford.

No one could understand how Mr. Manson had become so evil. Those who looked into his background found that his early years were spent only in Cincinnati. Mr. Manson was born "Charles Milles Manson" in 1934 at the old Cincinnati General Hospital on Burnet Avenue. His mother was an underage prostitute runaway from Kentucky. Does anyone know where the young Charlie Manson spent the first five years of his life? He lived quite near our Literary Club, on nearby Pike Street just south of Lytle Park. If members of the Literary Club in the mid-1930s had occasion to walk past Lytle Park, they might have seen little Charlie Manson playing on the swings and slides that were a part of the park in those days. No one would ever have suspected that he would have gone on to orchestrate mass murders at four different locations in 1969. Where did someone like that have his beginning? Only in Cincinnati.

The aforementioned Mr. Warner had amassed a fortune in the business of construction, financing, developing, and leasing related to a multitude of federal housing projects. He had been a part owner in major sports franchises such as the New York Yankees in baseball and the Tampa Bay Buccaneers in football and had been a major donor to a host of philanthropic and political causes. He significantly helped to elect Jimmy Carter as President in 1976 and was later rewarded with the ambassadorship to Switzerland.

Mr. Warner was quite adept in matters of finance and banking. He had owned Eagle Savings Association and later Home State Savings Bank, which became a symbol of the failure of the savings & loan industry across the United States in the 1980s. When there was a run on his Home State Savings Bank, the national media made it the prime story at prime time on the prime news networks. Where was all the attention directed? Right to Cincinnati. All of the politicians he had supported and helped elect could not be found as they all ran for political cover. Although Mr. Warner correctly stated that he was the biggest loser of all in the failure of Home State, the politicians, the media, and the public had no mercy.

Not to be outdone by Mr. Warner in terms of publicity concerning the collapse of a major financial institution, another Cincinnatian,

Mr. Charles H. Keating, drew even more attention. Mr. Keating was a person who could do it all and had done it all. He had been an outstanding athlete and an All-American swimmer at the University of Cincinnati and elected to the UC Athletic Hall of Fame. He had been a jet fighter pilot with the U. S. Navy. He was an accomplished lawyer who established the firm of Keating, Muething & Klekamp, which became one of the most successful and influential law firms in Greater Cincinnati. Mr. Keating was also quite adept at raising money and arousing public opposition.

However, his high profile was nevertheless surpassed by Mr. Keating's ownership and operation of Lincoln Savings Bank, based primarily in California, which brought the entire savings & loan industry to a crashing halt. Upset by federal regulators and never one to back down, Mr. Keating engaged the support of President Jimmy Carter and five of the most prominent members of the U. S. Senate, which became known as the "Keating Five." The group included John Glenn of Ohio, Alan Cranston of California, and John McCain of Arizona, three of the most highly influential and respected senators. They were not able to help.

People nationwide wondered how could Cincinnati have produced both Mr. Warner and Mr. Keating? Out-of-towners asked if there was something in the drinking water. Some good Cincinnatians were embarrassed by the adverse publicity cast upon Cincinnati by these two gentlemen. Many of them expressed relief when Bernard Madoff brought about an even greater and more outlandish financial scandal which led to his investors losing more than $60 billion. They were relieved that Mr. Madoff, based in New York and Palm Beach, had created an elaborate Ponzi scheme that might direct attention away from Cincinnati and the financial collapses of Mr. Warner and Mr. Keating. However, it was not possible to shift the focus away from Cincinnati, as Mr. Madoff got his start in the investment business at the former Cincinnati Stock Exchange in the Dixie Terminal Building on Fourth

Street just a few short blocks west of our club. Was it a mere coincidence that Mr. Madoff had Cincinnati connections? Is there something in the drinking water of Cincinnati?

The aforementioned Mr. Keating had an impact on Cincinnati politics. He served as the campaign chairman for his beloved brother Bill, who successfully ran for Judge, City Council, and the U. S. Congress. He also strongly backed Simon L. Leis, Jr. for his three terms as Hamilton County prosecutor. Mr. Keating brought national recognition to Mr. Leis for his prosecution of pornography cases. Mr. Leis became the highest profile anti-pornography prosecutor in the United States, and had the full support of Mr. Keating and his huge CDL organization. Mr. Leis first became prosecutor in 1971 after the turbulent 1960s.

Thus, when Mr. Leis came into office as prosecutor, he faced numerous challenges. He never shied away from controversy, but actually sought it and embraced it. As a former Marine, he was fearless in the face of conflict and strife. It would only be a matter of time before he would go after the "King of Smut," Larry Flynt, who based his Hustler operations in Cincinnati. His Hustler bar on the lower level of the former Metropole Hotel on Walnut Street was a known den of iniquity. What took place there is better left unsaid. The raw coarseness and extreme vulgarity of his Hustler Magazine exceeded the limits of First Amendment protections.

One of the most dramatic scenes to ever occur in a courtroom in Hamilton County was during the prosecution of Mr. Flynt by Mr. Leis. When making his arguments to the jury, Mr. Leis pulled a piece of chalk from his pocket and drew a long line on the floor of the courtroom in front of the jury box, telling the jurors that there is a line when it comes to acceptable and protected speech, and Larry Flynt had crossed that line. Both Mr. Leis's supporters and detractors in that courtroom were moved by this dramatic scene, and still to this day talk about it. Whenever Mr. Leis was challenged about his motivation for prosecuting the peddlers of smut, he dramatically would respond: "If you do not want me to enforce obscenity laws, then have the legislature repeal those laws."

Some years later, when Mr. Leis was county sheriff, he led an unprecedented raid on an art museum along with the then-prosecutor Arthur Ney and Cincinnati's chief of police, Colonel Larry Whalen. On display at the Contemporary Arts Center south of Government Square was the exhibit of artist Robert Mapplethorpe known as "The Perfect Moment." The exhibit featured a series of homoerotic photographs. The ensuing publicity was loud and widespread, resulting in thousands of Cincinnatians visiting the Contemporary Arts Center to view the exhibit, far exceeding the attendance for the display in Boston, New York, and Washington combined. CNN News covered the trial, giving it national attention and raising the profile of Cincinnati as the unofficial controversy capital of America. Where in the United States had there ever been a raid on an art museum and the bringing of criminal charges against the art museum and its director? Only in Cincinnati.

Cincinnati Vice-Mayor David Mann expressed at the time that this raid and criminal trial made Cincinnati the "laughingstock" of the country. This is quite a remarkable statement from a member of City Council, considering the council's history. Recall the time when the City Council held a public hearing on the propriety of having flying pig statues at Sawyer Point. The pro-pig advocates and the anti-pig zealots came out in force. With people wearing pig noses, pig hats, and pig masks, and making pig noises and snorts, a raucous free-for-all ensued. Council voted pro-pig.

Speaking of Mr. Leis, ironically and coincidentally, it was his sister who was known to be the only person in Cincinnati who could exert any control or influence over a certain prominent Cincinnati female who had the reputation of being uncontrollable. These two girls had grown up together in Westwood. That female was Margaret Unnewehr Schott, more commonly known as Marge Schott. When Mrs. Schott became the majority owner and president of the Cincinnati Reds, she was hailed as being an accomplished businesswoman, a pioneer of women's advances in sports and business, and a person to be beloved and praised. She was president of the Reds in 1990 when the team went wire-to-wire in first place and swept the vaunted Oakland A's in four straight games in the World Series. She was lauded by national publications such as Sports Illustrated, and even featured on the CBS television show "60 Minutes" by Morley Safer.

All of this came crashing down because of some of her frugal business practices, such as cutting off the free and elaborate buffets of food and alcoholic beverages at Reds' games that her predecessors offered to members of the press, and her occasional slips of the tongue after a few too many cocktails involving racial, ethnic, and a whole host of other slurs which led to suspensions. Her defiance of the city's anti-smoking ordinance at Riverfront Stadium prompted Pulitzer Prize winning cartoonist Jim Borgman to show City Councilman Charlie Winburn, who advocated for reintroducing paddling in the public schools, whacking Mrs. Schott on her bare behind. Another cartoon mocked her comments about Adolph Hitler, showing a scene in Hell with Lucifer asking Hitler what Marge Schott was like, and being told that she was good in the beginning, but she just went too far. When the anti-Marge Schott publicity went viral and nationwide, she had the perfect defense. She said that she was being discriminated against because she was a woman. Where could such have happened? Only in Cincinnati.

Was it a mere coincidence that, during her reign as president of the Reds, baseball suspended Pete Rose for gambling. Mr. Rose was a classic case of Cincinnati extremism and controversy. On one hand, Mr. Rose is one of the greatest success stories in the history of baseball, while on the other hand he is the epitome of one of the greatest falls from grace. Is it a mere coincidence that the crashes of Mrs. Schott and Mr. Rose coincided. Where in the world could such a joint meltdown of once highly regarded figures in the game of baseball occur at the same time? Only in Cincinnati.

Somewhat surprisingly, one of Mrs. Schott's defenders was a very prominent attorney who represented her in disputes with her limited partners to whom she would not distribute the profits of the team. The supporter was lawyer Stanley M. Chesley, one of the highest-profile and most controversial figures in the history of Cincinnati. He was known nationally for his major class action lawsuits and was referred to by Forbes Magazine as the "Master of Disaster." His multitude of nationally known mass tort cases included the deadly fire at the Beverly Hills Supper Club in Northern Kentucky, the MGM Grand Hotel fire in Las Vegas, the explosion of the Pan American Airlines jet over Lockerbie, Scotland, the Fernald Uranium contamination in Crosby Township, the Union Carbide pollution in Bhopal, India, the case against Dow Chemical Company for the use of Agent Orange during the Vietnam War, and most notably the billion dollar litigation against big tobacco companies which only could have been achieved with the assistance of the United States Government through his friendship with President Clinton. Somehow, Mr. Chesley was able to overlook the ethnic slurs of Mrs. Schott and represent her interests.

Unfortunately, Mr. Chesley subsequently faced major problems of his own, arising out of the fen-phen diet drug litigation wherein he reached a walkaway settlement of $200 million from the drug manufacturer. The plaintiffs in this case, who were the victims injured by the drug, were to receive two-thirds of the settlement funds, but only received a far lesser amount after secret meetings involving Mr. Chesley, his co-counsel, and the trial judge. When the plaintiff's victims hired their own counsel and exposed the fraud, criminal charges were brought against the attorneys with the exception of Mr. Chesley, who was granted immunity from prosecution. As the criminal case moved to trial before Presiding Judge William O. Bertelsman of the Federal District Court, Judge Bertelsman was quoted in the press that the legal system was on trial. It certainly appeared that the legal system had lost.

Not surprisingly, this case garnered national attention, including editorials in the Wall Street Journal and other publications, as well as features in television documentaries involving crime and justice. Mr. Chesley was eventually disbarred. Where in America could such occur? Only in Cincinnati.

It seems that there is no end to the controversies arising out of Cincinnati, and it seems that a number are still brewing and waiting to explode. In this light, it certainly appears that City Hall will generate more controversies that will bring national attention and negative publicity to our fair city.

In closing, it is hoped that this paper is found not to be offensive or embarrassing, but rather entertaining and amusing. Controversy is a part of our heritage. It should be accepted and embraced with a sense of humor, rather than the need to feel defensive or apologetic for any of the above-mentioned behavior that may have generated unwanted attention.

As a final warning, it is not wise to seek to understand what is responsible for the bizarre and extreme behavior of some of our most well-known citizens. Although people have questioned from time to time whether it is "in the water" that Cincinnatians drink, this question should never be asked. A number of years ago, questions were raised at City Hall about whether the high incidence of cancer in the residents of Cincinnati was caused by the river water which was processed by the Cincinnati Water Works and then consumed by Cincinnatians. When this issue came up years ago, the City Council became alarmed and hauled the director of the Water Works before the council, demanding a complete investigation and submission of a written report. The director was informed by members of Council that river cities like Cincinnati, Pittsburgh and St. Louis all had high incidence of cancer. The director proceeded to undertake and complete a comprehensive study, and so informed the council which set the matter for a public hearing. The council chamber was packed. Every Council member, city administrator, staff official and citizen present was on edge, waiting to hear the director's report which featured elaborate charts and graphs.

The director explained in detail that cancer was not caused by the river water, but rather by major league baseball, as every city with a major league baseball team had high rates of cancer. What would normally be a serious subject was reduced to guffaws of laughter throughout the council chamber. Where in the world could such a performance occur at a public hearing on a matter of life and death with elected officials, city administrators and members of the public all rolling in the aisles in uncontrollable laughter? Only in Cincinnati!

C. Francis Barrett is a 28-year member of The Literary Club of Cincinnati. He has practiced law for over 50 years, having been admitted to practice before the Supreme Court of Ohio and the United States Supreme Court. Mr. Barrett has also served as an officer, trustee, and/or director of many charitable and civic organizations including the Board of Trustees of the University of Cincinnati, the Health Alliance of Greater Cincinnati, UC Health, the Commercial Club of Cincinnati, The Seven Hills School, Mercy Health Partners Foundation, the Dan Beard Council of the Boy Scouts of America, the Cincinnati Club, the Cincinnati Tennis Club, the Ohio Building Authority, the Convalescent Hospital for Children, and Cincinnati Cancer Foundation.

2 Vanished Gold

WILLIAM BURLEIGH

THE 1946 spring issue of the Sears catalogue paved the way for my entry into newspapering. There on page 594 I found a Copy King hectograph selling for $1.88. I couldn't wait for my mail order to arrive. On the gelatinous surface of that copying device I was able to duplicate the first edition of my *Neighborhood News*. In it I reported on happenings up and down Gum Street and sold ads for a quarter a page. At 10 years of age, I thus became a newspaper publisher, affirming Alexis de Tocqueville's observation on his first visit to the pioneer precincts of this land that "the creation of a newspaper is a simple and easy undertaking."

For the next half century and more, through the boom times to the death rattles, I spent my working days in and around newspapers, inhabiting newsrooms, inhaling the heady aroma of printer's ink, and relishing those rookie moments pounding the keys of a Royal typewriter on deadline. Once I even rushed into a pressroom shouting "stop the presses" and surprised myself to witness them actually grinding to a halt.

It was a great span of time to have a newspaper career, that last half of the 20th century.

Some have called those years the Golden Age of the American newspaper. To be sure, all manner of eras and events get known in the

"You know that morning newspaper you used to hold in front of your face? I miss that."

history books as "golden," some of them pretty frivolously. But for newspapers of that period, it was truly the case. There was gold aplenty, if not in a reporter's paycheck.

In their heyday, successful papers became rich, influential hallmarks in the communities they served. It was a rare crossroads village that didn't have a paper. Scores of mid-size towns typically had two, and they were usually fierce competitors. More populated centers such as Cincinnati even had three. At one point early in the century, New York City counted 17.

With their business models panning for the gold of the local marketplace, a well-run paper could routinely produce profits exceeding 30 percent year after year. Advertisers paid dearly for the audiences that papers delivered. A playful series of New Yorker ads famously boasted, "In Philadelphia nearly everyone reads The Bulletin." At their peak, American newspapers circulated 63 million copies every day.

There was a time when readers treated their local paper like it was part of the family. They told Gallup pollsters that while, yes, they grew increasingly skeptical of the so-called national media, they trusted their hometown product. After all, it kept them up to date on what was happening around them — the goings-on at city hall and the schools, who was running for office, how much they were going to pay in taxes, who was dying and who was getting born, the ball scores, the arts and culture scene, and all sorts of tidbits from their neighborhoods. Sharing the daily news created common ground among them.

Over time, however, those bonds would be broken by forces that gradually surfaced in laboratories of discovery, at places like MIT, Stanford and Bell Labs. By 1972, computer wizards had conceived an information infrastructure for handling data. They called it the internet. A computer world was coming into being, introducing an all-encompassing information age the likes of which the world had never before experienced.

By the dawn of the 21st century, that digital revolution had America's newspapers in its crosshairs. Someone had built a better mouse trap.

Throughout the nation's history, businesses and even industries have come and gone. Newspapers were turning out to be no exceptions. The forces of predatory capitalism were at work.

The internet could be used to do many things better than newspapers ever imagined. As a result, advertising dried up and one-time readers drifted away. Based as it was on costly printing presses and boxcar loads of newsprint, the industry became a modern-day dinosaur headed for extinction, even if some doubting Thomases were slow to admit it.

A marvelous new instrument called a personal communications device became Everyman's prized possession. It was better known as the smartphone and was so smart that it allowed users to be their own reporters, their own editors, their own publishers. The whole wide world was their apple — and that world had turned digital. Who needed a newspaper when there was social media with Google, Facebook, Twitter, Instagram and an ever-growing array of other choices?

Faced with the resulting wholesale exodus of readers to the internet, newspapers tried to respond by offering digital versions of their print content. In the early going, those awkward efforts lacked the pizzazz of their digital competition and were thus unable to recover advertising that had found better places to land. The public, charmed by the free offerings of the internet, was in no mood to pay for news content it could obtain for nothing. The dirty little secret was that these new sites were at the same time purloining their content from traditional newspaper sources while also paying nothing.

Caught in this chokehold, papers responded by frantically cutting costs. They jettisoned payrolls. Thousands lost their jobs. Newsrooms were decimated. Within less than a decade, more than half of the nation's news force was furloughed. Too few reporters and editors, who were once dedicated to bringing news to their communities, were still around to do it. So devastating has been the onslaught that some local newspapers today no longer have a single reporter on staff.

By 2005, conditions had grown so ominous and revenue so scarce that both daily and weekly papers across the breadth of the nation started shutting their doors. Since then the shutdowns have

reached a casualty rate of about two every week over the past two decades. By today's accounting, about 2,900 papers — almost a third of the total — have gone out of business. More ominously, 204 entire counties across America — roughly 7 percent of all of them — are now complete news wastelands, with 3 million residents lacking access to any paper of any sort, daily or weekly. The largest city today without a daily newspaper happens to be in Ohio, in Youngstown.

Despite this toll, there are newspapers still around, even if many of them are starved images of their once robust state. Too often there is little left to identify them as distinctly belonging to the communities whose names they bear. Especially is that the case among the two largest groups of papers, which are in the hands of corporate operators -- one a hedge fund, Alden Global Capital, known in some quarters as the grim reaper of American newspapers, and the other a debt-ridden Gannett, one of the last of the newspaper chains, with a reputation for turning the screws until it hurts.

As the digital revolution has gained momentum, with more efficient, exciting means of communication taking the place of the old newspaper, the vital ingredient that has been largely lost is the local news content. Local news, the vital nitty-gritty of community information, the grease on the wheels of the democratic way of life, has all but disappeared in many places.

In the constitutional scheme of things, newspapers have been seen historically as something more than commercial enterprises. They once enjoyed a popular reputation as "watchdogs of democracy" and were accorded a kind of legal protection.

I once sat in a Columbia University symposium listening to a legendary journalist, Ben Reese, exhort a room of editors. "There's a scandal in every public office and it's your job to smoke it out," he snorted. Reese was a former editor whose St. Louis Post-Dispatch during his tenure had won a record number of Pulitzer Prizes for public service. It was said of him that "once Old Ben is on your tail, there's nothing but jail or suicide." The first of the Pulitzers he garnered, by the way, exposed fake voter registration rolls. Sound familiar?

The cognoscenti has often dismissed this fire-breathing aspect of the press, calling it "yellow journalism" and claiming it is built on "sensationalism, trash and filthy lies." But the tradition has a more serious pedigree. Going back to his examination of the young nation, Tocqueville found value in the free rein accorded the press, as had the Founding Fathers. He famously wrote: "I do not hold that complete and instantaneous love for freedom of the press . . . is unqualifiedly good. I love it out of consideration for the evils it prevents much more than for the good it does." He paid particular attention to the local papers in the towns he visited, going so far as to say they helped to "maintain civilization" by protecting the citizenry from charlatans and crooks in public life through the information the papers delivered.

Generations of journalists took this responsibility seriously. In my time, the reporters and editors who populated newsrooms may typically have constituted a motley crowd, considered by many outsiders as a cynical lot of eccentrics and lowlifes. But beyond the airs some of them may have pretended and the ideological baggage they may have carried, at heart I found them mainly to be idealists on a mission, not just to smoke out scandal but to report on the everyday life of their communities, giving it a texture unavailable anywhere else.

Peggy Noonan, the columnist, recently sought to describe the type. "The best journalists," she wrote, "are and always have been professionals. They want to tell people what they have a right to know about the world they live in. That is why you break the story, unearth the lie, ask the question, tell the yarn. You're trying in your way to make the world more just."

My friend Lance Morrow, now an octogenarian still writing wise essays for *The Wall Street Journal*, recalls his newsroom days when "journalism was a rascal, a smoker and a drinker. The pay was bad. You were broke half the time, and often hung over. But you were young enough to enjoy the scruffy mystique and a winking intimacy with history itself."

James Bennet, a fallen angel from the *New York Times* heavens, writes of his reporting days that "unlike the dueling politicians and advocates of all kinds, unlike the corporate chieftains and their critics, unlike even the sainted non-profit workers, you did not have to pretend things were simpler than they actually were. . . you did not, in other words, ever have to lie."

The redoubtable Maureen Dowd still relishes her early newsroom memories — "the incredible camaraderie and panache about the whole endeavor, whether you were pursuing stories about murder, politics or the breeding woes of the pandas at the National Zoo." The rookie Ms. Dowd was once sent out on deadline to get beer and claims she was nearly fired when she returned to the newsroom with Miller Lite.

It's worth recalling these times to realize what goes missing from the warp and woof of community life when newsrooms are emptied out and the mission of so many journalists is aborted.

I know the ache it leaves. Our company's papers used to carry a lighthouse logo in the upper left corner of every front page with the motto, "Give light and the people will find their own way." Sadly, the directors of Scripps chose to dim those lights, to fold its newspaper tent, and instead to chase digital treasure in other venues. The gold didn't vanish but a noble mission of more than a century did.

In this era of upheaval, there are a precious few prominent U.S. papers still widely available that can be trusted for news of national and world moment. Despite the admitted excellence of these few organs in covering the big picture, such as *The Wall Street Journal* and the *New York Times,* they nonetheless fail to provide the balance that an added mixture of news closer to home would bring. In the view of Tim Franklin, who runs the Local News Initiative at Northwestern University's Medill School,"When there's this void of local news, people revert to the blue and red echo chambers."

Of course, television stations do continue to serve up a local menu, even if it's generally a predictable one. Their version of local news is the easy-to-get stuff. It consists of skimming the headlines and not much else. More days than not, there's plenty about the weather, something from the local police blotter about the latest triple ax slaying, another of those demonstrations carefully staged for the camera, and in this election season a string of paid political ads where truth is no welcome guest. But for reporting truly meaningful, useful information about the polis, TV budgets are thin. Ominously, the stations themselves are now endangered by the same forces that stilled the newspapers' voice.

It's been a long time ago, but I was with a group of editors in the 1980s listening to Walter Cronkite as he retired from a career in broadcast journalism that had made him the news voice most trusted in America. "Uncle Walter," himself a hard news man, told us what worried him most was that television news was being turned into entertainment. He spoke with a prophetic voice. While current Gallup numbers show only 16 percent of the public has any degree of confidence in the newspapers that remain, even fewer — 11 percent — harbor trust in television's news-as- entertainment, as it is inevitably delivered by chatty anchors sporting the latest fashion in woke points of view.

Not to be too quick to find fault with electronic journalism, however. Candor requires one to admit that many of today's practitioners of the print version exhibit the same biases, or worse.

They seem to consider their craft as a license to advance a social agenda at odds with the age-old requirement of traditional journalists to be honest umpires calling balls and strikes without fear or favor.

Old-line editors would quake over the very idea of blue or red brushes blurring the reality of an honest report. The choicest words of opprobrium from the newsroom lexicon would await the lowly reporter trying to inject personal opinion into a story. Woke my eye!

As this century's battle lines of ideological debate in American political life have grown more rigid, television watchers have chosen up sides, migrating from traditional television networks to the cable channels that serve up their own peculiar political stew, where incessant babbling pierces decibel levels and where demagoguery is on full parade. Only today, in the latest fad in screen watching, entertainment-hungry audiences are found moving away in growing numbers from channel viewing to stream content of their choosing. Streaming is the magic word.

At the same time, Americans, always an opinionated lot, have learned to talk back.

Newspapers and television only offer a one-way method of communication. It is in the very nature of the new social media that it is two-way, a back-and-forth exchange. So the multitude of social media sites, resembling a modern day Tower of Babel, are used to publish just about anything from anyone — and with lightning speed and often with reckless anonymity. There's no fact-checking, no confirming of sources, no standards of fairness, none of the lie detectors once routinely employed by professional journalists to assure a measure of accuracy. However useful and habit-forming these platforms have become, they are — as we have learned only too well — a decidedly mixed blessing.

With them has come endless instances of misuse — hacking, spam, the infamous "fake news" and countless other methods of tarnishing supposed enemies while misleading vast sectors of society.

Not long ago my wife, looking over that day's computer output, excitedly exclaimed that "Putin has cancer and he won't be around long." How do you know that, I asked. "It says so right here on the screen." It didn't take much checking for us to determine that the so-called news of Mr. Putin's impending demise, which had spread over the internet like a Maui wildfire, was but the latest in the stream of misinformation that spews daily from social media sources.

Geoffrey Hinton, often called the godfather of Artificial Intelligence, told the *New York Times* that the average internet user might soon "not be able to know what is true anymore."

Reflecting back, it seems downright incredible that it was only in 2005 — not two decades ago — that social media first began to take shape. Countless platforms and networks quickly appeared for people around the world to communicate with each other. Whole new forms of conversation ensued, especially ones with 280-character limits and abbreviated vocabularies translatable only by insiders. Last year Facebook, the top-rated site, counted three billion users each month — three billion — followed closely by YouTube, WhatsApp and Instagram, all boasting similar gigantic communities.

Despite the unreliability and the episodes of misuse that characterize the social media world, it's now estimated that 8 in 10 Americans use a digital device to access what can loosely be defined as news found on social media. The Pew Research Center recently reported that 14 per cent of American adults say they regularly get news from TikTok, the Chinese-owned site which boasts 150 million accounts in the United States alone. Among the young in GenZ, where there's little appetite for news of any sort, the polls show only 5 per cent of this group bothering to read a newspaper.

The traditional free press of my life's experience is in free fall, certainly where it comes to serving the local needs of an informed community. The genie is out of the bottle. The largest tech companies now say that hosting news on their sites is more trouble than it's worth, so they have decided to bury links to news publications, thus drying up any sources of advertising income for publishers from social media. What's even worse, the technology that makes Artificial Intelligence possible has, in the eyes of some, the potential simply to destroy journalism and media brands as we know them.

Perhaps 21st century America has become so hardened and jaded, so me-driven, its sense of citizenship so shriveled, that citizens no longer care about whose elected finger is in the courthouse cookie jar. Or perhaps it's the case of being so accustomed to using social media to find out in an instant whatever itches one's curiosity that there's no particular concern for undertaking the harder work of being responsible modern citizens, whose tool kits need to be filled with reliable information about the world they live in. Are we turning our heads away from a building block of democracy?

Or has the muscle memory of local news simply atrophied, as someone recently asked. So what if there are no longer qualified journalists whose jobs were to ferret out the daily happenings that tie a local community together? Why is one to care? What difference does it make?

Quite a bit of difference, in the judgment of careful students of the body politic. A chorus of alarmed voices has arisen, pointing out that however much the American landscape has changed, an informed electorate continues to need the nourishment of truthful information to shape intelligent opinion and to form consensus on public issues. For most of the life of this country, the local newspaper was a lightning rod around which a community was gathered for the information it needed. It wasn't a community's sole organizing force, but it served as one bulwark of how Americans governed themselves.

Margaret Sullivan, a one-time newspaper ombudsman, is outspoken. "The demise of local news poses the kind of danger to our democracy that should have alarm sirens screeching across the land." Her one-time employer, the *Washington Post*, has written that "when we lose local journalism, we lose a fabric that holds together communities. We lose crucial information that allows democracy to function. We lose stories that need to be told."

Or listen to Timothy Snyder, a Yale professor who wrote a book on the threat of tyranny: "When local news goes away, then our sense of what is true shifts from what is helpful to us in our daily lives to what makes us feel good."

The Brookings Institute has found that "as Americans have shifted away from local news, turnout in state and local elections has fallen and communities that have lost reporters have seen fewer candidates run for local office." . . .

A sense of isolation creeps in when residents are left without reliable access to information about the communities they live in. They can grow anxious, even depressed. As Tocqueville pointed out long ago, the intermediating institutions he found in American society, such as newspapers, act as important buffers protecting individual citizens from Big Brother intrusion into their private lives.

Not to pick at scabs, but the *Cincinnati Enquirer*, a newspaper with a proud, rich history, has been stripped of so many resources by its present owner that it is among those now known in the trade as one of the "ghost" papers, those starved for local news. Like others in this category, the Grand Old Lady of Vine Street is but a shadow of her former self. Her owner seeks to masquerade her diminished resources, but glitzy marketing and empty promises hardly hide the short supply of once-vital local content found in either the print or digital versions that are now offered.

The Grand Old Lady is not even printed in her home city any longer. She joins other Gannett titles taking their turn getting published overnight at a central site elsewhere, then trucked to Cincinnati for distribution the next morning. This means that to accommodate publishing schedules the flow of news for the next day's printed edition is shut off by mid-afternoon of the previous day. Thus, readers can find nothing in print to go with their morning coffee that happened in the previous late afternoon or evening — no Reds' score, nothing about a school board's evening meeting on book choices, nothing of what a mayor said about putting a hot tax issue up for a vote. They do find pages of material identical to what is found in other papers in what Gannett terms "a network of shared resources."

So much for immediacy. I am reminded of an editor in my experience who would growl at any reporter who dared to be delinquent at deadline: "Wha'da'ya think we're running here, a seed catalogue?"

Today's ghost papers — fine-tuned to the latest marketing tastes — tend to be built not on breaking local news of timely importance but on a diet of bread and circuses, the feel-good stuff. They devote their admittedly diminished resources not to local news coverage so much as to items geared to attract the sports fans and the foodies.

It's no wonder that in the four-year period from 2018 to 2022, the Sunday circulation of the *Enquirer* — both print and digital — shrank 67.2 percent, according to a report from the Nieman Foundation at Harvard, whose Joshua Benton claimed that "the scale of local news destruction in Gannett's markets is astonishing." One can only mourn for the Grand Old Lady on Vine Street.

My boyhood hero, the late small-town editor William Allen White, once wrote a famous editorial, "What's the Matter with Kansas," railing against the "gibbering idiots" he thought were ruining his state. His century-old classic came to mind last summer as I read about a latter-day group of Kansas "idiots" who, armed with a storm-trooper search warrant, raided a small newspaper in Marion, a town of hardly 2,000, and confiscated all of its computer equipment and cellphones.

This egregious assault on a lonely outpost of a free press was motivated by the local police chief and others seeking payback for the aggressive editor poking into their past misbehaviors. So stressed by the police invasion of her home was the paper's 98-year-old co-owner, the editor's mother, that she died the next day. The case drew national outrage, and even though it was eventually resolved in the paper's favor, many townspeople, not welcoming all the ballyhoo, considered the editor a "pot stirrer." Such can be the way of life in small town America with a rambunctious editor, but those places are better for the trouble.

The Kansas tempest served to call attention to the plight of other small, courageous newspapers, mainly weeklies, which still hang on but are being targeted in new ways for their work in calling local officials to account. Taking a page from the Trump playbook, agitators have resorted to social media and defamation laws as cudgels against vulnerable editors, as have ambitious prosecutors anxious to make a name for themselves. It's the fashion of the times to broad-brush journalists as "enemies of the people." Beating up on the media has become a popular game of outrage.

By the very nature of their work, editors don't ordinarily win many popularity contests.

They are easy targets, especially in this era of culture wars. In one recent case in Wausau, Wisconsin, an editor who refused to buckle ran up legal bills of $150,000 — nearly her entire annual budget -- trying to fight off the assault of a wealthy state senator offended by her paper's coverage of remarks he claims he didn't utter (but which witnesses said he did). When a judge threw out his suit, he stubbornly appealed. His apparent aim is to make it too costly for the paper to continue publishing because he doesn't like what he thinks it stands for.

"News organizations can be sued into oblivion," points out the executive director of Aspen Digital, a non-profit organization that is seeking to help endangered local news outlets.

Andy Alexander, a one-time Washington newspaper ombudsman, thinks local news organizations are in a race against time. He poses the question: "Can we save papers before they vanish? If they do, you've left a huge societal vacuum."

Aroused by the threat, a whole army of old names and Johnny-come-lately's-think tanks, foundations, study centers, philanthropists — has jumped into action, launching an array of experiments hoping to revive journalism at the grassroots.

Last fall a coalition of 22 donors pledged more than a half-billion dollars to create a project titled *Press Forward* to strengthen what is now fashionably termed civic media, calling free and independent local voices a "key pillar of American democracy."

Northwestern's Tim Franklin, whose mission is to keep tabs on the battle, says he is more optimistic than he was five years ago that local journalism can be revived. He admits, though, the situation remains "dire." . . .

And then there's talk of Artificial Intelligence chatbots being employed to produce local news. I wouldn't know an algorithm from an albatross, but I am hard-pressed to understand how robots from the metaverse can become reporters on the local beat.

As all of the activity responding to the crisis does make clear, there's no lack of effort trying to revive the American news gathering tradition and, in the process, to shore up our democratic ways of running things. Whether any of it works, now that remains to be seen.

Meanwhile, for this aging ex-city editor, maybe it's not getting too late to hunt up a digital version of the old hectograph machine.

Bill Burleigh joined his hometown newspaper staff at age 14 and spent more than a half century in journalism jobs, ending as chairman of the E.W. Scripps Company, America's oldest media chain. In another association he cherishes, he joined The Literary Club in 1978 and was privileged to serve as its president in 2001-02.

3 *The Very Short and Mostly Disastrous Career of Lt. Tom Cuni as a Drug Counselor*

THOMAS L. CUNI

IT was 1971. The American involvement in what had been a long war in Southeast Asia was winding down. I was a First Lieutenant attached to Charlie Company as its artillery forward observer. It was a very understrength infantry company in the 101st Airborne Division. Our area of operations was in the mountainous jungles east of the Laotian border and five miles or so south of the Demilitarized Zone, which once separated North Vietnam from South Vietnam. After more than three weeks of sweating and swearing our way through that particularly unpleasant little corner of the war, we received a message in the late afternoon from battalion headquarters. It was Charlie Company's turn for a three-day stand-down at Camp Evans. Helicopters from the aviation battalion were to lift us out at first light on the following day.

That evening, Billy asked if he could have a word with me. He was a quiet private first class. He was of slight build with blond scraggly hair that was a good deal longer than Army regulations permitted. Although he was from the Midwest, Billy had a laid-back Southern California attitude. He carried one of the machine guns. The M-60 machine gun was a heavy piece of steel. It was nearly as long as Billy was tall. It was often referred to as the Pig. Billy did his job without complaining. This story is about Billy and the advice that I gave him that night.

I had never been a heavy sleeper. Sleeping on the ground did not improve my already peculiar sleep pattern. On most nights I would wake up at two o'clock or so and stay awake for the rest of the night. Billy seemed to sleep even less than I did. We were the obvious candidates for the 2 a.m. to 4 a.m. radio watch. To pass the time, Billy and I would often talk quietly during the watch. After a time, we knew each other's life story. I believe that since we had talked so often, Billy was comfortable asking me for advice about a drug test he would have to take during the upcoming stand-down. Billy was scheduled to leave the country for seven days of Rest and Relaxation ("R&R"). Before he could leave for R&R, the Army required that he take and pass a urine test. It was common knowledge that I had a pretty laissez faire attitude about alcohol (juice) and cannabis (weed) when we were in the rear areas. So long as someone was not stoned or drunk in the field, I was pretty much okay with whatever made his life just a little more tolerable in that unpleasant little war.

At the time I gave it, I believed that my advice to him was both practical and sound. I advised him to not take a chance on spoiling his R&R by smoking weed at all before he took the test. I suggested that he juice it for a couple of days at Camp Evans, and then smoke his brains out in Bangkok during his R&R. The dope in Thailand was reputed to be better than anything he could get where we were.

Early the next morning we flew to Evans. The universe sometimes provides a lesson in humility. It was my turn to have such a lesson. I was scheduled to be the Duty Officer for the Company on the first day and night of the stand-down. Being the Duty Officer required that I stay around the Company area. I did not care. After taking a shower and putting on a clean uniform for the first time in several weeks, I drifted over to the mess hall to drink several cups of freshly brewed coffee. A sandwich on fresh bread tasted like a gourmet meal after having eaten field rations for weeks. I enjoyed a lazy afternoon lying on my bunk and reading a book. It was a pleasant day by any measure.

Shortly after dark, my pleasant day took an unpleasant turn. The screen door slammed shut behind him as the Company Clerk ran over to my bunk to wake me. I needed to get over to the MP station immediately. Having been a Duty Officer on several previous occasions, both in the States and during my tour, it had been my experience that a summons to the MP station was rarely a good thing.

Drunken behavior was not new to me or any other grunt. After being sweated down to about 150 pounds, it only took about three beers (at 10 cents each) and one shot of whiskey (at 25 cents) to pretty much put me away for a night. I was not alone in that weight related loss of tolerance for alcohol. I expected to find one of the men sobering up in the lockup. MPs generally just wanted the Duty Officer to take a drunken soldier back to the barracks to sleep off a drunk. Sometimes it could be worse. This was one of the "it could be worse" times.

When I walked into the MP station, Billy was engaged in a brawl with three MPs. Before I could come to grips with the situation, Billy lunged at me with what appeared to be the intention of inflicting severe injury to my young ass. At the last moment, he stopped short of punching me. With an obvious effort, he focused on me and said something to the effect of "L.T. It's you." Everything changed at that moment. The ranking MP asked me if this guy belonged to me. I could not deny ownership. He told me to take him with me and leave.

As we were walking back to the Company area, I noticed that Billy's right arm had a sizable bandage on it. There seemed to be no future in asking him what had happened since he was mumbling something that I could not understand. It also seemed to me that most of Billy's attention was focused on the task of walking upright. A couple of the men from his squad had called it an early night, so I left Billy in their care. I walked over to the aid station to find out what I could learn about his injury.

What I knew to that point made no sense. Billy, in the time I had known him, was not at all pugnacious or even disagreeable. Fighting three MPs seemed far outside his usually calm demeanor. The medics provided me with a piece to the puzzle. Billy had been brought into the aid station with a deep and long cut in his lower arm. It had taken four soldiers to haul his struggling, belligerent ass to the medics. He was less than cooperative with the medics who were trying to sew him up. It took several of them just to hold him down on the table while they tried to sedate him. The first shot had a negligible effect on Billy's agitated state. They gave him a second shot of sedative, and he began to calm down. One of the medics must have been holding Billy's arm at a pressure point. When he let go of Billy's arm, circulation was restored. Most of the double shot of sedative hit his heart at one time, and his heart stopped. The medics revived him and sewed him up. They left Billy for what they thought would be a long, deep sleep. In less than an hour, Billy was on his feet and the game was on again. It had been at that point that the MPs came on the scene and hauled his angry ass over to the lockup. I had walked into the MP station as they were trying to get him into a cell.

When I returned to the Company area, I walked around asking the few men who were not still out getting drunk if they knew what had started this mess. I learned that Billy had left the enlisted men's club with the expressed intention of kicking the asses of every single motherfucker in Alpha Company.

A short digression is required. The company commander of Alpha Company was a West Point graduate in his first combat command. Shortly after he became a company commander, his unit got a black eye. Getting a black eye was a euphemism for losing an entire unit. In this case, a platoon. Everyone knew that we were getting near the end of America's participation in the war. Following our wars there is typically a sizable reduction in force — RIF. The Army usually shed officers and NCOs who did not have good efficiency reports. As a Ring Knocker, that is, a West Pointer, there were officers of higher rank who looked after the careers of fellow graduates. The name 'Ring Knocker' referred to the way West Pointers were reputed to hit their heavy class rings on a table to signal each other that they were from the Academy. The rehabilitation of the good captain's career was centered on not letting him fuck-up again in the field. The net result was that Alpha Company became the "Palace Guard" which meant that it was kept behind the wire at Evans or on a firebase. For the other four companies in the battalion, it meant longer intervals in the field. I have no idea if any of this was true, but it was widely believed - especially by Billy who was particularly unhappy about it.

When I walked over to Alpha Company's area, I learned that Billy had indeed succeeded in starting a fight with several guys - all at the same time. It did not go well for him. At one point Billy took a wild ass swing and cut his arm open on the lower edge of the corrugated metal roof of the small, frame barracks next to him.

When I had the whole story, I decided to get some sleep. I returned to my barracks and hit the bunk without taking my boots off. It was not a long rest. One of the guys who had been keeping tabs on Billy woke me up with some alarming news. After having passed out on his bunk for a few hours, Billy had awakened and set out to complete his mission to punish Alpha Company. As he was leaving the barracks, Billy had said something about getting his rifle to finish the job. Shortly afterward we found Billy passed out in front of the steel CONEX box which was used for the storage of the company's weapons when we were in garrison. We found him asleep in front of the CONEX container. Apparently, Billy had not been able to knock the lock off the door. At some point, he had passed out in front of the door. We managed to get him on his feet, and between the two of us walked him back to his bunk. It was finally the end of a long but interesting night.

It was also the end of my career as a drug counselor. Who would have believed that alcohol could produce such a dramatically different personality in a guy who just liked to smoke a little weed and chill out?

I made a minimal entry on the Duty Officer's log that omitted most of the details of the incident. I did not want Billy to get in trouble and ruin his R&R. I also understood that I bore some of the responsibility for the whole mess because of my misguided drug counselling effort.

Some degree of violence was expected by the Army in a war zone. I was not called to headquarters to explain the incident. A day later Billy left on his R&R. The rest of us returned to the task of harming someone other than each other.

In 2016, on a small farm in central Indiana, I joined a group of no longer young men. We sat in the shade of several big trees on a warm summer afternoon and talked about our experiences in a long-ago conflict. Someone asked, "Do you guys remember the time at Camp Evans when Billy....?" The memory of that day returned to me in perfect detail. It was a small part of the most transformative event in my long life.

As a postscript of sorts, Billy made it home in one piece. He has lived a good life without any more advice from me.

Thomas Cuni was a paperboy for the Charleston WV Gazette, a stockboy and delivery truck driver for the Man, West Virginia Piggly Wiggly, and an apprentice miner, hard rock driller and powder monkey at various sites in southern West Virginia—and a member of the 101st Airborne in Vietnam. After studies at the University of Cincinnati College of Law, he has been an attorney practicing in business transactions and related litigation. The husband of Sally and father of Zach and Seth, he volunteers as an attorney for ProKids.

4 Metropolitan Transportation

JACK DAVIS

THE Metropolitan Museum of New York has one of the finest collections of Greek and Roman antiquities in the world. Galleries stretch expansively along a long corridor on the south side of the ground floor of the main building, left of its Fifth Avenue entrance hall. Galleries are named for major donors to the museum, members of its Board of Trustees. The rooms change their names from time to time. A friend of mine, Malcolm Wiener, long ago endowed a gallery in his name alone, but later changed it to include his wife and four children. As he told me at the time, otherwise his body wouldn't be cold in the ground by the time a mercenary Met with a corporate mentality would rename the gallery for someone else. This is the way of modern American museums that are not state funded, as are European.

But our museums are in other ways similar to European museums. They too began to form their magnificent collections at a time when many eastern Mediterranean countries operated on a system of partage, according to which the fruits of archaeological excavations were split between the discoverers and a host country through a process of negotiation. An archaeologist would divide his spoils into two piles and a local government representative would decide which could leave and

Marble column from the Temple of Artemis at Sardis. Metropolitan Museum of Art. Public domain image.

which would stay. Partage was particularly characteristic of the Ottoman Empire, and was in 1937 the means by which Literarian Nelson Glueck legally brought Jordanian antiquities to our own Cincinnati Art Museum.

But our museums are in other ways similar to European museums. They too began to form their magnificent collections at a time when many eastern Mediterranean countries operated on a system of partage, according to which the fruits of archaeological excavations were split between the discoverers and a host country through a process of negotiation. An archaeologist would divide his spoils into two piles and a local government representative would decide which could leave and which would stay. Partage was particularly characteristic of the Ottoman Empire, and was in 1937 the means by which Literarian Nelson Glueck legally brought Jordanian antiquities to our own Cincinnati Art Museum.

But outright theft also enriched the great museums of Europe and America. Consider the means by which the so-called Elgin Marbles reached the British Museum. Now more properly called the Parthenon Marbles, these substantial elements of the decoration of the Temple of Athena on the Athenian Acropolis were removed by workmen in the employ of Thomas Bruce, 7th Earl of Elgin, British ambassador to the Sublime Porte, 1799-1803. Elgin claimed he had received a Ottoman *firman*, a permit, to "fix scaffolding round the ancient Temple of the Idols, and to mould the ornamental sculpture and visible figures thereon in plaster and gypsum," and "to take away any pieces of stone with old inscriptions or figures thereon."

The original permit has never been found in the Ottoman archives in Istanbul and exists only in an Italian translation. The current Greek governmental position is that no such permission ever existed. A recent director of the Acropolis Museum has written that "the document that has been saved and called a firman, and which was cited by Lord Elgin ... is, in reality, not an order by Sultan Selim III," but rather an administrative letter sent to Ottoman authorities in Athens. Permission was granted to dig into earthen mounds created around the Acropolis after it was bombed by cannon fire in 1687 by Venetian general Francesco Morosini.

Elgin's loot was first displayed in his Scottish estate, then sold to the British Museum in 1812. Not all English approved. Lord Byron considered Elgin a vandal.

American museums in any case had a lot of catching up to do. While museums in Europe were building fabulous collections of antiquities, by legal and illegal means, museums in America were newcomers to the game. The 19th Century saw their advent, first as collections of curiosities, such as Charles Willson Peale's Cabinet in Philadelphia, built around a desire to document the history of discovery in the New World. Peale was both a painter and a collector, and in 1786 filled his museum with his own portraits of George Washington, and later with bones of a North American woolly mammoth. Meanwhile, other museums were springing up in private homes, and in the inns of any town where someone might believe a sign saying "George Washington Slept

Here." P.T. Barnum bought out Peale. The Smithsonian Institution followed in 1846.

The Met opened its doors only in 1872, after the golden age of looting in the Mediterranean. By then Greece, Italy, even the Ottomans, had codified their laws concerning antiquities, so as strictly to regulate, even to forbid the export of any items considered to constitute cultural patrimony. How were American museums to emulate, indeed compete with the European? It is at this point that I turn to my principal tale.

At this very moment, for the paltry sum of $125, anyone can buy over the internet from the gift shop of the Metropolitan Museum a pair of graceful bookends modelled on a 4th century B.C. Ionic column from the Temple of Artemis at Sardis. The Met describes them as follows:

"An eye-catching pair for home or office, our bookends celebrate the magnificent Sardis column in The Met. The capital, base, and portions of the shaft of this great Ionic column come from a monumental temple constructed at Sardis (in today's Turkey) and dedicated to Artemis, the Greek goddess of the hunt and the moon.

Shortened from its original height of 56 feet, the Met's massive column on display in the Greek and Roman galleries lets viewers admire the fine carving of the foliate ornaments on the capital and the fish-scale pattern on the molding at its base. These same decorative details appear on our handsome bookends."

The story of how this column ended up in the Met (and why it is shortened!) is more interesting than the bookends themselves, however worthy of admiration they may be. Hint: the column was not shortened so that visitors could view its fine carving.

(It is also important to note immediately that the Temple of Artemis is not only in "today's Turkey," but was already in Turkey when the Met's column left Sardis.)

The journey of the Sardis column to New York City is intertwined with the fate of a zone in western Turkey administered by Greece following the First World War.

Between 1919 and 1922 the Greek state realized what former British Ambassador to Greece Michael Llewellyn Smith has called Greek Prime Minister Eleftherios Venizelos's "Ionian Vision." Following the surrender of Ottoman Turkey in October 1918, Turkey had allied with Germany, Austria, and Bulgaria in the war. Istanbul, the capital, was occupied by the Allies, with Admiral Mark Bristol, American High Commissioner, protecting U.S. interests there. The Allies had divided coastal Anatolia into mandates with Greece installed in the district of Smyrna, modern Izmir. In accord with this agreement, on May 14, 1919, Allied troops moved into Smyrna and rumors circulated that the city was to be handed over to Greece. The following day an Hellenic army arrived, blessed on its landing by Chrysostomos, the Greek Metropolitan bishop of Smyrna.

At this time Greek influence was so strong in the area of Smyrna that the Turks called it "Smyrna of the infidels" (Gavur İzmir). During the late 19th and early 20th Century, the city was an important financial and cultural center of the Greek world. Out of the 391 factories, 322 belonged to local Greeks, while three out of the nine banks were backed by Greek capital. Education was also dominated by the Greek communities.

Venizelos purposely chose a civilian governor for the Smyrna district, a lawyer named Aristeidis Stergiadis, a fellow Cretan, previously the governor general of Greek Epirus—an area of northwestern Greece best known in Ohio as the birthplace of Cincinnati chili. Stergiadis, an expert in Islamic jurisprudence, had won a good reputation for his even-handed administration there. Chief among his goals in Smyrna was the restoration of order and the establishment of an efficient and impartial local government. The Greek administration was in principle not intended to replace Turkish sovereignty; both Greek and Turkish law were to be recognized.

Two American archaeological digs operated in Turkey under this Greek mandate, one at Sardis, the ancient capital of Lydia, seat of Croesus, whom we know well from Herodotus, and the expression "rich as Croesus." The other was at Colophon, one of the cities of the ancient Greek Ionian league on the western coast of Turkey. At Sardis an expedition excavated under the direction of Howard Crosby Butler until World War I and then resumed its work in the spring of 1922. Butler, a Princeton professor, was supported in his efforts by the American Society for the Excavation of Sardis, an organization consisting of prominent industrialists, art collectors, and philanthropists, including members of the board of trustees of the Met. Sardis lay 70 km inland to the east of Smyrna, and the eastern border of the Greek mandate passed along its acropolis—placing it in a particularly vulnerable position in case of armed conflict.

The concerns of Harvard University were, on the other hand, the driving force in promoting the organization of a newly launched program of fieldwork at Colophon, aiming to enrich the collections of its Fogg Museum. In collaboration with the American School of Classical Studies at Athens, a dig of some sort had been discussed at least since 1915, when Paul Sachs, assistant director of the museum, wrote to his cousin Hetty Goldman that there "is no reason whatsoever why you should not head a Harvard expedition to excavate in Greece at the proper time." (They both were offsprings of the founders of Goldman-Sachs.)

But momentum was broken by World War I, and there is no mention of an expedition again until late 1920. Goldman was attracted by the possibilities of excavating in areas of Anatolia that had just come under Greek jurisdiction. She wrote Sachs that "I will not give up Asia Minor without a struggle." Sachs wrote in the spring of 1921 that "we want, if possible, to get a site in Asia Minor, since we all feel that that is where important discoveries may be expected."

Sach's "important discoveries" was obvious code. Harvard's decision to excavate in Anatolia was ultimately influenced by the desire to add antiquities to the collections of the Fogg Museum. This is clear from correspondence between Sachs and Goldman. Goldman wrote to Sachs in November that "Greek sites will not yield the opportunities for exportation of finds that sites in Asia Minor might."

A desire to acquire new antiquities was also a goal for the Princeton excavations at Sardis. In the spring of 1922, members of the Sardis Expedition saw their opportunity, and moved architectural members and other finds to Smyrna, including parts of the Ionic column now in the Met. All expected the Greek administration in Smyrna to hold firm. Major William R. Berry, a member of the Sardis team, wrote: "I have deemed it wise to go on to Constantinople for the purpose of attempting to enlist Admiral Bristol's sympathies in transportation—if you understand what I mean— i.e. to say, 'Metropolitan' transportation."

The United States consul in Smyrna, George Horton, did his utmost to ensure that antiquities would leave Turkey for America under the Greek administration, as described in a letter to U.S. Secretary of State Charles Evans Hughes. A representative of the Sardis excavations, Leslie Shear, had asked for help in arranging export of finds. Cyrus McCormick, the Chicago industrialist and son of the founder of the International Harvester Company, had tried in person to negotiate terms, but unsuccessfully. Shear was "truculent," according to Horton, and disputed any Greek claim on the antiquities. He demanded an audience with Stergiadis, accompanied by Horton.

Wisely Horton went alone. He convinced Stergiadis of the wisdom of allowing the export of antiquities on the grounds that the finds might otherwise be destroyed—implying also that Greeks would in that case be blamed. He argued with some sophistry that the U.S. deserved these finds since, unlike European countries, its museums had not been able to be filled with finds from Greece itself. Greek culture would in this way be better known in the U.S. and that will be good for Greece.

From Princeton, Professor Edward Capps, had been pushing hard for permission while Horton was at work in Smyrna. As the former U.S. ambassador to Athens under President Wilson, his network of connections to influential Greek politicians and to members of the Greek royal family was extensive. Capps, like Shear, was clear in his mind that the antiquities of Sardis did not belong to Greece. Greek law was thus not applicable, and consequently the removal of artifacts from the site should not be impeded by Stergiadis. He encouraged the director of the American School in Athens to take the matter to the highest levels of government. By using Capps's name freely, the director managed to obtain an audience with King Constantine and a meeting with the Greek foreign minister. Both the King and the foreign minister promised to advise Stergiadis to exercise "the utmost possible generosity" in dealing with the matter.

The results of these protracted negotiations were welcomed in Harvard, as well as in Princeton and New York. Goldman's fears must have been allayed by the following news conveyed to her by Carl Blegen, later professor at the University of Cincinnati and a Literarian:

> "In case of evacuation of Colophon by Greece we are to be free to carry off everything our conscience permits to America or where we like. So Stergiades told me. This is private to you and Miss G."

The collections of Harvard's Fogg Museum would indeed be enriched.

Not everyone was so complacent, and some predicted trouble ahead. Allen Welsh Dulles, of the State Department, Division of Near Eastern Affairs (and later the first director of the CIA), wrote that a letter he had received from Capps raised problematic issues. Whether or not the State Department should approve Horton's "complicity in this classical looting" was a "matter of policy."

But operations in Smyrna went into motion in summer 1922. The Sardis Excavation first tried to arrange the dispatch of antiquities to New York on a ship of the Standard Oil company, but Standard Oil had gotten cold feet. Instead the loot was boarded on the S.S. Ossa. Fifty-eight cases left Smyrna when conditions in the district were still militarily settled, and on arrival in New York were stored at the Met. Some had been labelled "For Princeton."

By autumn, New York newspapers were crowing over such spectacular additions to the Met's collections. Horton would later write that "I took keener satisfaction in bringing these remarkable antiquities to the United States than in any other single act of my entire consular career." He had been promised that his bust would be installed in a new gallery at the Met.

The hammer fell on the Greek administration unexpectedly on September 8, 1922, and its headquarters in Smyrna were evacuated. Turkish cavalry entered the city the next day. On September 11, Smyrna was set on fire.

Harvard's expedition suffered no political difficulties, and the zone of Colophon had been militarily secure. It was, in fact, the very abruptness of the collapse of the Greek administration that baffled the civilian population and archaeologists alike. Blegen wrote the director of the American School on September 10: "What is the inside story of the disaster in Anatolia? I don't understand it. All speed records seem to have been broken."

Members of the two excavations and officials of the American School focused immediately on "damage control," since the rules of the game had changed overnight. Turkish, rather than Greek, authorities needed to be courted and their pique assuaged. In February 1923, Blegen departed for Smyrna and Istanbul in the interests of the Harvard project. Although he found general good will toward Americans, he concluded that any resumption of excavations in 1923 was out of the question. Blegen wrote that in Istanbul, "I saw Dr. Halil Bey, Director General of the Museum... He said frankly that he felt hurt... when he learned that the dig at Sardis had been resumed..." under the Greek administration. Later that year Goldman wrote to Sachs that the situation had become very complicated. Halil Bey considered the past work at Colophon to be illegal. He professed to be deeply offended that the Americans had recognized the authority of the Greeks since they were "invaders who came to rob and pillage the country."

At the heart of the matter lay the 58 cases of antiquities taken to New York City. The Turks were quite aware that antiquities were stolen, aided by the many triumphant articles in American newspapers.

In addition to the crates of antiquities shipped to New York, there remained the matter of 30 gold coins from Sardis that surfaced in Athens, after being given to Horton for safekeeping in Smyrna. Capps repeatedly asked the State Department to transport them to America in a diplomatic pouch, but his request was refused. In the end Horton himself carried the coins to New York.

The first steps toward a formal resolution of the dispute between the American excavators and the Turkish authorities were finally taken in 1924, with Admiral Bristol mediating. Permission was given to reopen the Sardis excavations as soon as Turkey was officially informed that the Metropolitan Museum had shipped back the finds in its possession. Bristol wrote on May 14, 1924, that a proposed settlement was accepted by Halil Bey. The antiquities would be returned to Turkey at the expense of the Turkish government, except for the capital and other column parts from the Temple of Artemis. (Not all the drums had been taken.)

In the end most Sardis finds were sent back to Turkey, and Turkey returned a selection of them to New York. But even so the Metropolitan Museum and the members of the Society were unhappy with the arrangement. Edward Robinson, director of the Met wrote to Bristol in early 1926 that the Society was deeply disappointed at what it had received. "A large proportion of the objects now in its possession could find no place in the exhibition rooms of any first-rate museum and have little or no educational value..." Members of the Society had not gotten their money's worth and that would discourage future attempts to raise funds in support of American excavations in the Mediterranean.

And so it is that the Ionic column stands in the Greek and Roman galleries of the Met today, described as follows, with no reference to its chequered past:

"The section of a fluted Ionic column in the center of this room stood over fifty-eight feet high in its original location at the Temple of Artemis..."—a "gift" of the Society for the Excavation of Sardis.

Now we arrive at my final chapter of this story. Surely nothing like Sardis could or would happen today. Probably not, at least not as so blatant and organized an enterprise. But museums are big business, attracting billions of tourist dollars, advancing science, and educating and amusing more than 850 million people annually. If we add up the attendance for every major-league baseball, basketball, football, and hockey game this year, the combined total will come to about 140 million people. That's a big number, but it is only a fraction of the number of people who will visit American museums this year.

New strategies have evolved to feed public appetites for antiquities. The Art Institute of Chicago established a Classical Art Society in the 1970s. Members were given professional advice by, and special access to, curators. Other museums organized days when members could bring their own antiquities to the museum for appraisal by curators.

The collecting of antiquities remains popular, and there is no lack of access to them. Where do antiquities come from? The vast majority are looted from archaeological sites and smuggled from their countries of origin. Some leave in the suitcases of dual nationals, their families hoping for remittances from abroad. At the low-value end of the scale, many, such as coins, go for sale on eBay. At the upper end they find their way to Swiss auction houses, and move from there to London, New York, and the Far East. They may hit the auction block with fabricated pedigrees, claiming they come from old private collections. And the system exalts when chaos reigns in antique lands. ISIS began mining antiquities even as it blew up archaeological sites. In Afghanistan our boys brought them home in knapsacks. Friends of mine tried to stem the tide in Iraq by lecturing at army and marine bases—with limited success.

I was in Albania during the civil unrest that followed the collapse of pyramid banking in 1997, and during the Kosovo War. I saw with my own eyes northern European buyers descend, offering local farmers exorbitant sums for pieces of ancient sculpture. The temptation was so great that even Albanian museums were looted of their displays. Here is the dirty end of a supply chain that well-heeled bidders never see in the swishy showrooms of Sotheby's in Midtown. Collectors create demand, but now investment groups also form portfolios of antiquities.

The middle ground of museums between collectors and those who deal in antiquities has been ambiguous. For the most part artifacts on display are ripped from their context—generally because nobody knows it. Descriptive text may be kept to a minimum. An artifact is transformed into art, the viewer challenged to admire it alongside works of other eras. But attitudes have gradually changed. When I first researched the story of Sardis decades ago I was chastened for wanting to sully the reputation of a great American institution. Now the Met's archives are open to researchers. When I was a student, the J. Paul Getty Villa Museum in Malibu opened its doors in 1974 and began to scour the markets for notable antiquities under the leadership of an unprincipled head curator. Following a particularly notorious scandal in the 1990s, when the extent of its illegal collecting was exposed, the Getty has remade itself under the leadership of a new, more ethical administration. Stolen antiquities have been repatriated to their countries of origin.

Even the Met has jumped on the bandwagon. In my first year of graduate school the big news in Classical art was the Met's purchase of the so-called Euphronios krater, an elegant mixing bowl for wine, painted in the Athenian red-figure style with a scene depicting the Homeric passage that describes Sleep and Death carrying the dead warrior Sarpedon from the battlefield at Troy. It is certainly one of finest surviving works of Greek painting and was the first Greek or Roman antiquity to command a million-dollar price, $1.2 million to be exact. The vase was repatriated to Italy in 2006 after its place of discovery was indisputably determined by the unit of Italian police charged with investigating antiquities theft. Now we know that it was found in a tomb near Ceverteri. Although produced by Greeks, the vase was intended as an export product, one with significance to the Etruscan nobles who acquired such things.

But, you may be thinking, who cares? You may even, as I do, favor the return of emotion-charged objects, such as the Parthenon Marbles, to their country of origin. For Greece they have become a national symbol, although designed in antiquity as a monument to the achievements of Athens, only one of hundreds of city-states. And then again, surely the bulk of antiquities that reach market have no such significance and might as well be displayed in our homes, treasured as investments, or given to museums to commemorate our families' names. That is the argument made every few years by coin collectors who urge our State Department not to renew memoranda of understanding with those European and Middle Eastern countries where smuggling is rampant. What difference does a little coin make in the greater scheme of things?

But even the context of tiny things like coins matters, since in the aggregate they help historians to understand patterns of trade among ancient city-states and, since they are often found in large numbers as hoards, the date of their deposition can help us understand even political events and to date them. Still more important is the damage that those who loot antiquities, even coins, can do to archaeological sites. Typically, in a given year hundreds of cases of illicit digging are documented in Greece alone, in only one of its provinces. The severity of the situation intensified with the worsening financial conditions after 2005.

I will conclude with an example from my own experience, one that occurred within the context of an intensification of that financial crisis in 2015. That year we accidentally made one of the greatest archaeological discoveries of all-time: the grave of the Griffin Warrior. Several thousand objects of gold, silver, ivory, and semi-precious stones, compressed into a deposit of only a cubic meter. The fact that we were able to excavate this intact burial has enabled us to construct much of the belief system, conceptual and political, ca. 1450 B.C., at the very beginning of the Mycenaean civilization. None of this would have been possible had the grave been disturbed by looters. It was only because we found it intact that allowed us to examine the pattern of associations of the individual artifacts with each other. The artifacts we found would bring millions in the art market, but the information lost to history would have been inestimable.

Ironically, our discovery of the grave of the Griffin Warrior encouraged looting in the nearby field where we now have excavated two massive Mycenaean tholos (beehive) tombs since 2018. In 2018 when we uncovered the first of the two we found that the previous owners of the field we had legally expropriated had tried to break into one tomb unsuccessfully. We found the wrapper of a chocolate croissant with an expiration date of September 2015 under a large stone block that they had dislodged with a backhoe.

At the risk of sounding overly didactic—a privilege I might claim since I am a professor—it is worth considering what we in America can do to stop the destruction of what is, after all, a heritage that we hold in common with the rest of the world. Law enforcement is largely outside our control and in the hands of Interpol and the FBI. But education is within our purview. We can ask our museums to educate consumers by allowing them to learn the object-biographies of artifacts on display. And we can ourselves not contribute to the demand for antiquities by collecting even very small and apparently innocent pieces like coins. There are so many other things to collect, things that were made to be sold and traded and collected. As for me, I have chosen dolls made by refugees who left Turkey after 1922. But that's another story.

Jack Davis left Apple Creek, Ohio for Cincinnati in 1972 and made Clifton his home. As a professor of archaeology he directs research in Greece on behalf of the Department of Classics at the University of Cincinnati. Most recently, he and his wife, Sharon Stocker, have been excavating at the Palace of Nestor, an important Greek Bronze Age site discovered in 1939 by Literary Club member Carl Blegen.

5 Witness

JOSEPH J. DEHNER

NEVER had I been asked to witness what Gregor sought. Oh, I'd notarized wills and trusts I'd prepared for clients, instruments designed to control beyond life who gets what's left. I would witness my clients pausing, staring into oblivion, then inking often indecipherable markings above the line I pointed out. From his seaside estate, Gregor called me on a landline that September morning (he refused even to touch a cell phone). What he asked in a raspy voice like that of an asthmatic Orson Welles made me shiver. He asked me to witness death.

Gregor Rabotnikov III roomed with Dean Abernathy and me sophomore year at Dartmouth over fifty years ago. Our college years featured assassinations and Vietnam, Motown and the Stones, psychedelics and Richard Nixon. Gregor lived as though the Bolshevik Revolution never occurred. With a Saint Petersburg accent, he spoke in poetry and formal prose. He abjured beer. He played chess (I was no match), using a punch clock inherited from his father, who acquired it from a Soviet grandmaster who fled to Paris to escape Stalin's purges. His angular face was like a Modigliani. His thick black hair received a daily caress of Sweet Georgia Brown Hair Dressing Pomade. During college most of us sauntered about in faded corduroys and oxford blues. Gregor wore coat and tie to class, always with a signature gold pin of a

double-headed eagle sprouting an Orthodox cross. Gregor was a Romanov from his father's side, part of the branch who escaped with their wealth to France in 1917. From his mother's lineage, he was related to Franklin Pierce, fourteenth President of the United States (the only president from New Hampshire unless you count The West Wing's Jed Bartlet). On his bookstand was a pen and quill set President Pierce used to sign the Gadsden Purchase. Above his desk was an eighteenth-century icon of Saint Michael the Archangel.

One Sunday night in 1967, Gregor hosted a tasting in our room. "Cognac Maison Prunier," he invoked as a priest might start a service. A graceful flick of his left arm with a gold cufflink blessed a lavish charcuterie. With his right he poured generous splashes into crystal snifters. "Winston Churchill's favorite. A la santé," he toasted. We clinked and imbibed. Cognac conjured transubstantiation, and beyond midnight we shared innermost dreams. Years later I would learn that the bottle cost about what I paid for the clunker of a VW bug I used to drive between New Hampshire and my Cincinnati home.

After graduation we reconvened every five years at reunions. Gregor led our class contingent in the alumni parade, pumping a silver scepter of the Class of 1969, costumed in an outfit authentic to 1769, when Eleazar Wheelock founded Dartmouth to educate "Indian tribes of this land ... English Youth, and any others." The rest of us dressed in green polo shirts festooned with images of Bullwinkle J. Moose, whom we adopted as an honorary classmate. Over the years, waistlines expanded, hairlines receded like melting glaciers, and canes and golf carts assisted perambulation. Gregor appeared each time almost ageless (had he found Dorian Gray's mirror?), until he summoned me to lunch two years before his September phone call. We met in Boston, where I was the senior of the law firm's estate planning group, recently renamed the private wealth team. He greeted me at the door of Fox & The Knife. I remember it vividly now — he was deflating, shrinking, that was what struck me.

He asked me to be his executor.

"Of course," I said, then added without a smile, "How are you, seriously?"

He confided that he had amyotrophic lateral sclerosis, a disease made famous by Lou Gehrig. "I may have a couple years," he said. "I need you to make my estate plan as tight as a tuned tympano." He told how Eleonora left him five years ago for an Uber driver. Despite his efforts, she refused even to acknowledge his letters beseeching her to return.

I said I understood, though I couldn't really. It's one of those things lawyers say as a substitute for empathy. I had done well over the years by acting like a Carl Rogers psychiatrist — "I hear you saying...." It was so reassuring to clients.

"I have never been understood, old man," said Gregor. "We're not divorced. Only rendered asunder by love's treachery."

"I understand," I said.

I took notes in my pocket binder as Gregor dictated the plan, leaving nothing to Eleonora except for two ancient paintings that she detested. These held sufficient market value that I assured him it was highly likely that a probate judge would restrict her inheritance to this largesse. If she contested the will, she could forfeit even the two despised art works.

My assistant and I witnessed the signing a week later. Other than that, I did not hear from Gregor again until the September call.

"Witness death?" I feared I might gasp the words but maintained composure. I hate the idea of death, fear it, want nothing to do with it. I was programmed by parochial school nuns and priests to believe life is sacred, and this meant avoiding death in all ways possible and certainly not assisting it.

"Oh, old man," he said, "I face eternity. A second opinion confirmed yesterday that brain cancer will take me before ALS can claim the credit. I will be a vegetable in a month — or worse, and then...."

I didn't know what to say, so I said nothing.

"Can you get to Hampton the morning of October 8? I am inviting Dean to be there with us."

I scrolled my phone calendar. "Yes, of course. But ... join for what?"

"I know you think me a bit ditsy, but it is the day that President Pierce died — in 1869, one hundred years after Dartmouth began. October 8 will be my turn."

Stunned, I was tempted to backtrack but instead sputtered, "Gregor, none of us knows...."

He interrupted. "Yes, that is the point of it. This way *I* decide. The new statute, you know."

I knew what he referred to — a recently passed law in the state whose official motto was Live Free or Die. To me it meant Live Free, as to die is not a proper choice. The statute allowed voluntary, self-administered suicide for those with a terminal illness, with strict conditions and very specific procedures. There could be no assistance by anyone for the person aiming to self-terminate. My religious upbringing branded suicide as a mortal sin. And the one thing I vowed I would never do as an attorney was to violate the law. Over the years, that meant never being put in a position where I could even be accused of that. Reputation is all in the law business. And what if word got around that as an attorney, I was available not only to prepare estate plans but to expedite their maturation?

I quivered. The statute required two witnesses to attend a self-administered death but did not define "witnessing." Could I become a criminal by accepting this invitation, be disbarred, jailed? Would I become a headline? The acceptance burrowed into my brain like a tick on a leg ready to inject Lyme Disease. Should I pluck it out with tweezers? Backtrack?

I called Dean. An Episcopal priest, he became Dean Dean when he rose to be rector of a cathedral. He confirmed that he would be there to pray and witness on October 8. No one could "assist" Gregor, except that a New Hampshire licensed physician could lawfully prescribe the fatal doses, and a pharmacist could fulfill the prescriptions if handed directly to the physician for delivery to the death desiring patient. Two doctors must swear that the person suffered from a terminal illness for at least three months before the chosen day of death. The terminator must sign a statement twice — within thirty and fifteen days of the deadline. Two witnesses to death must sign a statement that the individual stated his willing desire to proceed on the chosen date.

"Our role? Aren't you concerned?" I asked, immediately ashamed that I was acting the lawyer, thinking more about myself than about Gregor.

"You tell me. You're the attorney," Dean replied. "It's my vocation to be present for death."

"I understand" was my reply. "I suppose we can sit and witness."

As October 8 approached, I scoured the statute again and again. I brooded over "assist." I struggled with what words mean as an attorney thinks about words — not what I personally think they mean but instead what a prosecutor, judge or jury might twist them to mean. The statute was a compromise between impossible extremes — not unlike what the country had come to on so many issues. Right-to-lifers brooked no escape from life is sacred, labeling proposal sponsors as murderers. Opponents declared — You wouldn't force a dog to endure what some people face. Give me liberty or let me die, trumpeted the Patrick Henry Society in promoting the bill.

The final version, which the Governor allowed to become law without her signature, was a muddle of provisions and exceptions, clauses and sub-clauses. The definitions section ran three pages, but there was no definition for "witness" or "assist."

I had not known Gregor to be religious in college or how he thought about suicide. We didn't ask in college because then we were immortal. Five decades later, we didn't pry into spiritual matters but freely shared troubles with prostates and hearts, hearing and hips. I attended mass occasionally but counted myself as more attune to "Who am I to judge?" than to what our Archbishop demanded.

I resolved to be there. Gregor had no children or other family of his own to surround him as in the Middle Ages, when a person summoned loved ones to join for the final bedside. We would witness only — no assistance. When the end came, Dean and I would sign a statement. I could call the funeral home and inform the coroner. This should work.

Dean and I drove to the estate that morning, arriving at precisely 10:00 A.M. as Gregor specified. A bow-tied butler met us at the enormous oaken door, greeting Dean as Dean Abernathy and me as Counselor. He led us to a dining room, where laid out on a table runner were two vials, a crystal glass, and two straws.

Gregor motored forward in a wheelchair and said, "Gentlemen."

The butler asked, "Shall I, sir?"

Gregor nodded with a slight dip of his head, and the butler bowed slightly and walked backward to exit.

"Thank you for coming," Gregor mumbled. He steered the wheelchair toward the end of a lengthy antique dining room table with its gold claws clutching a Persian carpet. Dean arose to help align the wheelchair closer to the table, but Gregor said, "No. No assistance." With a slight smile, "None required."

We conversed. Yes, travel went well. Yes, families are fine, except a daughter is getting divorced, a son is in rehab, Sally had a stent inserted.

"You read the instructions," Gregor said. "They are for my protection and yours."

I asked Gregor to confirm to Dean and me that he truly wished to proceed of his own voluntary act, as the statute required of us.

He said in a clear voice, "Yes."

He stretched toward a vial. I could see the label's brand and Morphine Oral Solution printed on it. His right hand quivered. His left arm was immobile. He tilted his head toward the table.

Can I help? flashed through my head, and immediately my brain ordered no.

Shaking, Gregor's right hand struggled to turn the cap clockwise. Very slow was the twist. The cap released. The vial almost spilled, but he clutched it and poured the fluid into the crystal glass. He deeply exhaled. He stared across the table for a moment, then tilted his head to a straw and sipped.

"They say I will be drowsy but ready for the next drink in about thirty minutes," he said. He looked at the grandfather clock as it chimed the half hour.

We held silence, as when entering an ancient cathedral and the organ's not playing and tourists aren't around, the still of moonlight, the quiet of a mountaintop climbed and only the view speaks.

Fifteen minutes into it, my cell phone buzzed. I had neglected to silence it. I glared at the screen to see a local number.

I muffled, "Yes?" It was Gregor's butler.

"Sir, Mr. Rabotnikov gave me your number. You see, I am carrying out his order for a final purchase with his credit card. The proprietor wishes to speak with Mr. Rabotnikov to authorize the expense."

I cogitated. Reasoning that it was not death "assistance" to connect the butler with Gregor, I clicked on the speaker icon and held the phone next to Gregor's right ear. He looked drowsy, but his eyes were alert. I explained.

"Put him on," Gregor rasped.

The proprietor introduced himself and seemed satisfied that Gregor was Gregor. "Do you wish to make these purchases?" he asked.

"Yes."

"Thank you, sir. Sorry for disturbing." Click.

That afternoon the butler apologized for not warning me this might happen. "You see, he insisted on having certain gifts delivered today. At six hundred eighty euros a bottle, the order came to over twenty thousand dollars."

The grandfather clock struck eleven deep-pitched tones. Gregor had slumped after the phone interruption. He came alert with the eleventh tone. He looked at us. "Thank you, gentlemen. It means so much."

We nodded without a word, ensconced in something we could not fully fathom.

He edged close to the table, straining to avoid slipping from an elevated cushion. The right hand extended toward the second vial. I could not read the small print. Fingers tried to twist the top of the small container. This time the vial resisted. He seemed angered, glancing at his left hand as though ordering it to assist, but it refused. The right hand tried again. Again failure. He winced. A third attempt. The vial lurched free of his hand and almost rolled off the table.

"May I?" I thought of asking but suppressed the thought.

He tried a fourth time. Again, the vial refused the right hand's entreaty.

I felt his desperation. A tear was welling in his right eye.

Witness, assist, what can I do? What will I do? I resolved to stay fast in my chair.

Gregor's right hand crumpled into a fist and thumped the table, as though embarrassed to fail its master. His head sagged. I thought he would collapse.

Dean's head was bowed, his lips moving in silent prayer.

I rose and took the vial. I twisted off the cap, poured the contents into the crystal glass, and placed the straw near his head.

Gregor's eyes met mine, glowing with what I believe was unspoken thanks.

He sipped.

The next hour was spent informing the authorities, summoning the funeral home, waiting. I began to wonder if I had done the right thing and troubled over what would happen next.

The coroner herself arrived first. She inspected the empty vials and sniffed the crystal glass, wincing. "He wrote me a week ago about this," she said.

I jumped when the door knocker summoned the butler.

An officer entered in dark green uniform with two yellow stripes atop each sleeve. All business, he whispered in the hall with the coroner. Dean and I stood alongside the table, where Gregor sat lifeless at the end. I suppressed a tremble.

The policeman entered the dining room and said, "Gentlemen." He waved his hand to invite us to sit. He glared at the empty vials. He picked up one and ridged his finger around its groove. "You were here as witnesses?" he asked.

We confirmed this was true.

He asked how it had gone, but before one of us responded, he added, "Mr. Rabotnikov informed us you would attend today - as witnesses, witnesses only. I take it that is all he asked of you."

I was the first to respond, "Yes." Dean nodded. It was the truth — to the question asked.

The officer seemed ready to ask the next question, one I dreaded.

Instead, he put down the vial, asked us for the signed statement that Gregor had confirmed his decision that day, and exited without more.

When we returned to the hotel, the concierge handed me a note. Gregor thanked me for handling the estate. As executor I would ensure that Eleonora would receive only her two hated paintings. The rest would be divided between Dartmouth and the revitalization of Ukraine after Russia's invasion.

Dean and I communed for a quiet dinner. To our surprise, the waiter did not ask for drink orders. He placed snifters before us and uncorked a bottle of Cuvee Number 1 Winston Churchill Maison Prunier.

"A la santé," we toasted.

Joe Dehner drove a Volkswagen through the Soviet Union during college, then traveled to 80 countries during a 50-year legal career. A past president of the Literary Club, he and his wife the Rev. Noël Julnes-Dehner have twin daughters and three granddaughters, all living in Cincinnati.

6 | *To Defend or Not?*

PHILIP M. DILLER, M.D.

I. WILLIAM PENN'S HOLY EXPERIMENT

THERE are likely some of us who can say that our ancestors were encouraged to come to America by William Penn, an influential Quaker who founded Pennsylvania and Philadelphia in the colonial era. This is true for my father and mother's ancestors who were Amish, Mennonite and Quakers. The setting for this story is Berks County in south-eastern Pennsylvania. The time period is 1700-1765 and involves an Amish community, three native American tribes, the Delaware, Shawnee and Iroquois, and the French, and English. My initial investigation led to troubling questions that pulled me into this distant past ten generations ago. An early family member who researched and wrote the initial story gave this advice, "to understand such a narrative, one ought to be familiar with the environments and the manners and customs of the Indians at that time."

William Penn was the oldest son of Sir William Penn Sr., who was an admiral in the Royal Navy, a politician in the House of Lords, and responsible for bringing back exiled Prince Charles from the Netherlands to assume the throne as Charles II in 1660. Admiral William

Penn had provided supplies from his personal funds worth eleven thousand pounds to the Royal Navy in the 1660s. This had never been paid back by the Crown, and by 1680 that debt had grown to sixteen thousand pounds. William Penn the son spent considerable effort over ten months in 1680 negotiating, working through parliament, and overcoming objections before he finally secured a royal charter granting him proprietorship of land in the New World on March 4, 1681 to cover the debt. Penn suggested the new colony be named Sylvania (Latin for "forest"), but Charles II insisted he add Penn-Sylvania in honor of Penn's father.

Before 1680 Penn traveled and spoke out on religious liberty both in England and Europe and with the charter in hand immediately began to promote the colony targeting specific religious groups in England and Europe that frequently suffered persecution from the State churches. In addition, he highlighted the economic opportunities that awaited those who would settle there. Because of his personal experience of persecution as a Quaker and witnessing intolerance for people of other faiths, the new colony would be founded on very specific principles of religious liberty. Those principles encompassed what came to be called "the Holy Experiment." As he said at that time, "I desire that the example may be set up to the nations, that there may be room there (in the new colony), though not here, for such a holy experiment." These principles included free and fair trial by jury, freedom from unjust imprisonment, fair elections, civil discourse, religious liberty, tolerance in matters of conscience, and, lastly, pacifism. He communicated to those already settled there that "you shall be governed by laws of your own making and live as a free and sober industrious people." To the native Americans living in the region, the Lanape, he reassured them that they would be able to continue to hunt and fish in the land and they should live together as neighbors and friends.

Who were the Lenape when William Penn secured his charter to begin the new colony? The Lenape, meaning "original people," first came into the region in the early 17th century. They were part of the Algonquin family of Indians and originally lived in land west of the Mississippi to the Rockies. The Lenape entered the Ohio Valley and, joining forces with the fierce Iroquois, drove out the Alligewi Indians who were living there. After securing and exploring the territory the Lenape decided to live around the four great rivers: the Susquehanna, Potomac, Delaware, and Hudson. They were subdivided into three clans: the Munsee, the Unami, and the Unalachtigo. The Munsee, most relevant to this story, were the most war-like and spoke dialects different from the other clans. It was the Munsee who settled in the area around the mouth of the Lehigh River northward into New York and New Jersey, and they also occupied the territory of the Blue Mountains, where the source of the Delaware River and Berks County, PA are located.

The Shawnee from South Carolina and Tennessee were invited in 1694 by the Munsee clan to settle in the Delaware river basin. Together they created multiple villages for the Shawnee in southeast Pennsylvania. Thus the Delaware and the Shawnee were the primary Indian groups living in the region between 1700 and 1765.

The Seneca, one of the tribes that eventually comprised the Iroquois Confederation, played an important part of this story. After driving out the Alligewi, the Seneca settled more north around the Great Lakes and in New York. In time the Seneca became jealous and sought to dominate the Lenape. Through a series of wars with the Lenape, the Seneca to gain advantage joined with the Mohawks, Oneida, Onondaga, and Cayouga to form the "Five Nation" Iroquois Confederation. In 1717 the Tuscarawas, displaced from North Carolina and Virginia, joined and created the Iroquois Six Nation Confederation. Eventually the Iroquois subjugated the Lenape. As a consequence, by 1700 the Lenape were forbidden to go to war or to sell land without approval from the Iroquois, and it was the Iroquois who served as the negotiators for the Lenape with the emerging white settlers. This arrangement would prove problematic for the Lenape.

William Penn called the Lenape the Delaware, because he first met them on the banks of the Delaware River. What were the beliefs, values and norms of the Delaware? From the English perspective, and even into subsequent generations, the Indians were viewed as inferior, simple, uneducated, unenlightened, and capable of torture, cruelty and were warring "Savages." In reality, this was far from the truth. A number of Moravian missionaries who had lived and labored among the Delaware Indians for over 30 years recorded their observations. Moravian John Heckerwelder wrote the following:

> "The Indian considers himself as being created by an all-powerful, wise and benevolent Great Spirit; all that he possesses, all that he enjoys, he looks upon as given to him for his use by the Great Spirit who gave him life. He, therefore, believes it is his duty to adore and worship his Creator and benefactor; he acknowledges with gratitude in his past favors, thanks him for present blessings, and solicits the continuation of his goodwill.

> "They believe the Great Spirit made the Earth and all that it contains for the common good of mankind. . . . It was not for the benefit of a few, but for all. Everything was given in common for the sons of men. From this principle, hospitality flows as from its source. With them, it is not a virtue, but a strict duty. Hence, they are never in search of excuses to avoid giving, or freely supply their neighbors' wants from the stock prepared for their own use. They are hospitable to all, without exception, and will always share with each other . . . even to their last morsel. [They would never be accused of] neglecting their duty by not satisfying the wants of the stranger, the sick or the needy.
>
> "They treat each other with civility and show much affection on meeting after an absence. They are not quarrelsome, and are always on their guard, so as not to offend each other. They do not fight with each other; they say that fighting is only for dogs and beasts... Contrary to the general supposition the Indian was not cruel by nature. His cruelty was confined to the times when he was on the warpath."

This was how the Indians treated each other in times of peace, and they welcomed William Penn's overtures of peace.

Penn's colony was one of the greatest anomalies of its day: an English colony that forswore the use of force against native peoples, but instead promoted peace and traded with them under fair and open terms. Penn's willingness to trade freely with the local Indians extended to providing them firearms and ammunition. In the absence of a militia or any organized form of self-defense among the colonists, the peace principles of the settlers offered the Indian a guarantee that they had nothing to fear from Penn and those settling in the colony. The Iroquois, Delaware and Shawnee became an effective well-armed defensive shield for Pennsylvania, and the Quaker province could safely dispense with a militia.

It became known among native groups that Pennsylvania offered a refuge from wars, and Penn's colony became a haven for the Indians as much as it was for the European immigrants. This ethos worked amazingly well, and it made Pennsylvania a successful, growing colony in English North America in the first half of the 18th century. The absence of warfare, the lack of military obligation for the colonists, religious toleration, and the comparatively cheap and fertile soil of the colony combined to attract thousands of immigrants, primarily from the lowlands of Scotland, northern Ireland, and the southwestern region of Germany known as the Palatinate. Following the end of the war in Europe of the Spanish succession in 1713, immigration accelerated, increasing the population 150 per cent each decade over the next 35 years. Prosperity kept pace with population to such a degree that 18th century Pennsylvania became known as the best poor man's country on earth.

After Penn died in 1718, James Logan, another Quaker, was designated by Penn's sons Thomas and John to oversee and manage their business operations in Pennsylvania, and Logan became the most powerful man in the colony. Between 1721 and 1732 Logan recognized the Iroquois were the likeliest group to provide defense and to serve as the diplomatic representatives for the Delaware and the Shawnee living alongside colonists in eastern Pennsylvania. Negotiating with the Iroquois simplified Logan's ability to purchase additional land for Penn's sons, and the Six Nation Iroquois was willing to sell the land where the Delaware and Shawnee had lived for over a hundred years. He was able to buy in quantity and then resell it to the white settlers at a significant profit that William Penn never saw. William Penn had died in debt, and when he had secured the charter in 1681 little did he know what would happen just 70 years later that his colony would be where the First World War began.

One of the seeds that would disrupt life for the Delaware and Shawnee two decades later occurred in 1737. James Logan and the Penn sons succeeded in buying more land known as the "Walking Purchase" that included Berks County. This was a major land fraud, and it cheated the Delaware out of nearly 750,000 acres near where the Lehigh and Delaware rivers join. The Iroquois were complicit in the fraud and prevented the Delaware and Shawnee from making any effective protest. This forced the Delaware who had peacefully lived among the settlers for over 70 years to move west to the Susquehanna Valley. In 1754 the Delaware and Shawnee would be displaced again when the Iroquois sold the area of the Susquehanna Valley in the Albany purchase, causing them to move even further west.

II. THE ENGLISH AND FRENCH APPROACH TO SETTLING AMERICA AND IMMIGRATION OF TWO AMISH FAMILIES

In the 1740s the region of Pennsylvania 60 miles beyond Philadelphia was the frontier. It was when France and England were on a collision course having different intentions and approaches to settle in America. The British were primarily located along the Atlantic coast and made inroads as far as Philadelphia and "Wills Creek," today Cumberland, Maryland. The English sought to possess the land. The French had been in the interior for well over a hundred years coming down through the Great Lakes. They were intent on building trading relationships with the Indians around the Great Lakes, into the Ohio Valley, and down the Mississippi all the way to New Orleans. They were more interested in trading than purchasing land. They traveled from their primary base settlements in Quebec [1608], Montreal [1642], Green Bay [1634] and Detroit [1701] around the Great Lakes and down to Mobile [1702] and New Orleans [1718]. "New France" was three to four times the land mass occupied by the British in North America, but was not populated by the French, such that by the 1750s, the British population in North America outnumbered the French twenty to one. The French enjoyed peaceful relations with the Indians, adopting the policy of recognizing them as naturalized Frenchmen (citizens) when they were converted to Catholicism by the Jesuits. They had little presence in Pennsylvania in the first half of the 1700s.

Two families, the Hochstetlers1 and the Hertzlers, members of the Amish community from the Palatinate region of southwestern Germany, immigrated to Pennsylvania in the 1730-1740s. Both families historically originated from Switzerland. In the late 1600s the Anabaptists were targets of persecution by the Swiss government. They were not considered citizens of the state and thus were unable to own land but still had to pay taxes and were often put into prison. As a result of this persecution many of the Anabaptist immigrated to other parts of Europe, particularly Alsace in France, Holland, and the Palatinate.

The Hochstetler and the Hertzler families first immigrated to the Palatinate region between 1700-1720. Jacob Hertzler was born in 1704 in Switzerland about 40 miles northeast of Bern before his parents immigrated. His family were Anabaptists farmers. Jacob Hochstetler was born in 1712 in the Highlands of Germany along the Rhine River in the Palatinate. Around the time these two Jacobs were born, there was a big rift going on between the Anabaptists, one faction led by Alsatian Mennonite Jacob Amman and the other faction led by the Swiss Mennonite Hans Reist. The followers of Jacob Amman became known as the Amish and dropped the Mennonite name to indicate they were more strict believers in not conforming to this world (Rom 12:2). The Amish urged the shunning of members who were excommunicated from the church, and advocated returning to the customs of Anabaptist leader Menno Simons a hundred years before—married men wearing full beards, using hooks and eyes instead of buttons on men's clothes. The division of the Amish and the Mennonites never healed and continues to today. The Hertzlers and Hochstetlers were Amish.

The Palatinate was not much better because of the four major wars in the period 1700-1748 fought there by the kings of France, Germany, and Spain: The War of Spanish Succession (1701 to 1714), the War of Spain

(1718 to 1720), the War of Polish Succession (1733 to 1738), and the War of Austrian Succession (1740 to 1748). The result of these wars led to recurring loss of population and an opportunity for Anabaptist refugees to live on the vacated land. This region was more tolerant of Anabaptists, and it was while eking out an existence in the Palatinate that Hertzler was sanctioned as a bishop of one of the Amish refugee congregations. Because of the ever-present threat of war, the region was not a stable or safe place, leading to the immigration of the Amish to America.

The first Amish came to America in the 1730s and began to settle in Berks and Lancaster Counties, PA. They began to send back encouraging reports of the ability to worship in liberty and of the economic opportunity to improve their lot in life. A letter from 1737 by one of the previous immigrants from the Palatinate said this, "If you are in Germany, Switzerland or Alsace and have no opportunities to follow our sect on account of the government, and you care for the salvation of your souls, in this country, here in Pennsylvania is a very good living." In 1737 Swiss Anabaptist landowner Durrs Thommen wrote, "I have low taxes to fulfill the requirement of the government, and we have good liberties in this land in all matters. There are many sects here, such as Reformed, Lutheran, Amish. Seventh day and Sunday Baptist, Mennonites, Pietist, and also Catholics. And all the nationalities are friendly and helpful to each other, as also the "wild people" or Indians are very friendly to the civilized people."

It was in 1738 when 36-year-old Jacob Hochstetler immigrated to the Philadelphia area, accompanied by his wife (name not known), and five-year-old daughter Barbara (b. ~1733) and three-year-old son John (b. ~1735). They departed from London on the ship *Nancy* arriving in Philadelphia on November 9th, 1738. Three months later (February 27, 1739) Jacob purchased one hundred acres close to other Amish families in Bern Township located in Berks County. The land was near the Northkill Creek that flows into the Schuylkill River that runs into the Delaware River through Philadelphia. Jacob later purchased another 130 acres and gave some of this to his son John when he married and started his family. Purchasing land was accomplished by putting a down payment on the property, noting key landmarks defining the boundaries, such as a big tree, a creek, or a large field stone, and followed by estimating the acreage. Once purchased, it would be surveyed to finalize the original deed. It was determined that Jacob had purchased a total of about 250 acres.

Jacob and his wife and the surrounding community built their homes, clearing the woods for planting corn, peach and apple trees, and raising animals. They also used their guns for hunting wild game. In time, Jacob and his wife had four additional children --e Jacob Jr. (?), Joseph (1744), Christian (1746), and then a young daughter (Franey?).

By 1740 about 30 Amish families had settled in the Northkill Creek region in Berks County at thc base of the Blue Mountains. They gathered in people's homes or barns to worship, not seeing a need for a building solely used for church. They believed that buildings should be simple, practical, and meant to serve specific functional purposes. The families desired officially sanctioned leadership, and sent out a call to the European Amish community for an "ordained" bishop to help them organize and teach principles of the faith. This is what brought Jacob Hertzler to America with his second wife, Catherine, and two of his children from his first wife, John and also Catherine. They subsequently had seven additional children. Hertzler arrived on September 9, 1749, coming over on the ship *Saint Andrew.* The war of Austrian succession fought in the Palatinate prompted a large immigration of members of the Amish community (some 400 in 1749) who settled in Berks and Lancaster counties.

Bishop Hertzler was a strong supporter of the Amish articles of faith, stressing the relationship that people had to God through Christ, and was known as a strict disciplinarian who defended the Amish fellowship's standards of "not conforming to the world." The Northkill Amish was the first organized, bishop-led Amish congregation in America, making Jacob Hertzler the first Amish bishop in America and the Hochstetlers one of the original founding families.

The Hertzlers, like the Hochstetlers, were able to secure land, begin farming and start raising their family. Because of the custom of marrying only within the Amish community, the children from the 30 families in this first Amish community ended up marrying. Jacob Hochstetler's oldest son John married Catherine Hertzler, and they lived on an adjoining farm that looked down on Jacob Hochstetler's house and farm buildings.

These families enjoyed religious tolerance and were able to build both spiritual and material wealth. They were excellent farmers, appreciating the importance of restoring the ground as part of their farming techniques. They were frugal and industrious, and they became self-sufficient with a ready market for their products in growing Philadelphia. In an area where threats of war were virtually non-existent, they could live "separate from the world." Anabapists historically did not engage in politics. Though they had firearms, they did not believe in using weapons to defend themselves. Much of this dated back to the Anapaptist confession of faith adopted at the Schleithein Conference in 1527, where they agreed to non-resistance, believing that "the sword is ordained of God outside the perfection, which is in Christ, and shall not be used to resist evil."

But life in the New World paradise was to change in the decade of the 1750s. The war experience on the European continent between England and France would spread to North America.

III. BUILD-UP TO THE FRENCH AND INDIAN WAR

With the acceleration of immigration from the 1730s to 1750s by the English to the colonies came the desire for more land, leading to westward expansion and opening of trade with the Indians. During this period beginning in 1745, the Anglo-Americans sought to block the regular supplying of New France/Canada by attacking and capturing the

French fortified town of Louisburg on Cape Breton Isle. This in turn caused a sharp decline in French trading with the Indians around the Great Lakes and created opportunities for English traders from Pennsylvania and Virginia to establish trading posts in southwest Pennsylvania and Ohio to compete with the French. The French found these new trading posts intolerable because they brought economic harm and undermined their alliances with the Indians. In June, 1752 the governor-general of New France decided in response to destroy the trading post at Pickawillany on the Great Miami River, near Piqua, Ohio, and encourage the Miami Indians of the region to return to Maumee. Five traders were taken captive, one killed, along with the chief of the Miami tribe, Memskia. The Ottawa Indians who participated in this raid ate the hearts of the killed trader and the Indian chief in a ritual ceremony. The Pennsylvania Assembly had no intent to rebuild Pickawillany or to defend the other trading posts. The Miami Indians of the region got the message and resumed trading with the French.

The Ohio Company supported by the Virginia House of Burgesses continued its trading efforts in southwestern Pennsylvania. French Governor Duquesne responded by fortifying western Pennsylvania with four forts built in 1753 and 1754: Fort Presque Isle (Erie, PA), Fort LeBoeuf (Watersford, PA), Fort Machault (Franklin, PA) and Fort Duquesne (Forks of the Ohio, Pittsburgh, PA). Governor Dinwiddie of Virginia responded by sending 21-year-old surveyor George Washington to gather intel on the French's fortifying efforts. Washington's report was shared by Governor Dinwiddie with the Duke of Newcastle and other leaders of King George II's government, who interpreted this as a defiant attempt by the French to seize lands that belonged to the King of England established by the Virginia Colony Charter in 1609. Dinwiddie received the authority to demand the French withdraw from the region, build English forts in the King's territory, and if necessary, evacuate the French by force. He asked George Washington to be his emissary to communicate this to the French. Washington traveled to Fort LeBoeuf in January 1754, meeting with the French captain who declined the demand to withdraw, saying it was not his decision to make.

Washington returned to Dinwiddie, who communicated the response to the Duke of Newcastle, who instructed Dinwiddie to build an English fort (Fort Prince George) with all haste and fortify it with 200 militia men. Dinwiddie once again chose Washington to lead this effort. By April 1754 Washington secured supplies and recruited 159 poorly trained militia. Upon arriving at Will's Creek he learned that the French had already built Fort Duquesne at the Forks of the Ohio. He traveled 60 miles south of Fort Duquesne to build Fort Necessity at Great Meadows, PA. There Indian scouts informed Washington that the French were only five miles away and planning to move toward him. Rather than wait, Washington took the initiative and traveled through the night in heavy rain, encountering the French as they were gathering for breakfast. Shots were fired in a brief skirmish, Washington's group had one killed and three wounded while the French had 14 casualties of the 35-member French brigade. One of the wounded, French Commander Jumonville, an emissary of the French governor, started to deliver his message: "The English were to evacuate the land of the King of France or suffer the consequences." As he was communicating this, a Delaware half-King in Washington's party, Tanaghrisson, stepped up and said, "Father, you are not dead yet," and with his tomahawk split open Jumonville's skull, killing him. With that the accompanying Indians proceeded to kill, scalp, and strip the clothes from all but one of the remaining French survivors. Washington, startled and inexperienced, did little to stop it.

Washington and his group returned to Fort Necessity. Over the next five weeks Washington deliberated whether he should attack Fort Duquesne. He sought help from the Delaware, but they chose not to join forces with him. Despite this, Washington moved to attack, unaware that a large number of French and Indian re-enforcements had reached Fort Duquesne. On July 3rd 1754, the French sent out 600 regular troops with 100 Indians toward Fort Necessity, which provided little defense. The French/Indian troops killed 30 of Washington's men while seriously wounding another 70. The next morning, miraculously for Washington and his men, the French commander offered a cease-fire and terms of surrender. Washington readily accepted and signed the terms, not knowing that in the document was an admission that he and his men had assassinated Captain Jumonville, the emissary of King Louis XV. Killing an emissary of the king was an act of war and could be used as justification by the French to declare war on England. In this instance the Indians did not inflict further casualties, and Washington and his surviving men were able to make it back to Virginia.

The British king and the Duke of Newcastle's response to the loss of Fort Necessity and the failure to take Fort Duquesne was to send British troops from England to Virginia under the command of Major General George Braddock. Braddock devised a comprehensive plan to respond to the French in North America, including capturing and occupying New France. One part of the strategic plan included dislodging the French from Fort Duquesne with Braddock personally leading the attack. In the spring of 1755 Braddock arrived in Virginia with 1,400 seasoned British troops and began preparation for the siege of Fort Duquesne. The colonies of Virginia, Maryland and North Carolina contributed another 1,000 men. Braddock traveled to Will's Creek, building Fort Cumberland there.

The Delaware, Shawnee, and Seneca Indians were eager to help Braddock's effort and brought maps of Fort Duquesne. They were also interested in gauging Braddock's intent and willingness to help them gain independence from the Iroquois and reclaim their hunting lands. Braddock was convinced he did not need their help, ignored the map, and saw them as inferior savages who should not inherit the land. The Indians leaders informed Braddock, "if they might not have liberty to live on the land, then they would not fight for it." Braddock later told Pennsylvania commissioner Benjamin Franklin, "Savages may indeed be a formidable enemy to your raw militia; but upon the King's regular and disciplined troops, Sir, it is impossible for them to make any impact." Respectfully hearing Braddock's intent, the Delaware and Shawnee withdrew and joined the French at Fort Duquesne.

It took Braddock six weeks to move his troops on newly built log roads to south of Fort Duquesne. They easily dispatched the few Indians they met, continuing to build up his impression that the force he was facing was no match for his troops. The French commander had sent out 900 men, including 617 Indians (Ottawa, Delaware, Shawnees, Seneca), 254 Canadian militiamen, and trained French troops to intercept Braddock's lead army. Early in the battle, the French commander was killed by a long-range shot, causing confusion among the trained French troops and the militiamen, but the Indians needed no direction and took their positions covered by natural vegetation. They began to easily pick off the red-coats, and within three hours the Indians and French troops killed two thirds of the 1,650 men in Braddock's army. Braddock was shot in the back, and his army began to retreat, carrying him on a munitions cart. Braddock died in route, and Washington, his one surviving aide, had him buried beneath the log road. Washington's uniform had four bullet holes in it and two horses were shot out from underneath him in the battle.

Colonel Dunbar, who took over command, was so demoralized that he retreated to Philadelphia in July to winter the British troops, even though he had 2,000 fresh troops that could have easily taken Fort Duquesne because the Indians were no longer there. The outcome of Braddock's defeat — the retreat of the British army leaving Pennsylvania defenseless — was all the Delaware and Shawnee needed to advance their goal of reclaiming their independence and their lands that the Iroquois had sold out from under them.

IV. A SERIES OF MASSACRES (1755-1758)

The Delaware and Shawnee were now firmly allied with the French, and the English were their enemy. The lands that the Delaware and the Shawnee targeted for reclaiming were those lands sold with the Walking Purchase of 1737 (eastern Pennsylvania) and the Albany Purchase 1754 (Susquehanna valley) Their goal was to induce the settlers to leave, using tactics of war honed over the previous one hundred-plus years. The first massacre occurred on Oct 16, 1755 at Penn's Creek in Snyder County, three months after Braddock's defeat, where six families were attacked over two days, leaving 13 dead including men, old women and infants. Eleven were taken captive. The Delaware were responsible. Over the next three years the Delaware and Shawnee would conduct raids on unsuspecting families, often known to the perpetrators. In the book, "The Indian Wars of Pennsylvania," there are recorded over 80 individual raids that resulted in 700 dead or taken captive in the first six months. The approach was similar: scout out the potential family, wait patiently for the surprise opportunity either day or night, kill swiftly using a tomahawk to crush the skull, shooting with a gun, or slashing the neck with knife; take scalps, select captives, and retreat as quickly as possible. Some captives arriving at the Indian village were made to run the gauntlet, a small number were tortured and burned at the stake in front of other captives, and the fortunate were adopted into an Indian family and treated as if they were native Indians.

These raids led to panic. Many families left the area for safer locations, but many stayed, even though it would take months for the Pennsylvania assembly to respond and shore up their defenses. It took concerned citizens bringing mangled dead bodies to Philadelphia on carts with placards reading, "The result of Quaker policies," for the legislature to raise taxes to fund a defense plan and be moved to take action. In 1756, 21 forts and 19 blockhouses in eight counties were constructed under the direction of Commissioner Benjamin Franklin in southeastern Pennsylvania. They were to serve as safe places for settlers and also as a buffer to Philadelphia 60 to 80 miles away. It was also in 1756 that the Pennsylvania Legislature passed the Scalp Act, authorizing payment for Indian scalps taken by the settlers.

However, these forts were not well fortified nor staffed with militia and in some instance became easy targets. The Northkill Fort was located in Berks County where the Hertzlers and Hochstetlers lived. Berks County was a target of the Delaware and the Shawnee with over 300 killed from 1755-1758 beginning a month after the first Indian raid at Penn's Creek. For those living in the Northkill area of Berks County, the families attacked by raiding Indians in the area were part of the larger community and acquaintances of the Hertzlers and the Hochstetlers.

THE HOCHSTETLER MASSACRE

The Northkill community was quiet after the June 1757 massacre of the Meyer family, until Monday evening September 19 when young people from the neighborhood gathered at the house of Jacob Hochstetler to assist in paring and slicing apples for drying. After the young people returned to their homes, the family retired to bed. About the time they were asleep, the dog began to bark awakening young Jacob, who went to the door and upon opening it was shot in the leg. He saw the Indians, realized they were being attacked, and managed to close and lock the door before the Indians could enter. The rest of the family rose, keeping the house dark. Looking out the windows they saw a group of eight to ten Indians (Delaware and Shawnee) standing near the bake oven about 20 feet south of the house. The Hochstetlers had plenty of guns and ammunition. With four shooters available and being good shots, the family would be able to put up a good defense. Joseph and Christian picked up their guns. Seeing this, the father Jacob, firmly believing in non-resistance, would not give consent to defend with the guns. The boys pleaded with him to use the guns, but Jacob said it was not right to take the life of another, even to save one's own life. (Joseph later claimed the family could have been saved if allowed to use the guns to defend themselves because the Indians always took cover when fired upon.)

The Indians chose to burn the house with the family inside. As the fire spread through the house the family moved to the root cellar where through the night they were able to use cider to control the flames. The oldest son John who lived nearby saw the fire and hid his wife and his four-year-old son Jacob in a thicket of brush a quarter mile from the house, and then ventured close to see what was happening.

At daybreak, it appeared the Indians had left, but a young warrior, Tom Lions, who knew the family, had stayed behind to gather peaches for his breakfast. As they emerged through a cellar window, Lions sounded the alarm to his fellow Indians. The mother being a fleshly woman had difficulty getting out through the window, and young, wounded Jacob shot in the leg, also needed assistance. Once out, the family was surrounded except for Joseph, who being fleet-footed ran up the hill into the woods initially eluding two Indians who gave chase. In time he chose to stay near, and the Indians eventually found and captured him too.

Young Jacob and his younger sister were swiftly killed with a tomahawk and scalped. Jacob's wife uncharacteristically was stabbed in the heart with a butcher knife and scalped. Death by a tomahawk or gunshot was considered an honorable warrior's death, but death by stabbing in the heart was dishonorable and disgraceful. Family tradition believed the mother was targeted for such a death because years before she had been brusque while refusing food to a few hungry Indians.

Before leaving, the Indians set fire to all the out-buildings. All this was witnessed from a safe venue by Jacob's older son John. As they were leaving, Jacob picked some ripe peaches and advised his sons to do the same. He also advised them to submit to their fate as far as possible. Jacob, Joseph (~15yrs) and Christian (~9yrs) were taken captive and then to separate Indian villages.

V. EPILOGUE

When I first read this story of the massacre, I knew little about William Penn, the native Americans living in the Delaware Valley, the establishment of the first Amish community in Berks County led by Bishop Hertzler, and the events leading up to the French and Indian war and the battle for the lands in Pennsylvania. There were parts of the story that troubled me. *Why did the Indians kill the most defenseless and vulnerable and make captives of the father and two sons?* I knew of the Amish stance on pacifism but did not understand Jacob's ready adherence to this principle in the heat of the moment and choosing not to defend his family and accept their fate that resulted in *watching his wife and two young children murdered and scalped in front of him.*

Reading through the multiple stories of Indian raids and massacres and about Indian warfare in this time period, I learned that the Indians often took captives and did not kill everyone. Jacob Hochstetler was so trusted in captivity that he was given a gun and bullets to hunt game and bring it back to the Indian camp. That trust allowed him to escape after nine months of captivity. Joseph and Christian were adopted into Indian families until they were exchanged seven years later at the end of the French and Indian War in 1764. They were so well treated that they struggled with leaving and assimilating back into the Amish community. The killing of the most defenseless in some instances was a practical decision based on those who would hinder swift travel. Where children or young women were taken captive it was at the request of Indian squaws who instructed the warriors to bring back a specific person to adopt into the tribe to replace lost family members or to have them help support the tribe. The manner of the massacres was typical of Indian warfare, and a scalp could come from a person of any age. Taking scalps contributed to acquiring a reputation as a warrior, akin to a trophy or award for others in the tribe to see. What the Indians did to the settlers was the same as they did to other Indians in time of war. Throughout history each people group has its own ways of being cruel in wartime.

Jacob's decision to adhere to the Amish principle of non-resistance and accepting one's fate was rooted the Amish belief that as the creator of all things, God alone decides when a person's physical life should end. The Amish do not question God's wisdom or authority on this matter and believe that the deceased leave the physical world to be with God and other family in the spiritual afterlife in heaven. They trust in God's omniscience. This trust in God's will extends to all areas of their lives. It is why the Amish do not believe in insurance. Any disaster is seen as an act of God, and even if not fully understood, accepted as part of his Divine Plan. This is one of many examples of devotion to God's overarching plan for their existence.

THE IMPETUS FOR THIS STORY

What was the impetus for this story? Back in mid-March of 2022, we had plans to build a pavilion to replace a 100-year-old barn on our property. We had a concrete slab poured and were having some asphalt work done to connect with the existing driveway. A woman who was delivering asphalt asked what we were doing. Telling her we were getting the site ready to build a pavilion, she mentioned she drove for an Amish man who put up pavilions, and she gave us his phone number. After trying for three weeks, we eventually connected. His name was Joseph Hochstetler. He said he would be interested in building the pavilion, and at the end of the call I asked him to spell his name. It was the same spelling as my great-great-grandmother Susanna Hochstetler Diller. He asked, "Do you know about the Massacre? It is described in the book *The Descendants of Jacob Hochstetler* (published in 1912)." The title jogged a memory that I had a copy of this book somewhere, but it was years since I saw the book. Finding it the next morning, I saw the book was inscribed by Susanna Diller and her son Henry Diller; it had been passed down to me by my father from his father. In it, I learned that Susanna Hochstetler Diller was the great-great-granddaughter of Jacob Hochstetler of this story. She descended from Jacob's oldest son John and his wife Catherine Hertzler, Bishop Hertzler's oldest daughter. This union produced ten offspring, and my great-great-grandmother descended from the youngest child, Jonathan Hochstetler. Joseph Hochstetler, our pavilion builder from Adams County, descended from John and Catherine's sixth child, David.

In the fall of 2022, my wife and I traveled to the site of the massacre and John Hochstetler's homestead nearby with my grandsons Wyatt and Everett, sons of our oldest Nathan and his wife Allison who live near Philadelphia. We found two memorial markers, one placed by the Pennsylvania Historical Society on Route 22 at the entry to the long lane leading to the house, and the second placed by the Hostetler family located near the house. We toured the grounds, stood on the foundation of the bake oven where the Indians stood, and saw the oldest part of the house built in the 1750s where the cellar and window into it could be seen. We included a visit to the Jacob Hertzler homestead (named Contentment) six miles east and walked on the property to the family cemetery where Jacob and his wife are buried. This experience opened up a new chapter in my family story.

To close, I have come to appreciate that Jacob Hochstetler's decision to not defend is an example of what Martin Luther King Jr. said on February 8, 1968: "*Conscience asks the question, is it right? And there comes a time when one must take a position that is neither safe, nor politic, nor popular but he must take it because conscience tells him it is right.*"

Phil Diller serves as the Sr. Associate Dean for Educational Affairs in the University of Cincinnati College of Medicine and as a family physician practices palliative care. He resides in College Hill and has been a member of the Literary Club since 2014. One interest is capturing and sharing stories of his family heritage.

7 A Witness to a Clowder of Witnesses

IGOR DUMBADZE

THEY stared at us. Although feral cats in the strict sense of the word, they were not emaciated or mangy, they were not aggressive nor were they afraid of us. I walked with my wife and son amongst ancient remains in the south of France, as our son got his first glimpse of ruins out in the field and not behind a glass wall in a museum. The cats stared at us, as though we were trespassing over something that was in their charge, much like a hostess casting a wary eye on children playing around heirloom china and antiques.

Several years later, on a sailing trip to the western coast of Turkey, I encountered the same experience as my fellow sailors and I toured ruins near the city of Ephesus. We had been to Hagia Sofia and the Blue Mosque that morning, had lunch consisting of freshly caught mountain stream trout, and now arrived at our afternoon destination: an agora with Turkish/Byzantine ruins. Columns in various stages of intactness, remains of old buildings and sections of walls were spread out over a wide expanse of land covered by red poppies blowing and swaying in the gentle breeze. A man of indeterminate age approached us as we were disembarking from the bus — "watch your step" he cautioned. His windswept appearance spoke to many years of exposure to nature's

elements. He collected an "admission fee" from us and then served as our guide, regaling us with stories of ancient days. These narrations entranced all of us as we carefully stepped amongst the ruins. It was surreal and haunting as I visualized people walking, talking and laughing in this very place some two to three thousand years ago, as they carried out the routine of their daily lives. But what was truly uncanny was the presence of the cats. They came out from behind the pillars, the walls, places I didn't even notice and then just sat there. They looked at us, shifted positions to get a better view, washed their faces with their paws, but with patience and perseverance, they never took their eyes off our group. Like their counterparts in France, they did not look mangy or sick and they did not manifest any aggressive tendencies. It was hard to count them as they seemed to be everywhere and in all imaginable colors: red, black, grey, calico and tabby. Sometimes one was nuzzled by a fellow cat, sometimes a cat would sit next to another cat, but their task did not change, as they continued to watch and observe us. I am an animal lover and have a strong affinity for cats. I had the urge to approach the cats and interact with them, but I had a strong sense that this was not an appropriate course of action. They were busy with their task. I tried to engage their eyes, a "staring contest," but that also was not meant to be. Their visual focus was on a much broader landscape, of which I was only one of the constituents. The cats stared even as we were boarding our bus to go back to the hotel. I do not know how long they sat and watched, nor where they went after the bus rounded the bend, but I suppose that they would reassemble when the next group of visitors came and wandered amongst the relics.

I remained haunted by my experience with the cats, and upon returning home I researched their history. From their "domestication" some ten to twelve thousand years ago in the Fertile Crescent and the Nile River valley, cats have held a unique position on the human-animal continuum. In ancient Egypt, cats achieved the status of a deity, principally due to their safeguarding the wheat in the granaries from rodents and snakes. Because wheat was the essential food source of the Egyptians, cats were venerated as guardians of things essential and important. I became more aware of my own cats as they observed the daily routine of life, showing up when I was doing something, especially if that activity was outside the normal routine: an open or a closed door, suitcases placed in the hallway, someone coming or going. They don't bark like a dog. They simply observe and record the event in some recess of their mind.

Do I know where these events are recorded? Do I know what becomes of these observations and notations? No, I don't. But I also do not understand quantum physics or particle physics, and yet I am told by the scientific literature that those are the very forces which hold the universe together. So just because I don't know what happens to a cat's observations doesn't mean that it isn't happening.

Yes, I am a "cat person," but mostly I am a "life person" intrigued by the infinite variety of the universe. There is an order to that universe, and although it seems at times to be chaotic, it may simply be my lack of understanding the underlying process. Perhaps there is a system of telepathy in the universe that conveys ideas through observations and then transports them throughout the galaxies.

Sometimes as I watch my cats, sitting on a window sill like an accomplished Yogi, deeply ruminative and mysterious, and what T.S. Eliot perceives as a "...cat in profound meditation...," I can't help but think that somehow the cats are witnessing the progression of our timeline, recording it in some great cosmic book, destined to be a story catalogued in some far reaches of the universe.

Walking among those ruins of civilizations past, I could not help but feel that I was not only a spectator, but also a spectacle. I was witnessing a connection with ancient mysteries. As those cats watched me stepping on their domain, there was a palpable concatenation between them, guardians of the ruins, and those mouse hunters of the Nile so many years ago.

Igor Dumbadze is a Literarian and a retired physician, who has two sons and one grandson. He lives with his wife, along with two rescue cats, in Hyde Park.

8 A Chicago Story

SAMUEL GREENGUS

I was born and grew up in Chicago during the middle decades of the 20th Century. If you ask me "what was Chicago like during those years?" I would invite you to re-read the poem "Chicago" by Carl Sandburg. Sandburg wrote his poem about Chicago in 1914; but even some years later, when I was a boy and then a young man, I could still perceive flashes of reality and truth in its descriptive lines.

> Sandburg began his poem with powerful imagery:
> Hog Butcher for the World,
> Tool Maker, Stacker of Wheat,
> Player with Railroads and the Nation's Freight Handler;
> Stormy, husky, brawling,
> City of the Big Shoulders:

The imagery of these lines has continued to resonate for me over these many years. I grew up on the South Side of the city, not too far from Lake Michigan. We had no air conditioning, so in the summer, we flung open every window, trying to catch a breeze. I recall how sometimes from the sprawling Chicago stockyards several miles inland, if the wind was right, we would get a whiff of the animals in those acres of

Permission: Meng Yang, illustrator

corrals and packing houses, being herded, slaughtered, and packaged. Chicago was a "Hog Butcher for the World — and more.

Chicago was a busy industrial center. From our house, I was able to walk to the sandy beaches on the shore of Lake Michigan; and when I stood on the beach and turned southward on a clear day, I could see the chimneys of steel mills as far as the eye could see. Turning to the north, I might just begin to make out among the tallest buildings the Chicago Board of Trade, where futures for grains, livestock, edible oils, and dairy products were being bought and sold. In the quiet of the night in my bed, I could hear the whistles of freight trains, and at quiet moments, during the day, in the morning and late afternoon, whistles of factories, telling shifts of workers that it was time to enter or quit working and go home.

The people of Chicago were hard working, devoted to their families, and supportive of their community institutions. But there were also "rough edges." And so Sandburg, in the next lines of his poem, turns his attention to some of the human flaws and failings that were manifest in the "stormy, husky, (and) brawling" city of Chicago. Sandburg goes on to say:

> They tell me you are wicked, and I believe them, for I have seen
> your painted women under the gas lamps luring the farm boys.
> And they tell me you are crooked, and I answer: Yes, it is true I
> have seen the gunman kill and go free to kill again.

Yes, there were flaws in the great urban center of Chicago. And in the era of my youth, Chicago still carried a conscious legacy of crime and corruption, which thrived and survived in popular imagination and memory. Chicagoans would mention the fatal shootout between John Dillinger and the FBI and point to the movie theater where it took place. There was the St. Valentine's Day Massacre in which Al Capone's gang eliminated a rival North Side gang and thereby extended his control throughout Chicago, over liquor production, importation, and distribution during the years of Prohibition. Capone lived on in folk memory for many years. My wife and I at times employed as a babysitter an older woman who recounted having a date with Al Capone when she was a young woman; she remembered that he was very nice to her and gave her a gift of $100 when they parted. My wife and I held back and did not ask for more details about that historic event.

Criminals of course also lived on in the American movies, portrayed by great actors like Paul Muni, George Raft, James Cagney, Edward G. Robinson. Hollywood brought to life the stories of famous criminals like John Dillinger, Baby Face Nelson, Bonnie and Clyde, Bugsy Segal,

Al Capone, Frank (the Enforcer) Nitti, Meyer Lansky, and more. I am not sure why gangsters, despite their crimes, were so fascinating and celebrated. Maybe, it was because their careers brought to the fore some of the challenging themes in American life of the 20th century. Stories of bootleggers resisting prohibition against alcohol, and bank robbers acting out forbidden and repressed responses to the Great Depression, and the poverty and hardship that many Americans were facing. In related fashion, stories involving casinos and gamblers stirred fantasies of unexpected riches gained through a lucky card, a winning bet, or hitting the jackpot. The human adversities that were widespread in the American experience somehow "softened" our attitudes and brought forward feelings of sympathy towards these criminals who violated the laws, even as we also realized that they needed to be apprehended and punished.

Why am I telling you all of this? It is to introduce you to an episode in my own life when I encountered a real-life gangster in Chicago.

It was an unlikely time and place. The encounter took place in a synagogue on Yom Kippur, the holiest day of the year for Jews. It was a mild, early October day in 1946 or 1947. I was attending worship services with my family. I was not yet 13 years old and thus formally exempt from fasting and saying all of the prayers. Still, I was trying to learn and take on the responsibilities of an adult man in our religious community.

Our synagogue was a large, rectangular, free-standing building. It had three levels. There was a basement level, partly above ground, and two more levels that were fully above the ground. The building was entered from one of the short sides, facing the street. Visitors walked up a series of wide stone steps to the first-floor level above the high basement. These outside stone steps were divided into two flights, with a landing between them. The landing was large; it extended to the full width of the stairway and created a wide resting place between the two flights of stairs. There was room for people to stand and linger on the landing itself, without going on to enter the building. People often paused on the landing to greet one another and chat. (I will say more about this landing shortly.)

Our synagogue was Orthodox; and thus, men and women sat in separate sections. The interior was designed like a music hall or theater. The first-floor level, entered by the exterior stone steps, led into a foyer. From the foyer one could follow one set of side stairs down to the basement, or a second set of side stairs to the second floor of the building, or proceed forward, through another set of doors, into the main section which filled the entire first floor interior. The first floor was for men. It was filled with rows of wooden theatre-style seats. The rows of seats were bisected by two parallel aisles, extending to the back wall of the men's section. In front of the back wall there was a podium or dais, ascended by side stairs on both sides. The podium was furnished with chairs and reader's tables, the larger of which faced the Ark, which was the focal point of the synagogue worship. The Ark itself was a large, ornamented cabinet, containing hand- written scrolls of the Torah—the Pentateuch, and a collection of scrolls upon which prophetic books and the Writings were inscribed. The doors of the Ark were covered by a large, embroidered velvet curtain hanging in front of the Ark. The large curtain could be pulled to one side, allowing the wooden doors of the Ark to be opened, giving access to the scrolls inside. There was also a smaller reader's table on the podium that faced the congregation; it was mostly used as a lectern for sermons. The podium and the Ark were flanked by two small rooms behind the back wall of the men's section; one of small rooms led to the back door of the synagogue building. There were also two outside fire escapes leading down from both sides of the women's balcony.

This first floor, as I have already said, was for men only. Women would go up the stairs in the foyer leading to the second floor. The women's section was smaller in area than the men's floor; it was actually a U-shaped balcony, going around the room, over the men's floor, but leaving the Ark, the podium, and a good part of the men's seating visible from the women's gallery above.

Below the first floor, in the basement, there were restrooms, a small apartment for the caretaker and his wife, and a large study hall, in which weekday and non-holiday worship took place. These services were attended mainly by male worshippers. Next to the men's study hall, there was a smaller, adjacent area for a small number of women who might attend. Sabbath and holiday services were held upstairs in the main synagogue.

Now the main synagogue was especially full of worshippers on Yom Kippur. I had been attending Sabbath services throughout the year, and so I saw many of the worshippers who were not in regular attendance for ordinary Sabbath services. Some of them I recognized; these included shopkeepers, tradesmen, professional men, and neighbors, but there were many whom I did not know. The crowd also included a cohort of boys, like me, not yet 13, but learning the responsibilities of adult men in a congregation. One of them, a buddy, stood at the edge of the aisle where I was sitting and tried to get my attention. He signaled to me that I should join him and go outside into the foyer. I followed his invitation, and in the foyer, he told me that there was something I needed to see outside of the front doors of the synagogue. There was a man with a gun standing on the landing of the front steps and I could see it for myself! We walked outside and I saw a burly man with a fedora, who stood in the middle of the landing opposite the front door. He slowly looked around to "check out" whoever was coming up the stairs into the synagogue. From time to time, he looked more closely at some of the men who walked on to the landing and into the synagogue. He ignored us boys, as well as any girls, and most of the women. He was wearing a dark grey suit, with a jacket that covered his upper body. But when he turned his body, I could for a moment get a glimpse of a shoulder holster strapped to his chest, holding a revolver. My friend whispered to me that there was another guy just like him, a stranger, covering the back door of the synagogue. We went outside and walked around the synagogue building in order to "check out" the back door. Sure enough, there was a second man, similarly attired as the man in front of the synagogue. There was much less traffic at the back door, but the man continued to stand and watch. We realized that both of these men were bodyguards, who came along to protect someone who was inside, attending our Yom Kippur morning worship services.

I later learned more about the man who came with the two bodyguards. His name was Ziggy Karnofsky. I was told by my aunt Ruthie that Karnofsky grew up in our neighborhood and that in his youth, he had attended our synagogue when he was a boy. He and Ruthie went to the same high school. I asked my aunt whether she had ever gone out with Ziggy; she laughed and said no, he was "too wild for me." Aunt Ruthie told me that Karnofsky had left school before graduating and took up with the gangs. Both of Karnofsky's parents were now dead and were buried in the synagogue cemetery. Karnofsky was their only child. It was customary to recite memorial prayers for deceased parents and other close relatives. These brief memorial prayers were in the liturgy of Yom Kippur morning.

I realized that I had noted Karnofsky coming into the synagogue earlier that Yom Kippur morning. He was walking down the aisle towards the front of the men's section. He did not have to walk too far. His progress down the aisle was interrupted by Mr. Tobin, the president of the synagogue. Mr. Tobin was evidently looking out for him; he met him, shook hands, and accompanied him to a seat in a row of seats at the left side of the synagogue, near the front of the men's section. Mr. Tobin and all of the men of course addressed him as Mr. Karnofsky.

I don't know how Karnofsky came to attend our synagogue on that Yom Kippur morning. There were, as I mentioned, the memorial prayers. But Karnofsky may also have heard that there was going to be a special fund-raising appeal held in the synagogue on that Yom Kippur in order to raise funds for the care and resettlement of Jews— "displaced persons" who survived World War II. The need for funds was pressing. There were over a million such displaced persons in Western Europe after the war; about 250,000 were Jews. They included survivors who had been in Nazi concentration camps, slave laborers, persons in hiding, members of resistance or partisan bands, as well as individuals who had survived under the Soviets, in places where the Nazis were unable to advance. But after the war, before the Iron Curtain sealed them off, they had fled to zones under U.S. and Allied control in Germany, France, Holland, and Italy. In the DP camps, i.e., the Displaced Person camps, they received medical care, clothing, and assistance in fashioning a new life, since most were alone, having lost parents, wives, husbands, children, relatives, and friends. Jewish charities in the U.S. were active in helping the rebuilding of Jewish communities in Western Europe and, with support from 20 countries, also resettlement abroad. The largest resettlements of Jewish refugees, from 1946 to 1951, were in the United States, Australia, and Israel (after 1948).

Our synagogue had in fact invited a younger rabbi to deliver a speech which they hoped would speak to the entire congregation and motivate them to donate money. Our regular rabbi was an older man; he was very learned, but he delivered his sermons in the Yiddish language. His sermons were directed at older congregants, most of whom were immigrants, who had grown up speaking Yiddish. The older rabbi understood English, but he spoke it with a heavy accent. By contrast, the younger rabbi was American born and was able to craft and deliver an inspiring message in idiomatic English, which made his message fully understood by the younger, post-immigrant generation. At the same time, the younger rabbi managed to sprinkle Yiddish words and phrases into his speech, which created a comfortable connection with the older, Yiddish speakers in the congregation. I don't recall the words of the rabbi's address; but I know that in it he urged the congregation to support the care and resettlement of the refugees who had fortunately survived and needed help from those who were spared and had survived the war, and who could give financial support.

When the rabbi concluded his address, Mr. Tobin, the president of the congregation, came up to the lectern to urge the members of the congregation to donate money and that the congregation would be ready to collect and channel donations from congregants to the Jewish charities that were involved in this effort to help and resettle the displaced persons. The congregation would also endeavor to raise gifts from congregants through the auction of important honors that would bring individuals into close contact with the Sacred Scriptures that would be read on this holy day of Yom Kippur.

The plan was to auction off honors, beginning with the honor of opening the Ark and allowing the removal and reading of the Torah scroll. I should note that this first honor did not require the holder to recite any prayers. The accompanying prayers would be recited by the cantor. So, there was no chance of someone stumbling over the Hebrew prayers and risking embarrassment. Holding an auction was not a usual custom; typically, someone was invited to take or perform the honor and that person would then later give a donation of his choosing without fanfare. But on this Yom Kippur day the goal was to raise as much money as possible.

Mr. Tobin, the president, then invited the shames, that is, the sexton of the synagogue, to come up to the dais and preside over the auction. Standing at the lectern facing the congregation, the shames announced the first honor that was the subject of this bidding, and an opening bid of $25 dollars. He called out in Yiddish: "Twenty-five dollars for opening the Ark."

It was exciting for me to watch this auction and hear a series of mounting bids. Then I saw Mr. Karnofsky raise his hand and make a gesture. The shames perceived his gesture and called out "one thousand dollars for opening the Ark." The congregation gasped and fell silent; and, after a pause, the shames intoned "one thousand dollars once" then "twice," then "a third time," slapping his hand on the wood of the lectern. Mr. Karnofsky's bid was final.

One thousand dollars represented an immense gift in 1946. To equal its purchasing power in our present day, it would require almost

$150,000. I was told that Karnofsky's gift was one of the largest if not the largest gift ever received within the congregation. Mr. Tobin, the synagogue president, was conferring with Mr. Karnofsky and motioned for the shames to come down and confer with them. The shames did so and then walked over to the opposite side of the synagogue and spoke with Mr. Arris, an elderly man who was a regular worshipper at religious services. Mr. Arris was small in stature and wiry, with a short, pointed beard. He was quiet but would respond with a smile when I or one of the boys at the end of Sabbath prayers would offer their hand to shake and wish him "Gut Shabbes," that is "Good Sabbath" in Yiddish. Mr. Arris otherwise gave full attention to the service and its prayers. On Yom Kippur, there is a custom for adults to fast for 24 hours; in other words, refrain from food or drink. But Mr. Arris went further and removed his shoes and stood in his stocking feet on the wooden floor for all of the prayers he recited in the synagogue on that day. Mr. Arris did not sit down even where the general custom was for one to pray while seated. Mr. Arris undertook these extra measures, in order to fulfill with extra zeal the biblical commandment to "afflict his soul" and thereby to seek forgiveness for his sins.

Everyone soon realized that Mr. Karnofsky had instructed the shames to invite Mr. Arris to perform the honor of opening the Ark, for which Karnofsky had just pledged his $1,000 donation. And so, the shames accompanied Mr Arris, who was walking in his stocking feet, and he slowly ascended the podium where, at the appropriate moment, the cantor nodded to Mr. Arris to open the Ark. The entire congregation then stood up from their seats in order to show their reverence and respect for the biblical scrolls inside that were soon to be brought forth for the scriptural reading of the holy day. Mr. Karnofsky retained his place among the other worshippers in the congregation.

Karnofsky and his bodyguards left the synagogue after the memorial prayers. The last time I saw him he was outside the synagogue, walking between the two bodyguards on the way to his car, which was parked down the street, out of sight. This was out of respect for the holy day and its strict observances by pious worshippers who did not ride to the synagogue.

I believe it was two years later, in conversation with my aunt Ruthie, that she told me that Karnofsky was dead. He had been gunned down and killed in front of his home, downstate from Chicago. His shooting appeared to be the result of gangland rivalry.

Karnofsky, however, remains in my memory until the present day. He was without question a gangster; and who can say what actions brought him to — and supported him in — his position of leadership in the mob. But his behavior on that Yom Kippur day truly demonstrated qualities of humility, respect, devotion, and yes, even of religious piety. Karnofsky paid a huge sum for the honor but declined to have it conferred upon him personally. Instead, he invited Mr. Arris, a person of modest means but unblemished piety, an elder of the congregation, to take the honor in his place. Karnofsky, after the scriptural readings, also recited memorial prayers. His actions would also have honored the memories of his deceased parents in that they brought to life values and sensitivities that Karnofsky would have learned from his parents, when he was a young boy. And finally, Karnofsky's behavior on that Yom Kippur brings home to me the truth of Rabbi Hillel's ancient teaching: "Hillel said . . . do not judge your fellow man until you have come to his place" (*Mishnah Avot* 2:4). This teaching does not tell us that we must become gangsters in order to judge a gangster; rather, it teaches us to recognize and reckon the good when we see it, even in persons who have committed wicked acts, deserving of punishment. I learned that lesson, years ago, from Ziggy Karnofsky.

Samuel Greengus, born, raised, and educated in Chicago, Illinois, has lived a life in close relationship to synagogues and rabbinical seminaries. He holds M.A. and Ph.D degrees from the University of Chicago. He was on the faculty of the Hebrew Union College in Cincinnati, Ohio, and taught in its rabbinical and graduate programs for 47 years. In retirement, he is the Julian Morgenstern Emeritus Professor of Bible and Near Eastern Literature.

9 Shooting

RICHARD HAGUE

1

ONE of my more vivid memories of growing up in Steubenville was the day a policeman who lived in our neighborhood—he bore the Looney Tunes name of Leo Lashley—gunned down a rabid dog in the middle of Dresden Ave. This was a year or two before *To Kill A Mockingbird* appeared on the cultural scene, so we were witnesses to a disturbing novelty. The noise, the smoke, the blood—strong stuff for a bunch of little boys. Later, when I was in high school, the father of a popular Italian American girl at our school was taken out in a mafia-style hit in the parking lot of a Las Vegas casino. For years, I tried to unimagine that distant yet unsettlingly close murder. Between the dog shooting and the father shooting, dozens of murders by gun took place in my hometown, known, since the early 20th century for its prostitution, gambling, and racketeering—as Little Chicago. Gunplay of all sorts—on television in that era of westerns like *Gunsmoke, Bonanza, Cheyenne,* Have Gun, Will Travel—occupied the zeitgeist.

At one time a little later in my boyhood, my father got himself into a feud with a neighbor. It was over religion and politics—the neighbor,

who worked in some administrative capacity for the Steubenville public schools, had opposed busing for Catholic school children at public expense. This was a project my parents had worked on for months. My father and he had some sort of argument, conducted loudly over the hedge separating our yards. (I long ago learned that the etymology of "Hague" comes from the Irish for "one who lives in a fenced or hedged enclosure, or one who argues over fences.") Whether my father ever knew that I have no idea, but there he was, enacting the essence of our family name. Shortly after that argument, snooping around in dad's top drawer among his handkerchiefs and socks, I was shocked to find a nasty-looking snubby .38 revolver. I had an almost physical aversity to it, and slammed the drawer shut. I think it was bought as a preemptive defense, never used. But after his death, it came my way, I still keep it hidden. Of course, there is no ammunition for it. It reposes in a sort of arrested time, just as my boyhood Remington one-shot rifle. When our first son was born, I hid the rifle in a crawl space and the bolt somewhere else. I haven't seen either since.

I mention all this because the ubiquity of guns in my life—in the most innocent of Americans' lives—is inescapable. The truck driver who delivered beeves and hams and sausages from Detroit to the meat shop I worked in as a kid carried what looked like a modern version of the Buntline Special strapped to his leg. Most of my dad's buddies were hunters, armed with shotguns and rifles they kept in corner cupboards or basement gun cases. My best friend Roger Swartz's dad belonged to a band of coon hunters, one of whose many hauls of cured skins is displayed in a photo of us boys taken in the family's backyard.

So what follows is not surprising. Depressing, yes. Aggravating, yes. Inevitable, given all the weaponry available to just about anyone, yes.

In the space of two months just a couple of years ago, four people were shot to death in separate incidents within four blocks of my home. Three were black men, and one an Asian-American police officer, shot by one of the black men in what at first seemed to be "suicide by cop." The latest incident, a multiple shooting at the local Elk's Lodge, happened at night; I heard the shots, and in my usual compulsive way, counted them, re-running the too-familiar *pop-pop-pop* over in my head. At least twelve shots, I reckoned. Coincidentally, by my clock it was exactly midnight. I also noted to myself that there were two different guns, each with a distinct sound. That I wasn't frightened out of my wits by this tells you that it was not an isolated incident. I would estimate that over the 40 years we have lived here, I have heard several hundred gunshots; it is difficult to be more precise because on New Year's Eve, Memorial Day, Independence Day, and even election night, the fireworks are a mixed volley of backyard pyrotechnics and semiautomatic weaponry. Right now, I have on the bookshelf next to my bed a spent .32 cartridge that I picked up in front of my house the day after the Fourth of July. My neighbor this morning tells me that when men came to work on his house a few weeks ago, they found a huge slug, as big around as his finger, in his gutter.

Back in the crack Eighties and Nineties, our neighborhood was a center of major drug activity. The largest cocaine bust in Cincinnati history took place next door; it happened after almost three years of calls to the police by myself, my wife, dozens of neighbors. You must understand that after the bust, though every adult male member of the family next door went to federal prison, we felt little relief. Our dread had been real and well-founded, nor did the arrests fix the deep problems of poverty, and desperation, and recklessness that underlay the lives of those arrested and their left-to-fend-for-themselves husband-less and father-less families.

In all of the busts or shootings I have been aware of over the decades in my neighborhood, not one was perpetrated by a woman. In my part of the world, at least, it's a seriously guy-only thing, shooting.

There are segments of American culture in which shooting is done for sport; I am fully aware of this. In general, I'm fine with it. After my father died, along with the revolver, I inherited his two shotguns; my sister was terrified by them. In a moment of really bad luck, after retrieving them from her home in Columbus, I left them under a blanket in the back of our van, intending to secret them somewhere in the house the next day. Before morning, they were stolen. The faces of the policemen who came to take my report were worried and drawn. I have had to fight back flashes of midnight imaginings of those guns being fired in violence against some human rather than an in-season squirrel. Such a mistake is difficult to forgive yourself for.

I saw a news article a few years back featuring a bunch of guys who enjoyed shooting fruit. They'd go to the supermarket and buy a bunch of watermelons and cantaloupes, then take them out into the boondocks somewhere and blast away at them with high-caliber rifles or absurdly heavy handguns. Then, after doing further research, I was led to write the following, during the initial outbreak of the pandemic. It was originally scheduled to be read on a Monday evening at the Literary Club of Cincinnati that happened to follow one of the most violent mass shootings of this century. Realizing the flippant tone of my commentary would be completely inappropriate for that evening's exercise, I substituted something else. Now, I offer this with regret and apologies, and not a little bit of ire.

2

In just the single month of June 2020, according to *The New York Times*, 2.3 million guns were sold in the United States. Before we go any further, this one-month number needs to be put in context. There were 620,000 deaths in the American Civil War. Let's say that each of the deaths represented at least one gun. Of course, huge numbers of men were killed not by handguns or rifles, but by artillery and by the rampant gangrene following limb-shattering engagements, not to mention other common infections, and in the prison camps especially, by disease and starvation. But let me repeat: 620,000 men, all of whom we can presume were armed at some time during the conflict with some sort of weapon, died in the Civil War, which lasted over four years. *In one month* of 2020, 2.3 millions guns were injected into the American population. Of the estimated 393 million total firearms in America, 392 million are unregistered. The mind reels. The palms moisten. The heart palpitates. Let us calculate a one-foot average length for those 2.3 million guns sold in June—many long-barreled ones offsetting the more snubby .22s, 32s, .38s, .45s, and nine millimeters. For example, the NRA claimed that as recently as a couple of years ago, the AR-15 was the most popular rifle in the US. So if all these armaments were laid out end to end, these Glocks, these Smith and Wesson Model 10s, these Colt M1911s , these Browning shotguns, these AR-15s, they would stretch from Cincinnati to St. Paul, Minnesota. I repeat: from Cincinnati to St. Paul, Minnesota.

From Cincinnati to Tallahassee, Florida.

From Cincinnati to Topeka, Kansas.

Imagine driving for hours to any of these cities, and all along the roadside you see, uninterrupted, this lined-up cache of live weapons.

Are you feeling safer yet?

Now I invite you to consider those numbers in the light of what I fear is a characteristically American pastime. I say "characteristically American" because of how it matches up with our rampant consumerism, our incredibly productive agriculture, and our national habits of ignorance and excess.

It is called "fruit shooting." It is reasonable to assume, that, as in other distractions, fruit shooting must be enjoying an increase in popularity at least as widespread as sourdough baking or knitting among prisoners, especially given the surging availability of guns.

To experience this phenomenon, visit this YouTube video: "S&W 500: Shooting Fruit." The S&W is for Smith and Wesson, and the 500 is the brand of their Magnum revolver, which is featured as the weapon of choice in this production.

Our shooter is a fellow named Don, in his thirties or so, a self-identified Hoosier, very possibly from Literarian Mark Schlachter's fictional Ersatz County. He is dressed in camouflage and wielding a revolver that reminds me of the Army-issue Smith and Wesson .45 my grandfather brought back from World War I, only this one is bigger. Mr. Indiana quickly announces that this program constitutes "Day Five of Shoot Something Every Day for A Month Month." His assistant, there for her good looks and appreciative laughter, is Jen. She could be his sister or his wife: not clear. But she is certainly game. By the end of the show, she has been besmeared, bedaubed, spattered and smattered with the remains of a whole shopping cart of produce.

Don begins with what he calls, twice, "squarsh. "Just in case the viewer doesn't get it, a chyron along the bottom of the screen informs us in capital letters: SQUARSH. The targets are actually three innocent long Waltham butternuts, garden standards, one of the heirloom varieties most commonly grown all over the east and Midwest, and one of the staples of my own garden in Madisonville.

Don stands the wobbly butternuts on their rounded ends on a small wooden table of the kind featured next to backyard grills: slats of thin wood over a frame of more slats, and all that attached to two x-shaped sets of metal legs. In other words, a square, foldable item you might see at Home Depot selling for, say, 17.99. Nothing fancy here, the table implies. Just regular folk.

Jen steps behind Don as he plants his feet and raises the gun. The camera pulls back, revealing another tiny camera riding on Don's head, clipped to the ballcap he wears.

The shot now is from his headcam.

Pow! or is it *Blam?* Neither word suffices, really: all that can be said is that there is an explosion and the middle butternut, gut-shot, sags to the table. Don turns and grins into the camera. He approaches the table, sets up the other butternuts which have fallen over and straightens up the gut-shot one, as best he can, then backs up again and aims. This blast not only puts the wounded squarsh out of it misery but knocks the other two completely aside.

Cut to scene two, "Canny lope." Don tells us twice what he is holding, so we can yuck it up a bit and enjoy some suspense. The chyron appears in capital letters: "CANNY-LOPE." Don sets it among the shreds of butternut flesh and clots of seeds and connective tissue on the table, steps back, plants his feet, and once again the big noise. The canny lope is replaced by a huge orange smear and fragments flying in all directions. Don walks to the table, leans over, and picks up from the lawn one of the larger pieces and takes a bite, and then another. Grinning, he says, "My pappy always told me, eat what you kill." Jen, off-camera, giggles in solidarity.

One more scene: the victims this time are four coconuts, lined up one behind the other. As usual, the title appears below them, so we won't be mistaken about what is about to be gunned down. This time, the effect of the shot is to explode all the coconuts, as well as the table they are sitting on. It is almost totally wrecked, and Don admits his long relationship with it. "Will you miss it?" Jen sadly queries.

Apparently not, because Don sets a bag of grapes on the wreckage and shoots it, as well as some papayers, "or whatever," Don says. (The title reads PRAPIE-A. It is fortunate for all involved—I guess—that Don is a somewhat better shot than speller.) These targets are transformed into mush on the final wreckage of the table, slats splintered and hanging, slobbers and drools of papaya and melon and grapes everywhere. In the final sequence, Jen and Don stand together, she laughingly complaining about the fruit shards and shot glop in her hair and on her face and shirt. Concluding with a broad smile, Don leans into the camera and invites his viewers to propose some interesting things to shoot for tomorrow's show. "A running lawn mower would be good," he suggests.

3

In August of 2011, my son Brendan had a gun pressed to his temple as he was helping re-open an heirloom Cincinnati restaurant in Over The Rhine. Grammer's had been a old-country style German mainstay of the Queen City, and was just finished with a deep renovation, to which Brendan contributed long hours of manual labor. Now he was bartending.

Three guys came in, ordered drinks with straws (Bee noticed this and thought it odd: later it became quite clear—no fingerprints.) When the manager and the other bartender stepped outside for a smoke, the three drinkers drew guns, muscled Bee to the ground, and emptied the contents of the cash register and Bee's wallet. They grabbed his phone. Brendan's personal cash, his night's tips, and his credit cards were gone. When the manager and other bartender came back in, they too were robbed and told to lie down on the floor and count to a thousand. Within 24 hours, the owner closed the place for good, never expressing any sympathy, or compensating Brendan for his losses, nor for the trauma of being held at gun point.

The one who held his gun on Bee was caught and he gave up the other two. At trial, Brendan pointed out the man who terrorized him, who was sentenced to 40 years, having built a long record of previous crime. When I checked these facts again with my son, I told him I was sorry for asking him to revisit this psychological mess. "No problem" he said with an unconvincing shrug. "It'll come up in therapy some day and I'll get over it."

4

So sorry: I struggle to find words for the frequent lunacy associated with guns, armed robbery of course, as well as the stupidity and waste of fruit-shooting (let alone its grotesque distortion of the gift of American agricultural abundance and its ironic underscoring of the availability of ammunition). It is even harder for me to find words for my absolute scorn for those legislators and lobbyists and citizen's organizations who continue to make it possible for guys like the ones who killed two of my neighbors and wounded five more—and this at a birthday party—to get an automatic weapon. Or for the ones that held up my son to be so dangerously armed.

I have no words that haven't already been said. Presidents have said them—to no lasting effect. Jim Brady and Gabby Gifford have said them—to no lasting effect. The kids from Parkland have said them. Is it not telling that most of the officials opposing getting real about guns in the hands of men and boys are themselves men? This is one root of the problem. Decades ago, Robert Bly, poet, citizen, leader of men's groups for peace and self-understanding and author of the best-selling *Iron John*, wrote: "The dark side of men is clear. Their mad exploitation of earth resources, devaluation and humiliation of women, and obsession with tribal warfare are undeniable. Genetic inheritace contributes to their obsessions, but also culture and environment. We have defective mythologies that ignore masculine depth of feeling, assign men a place in the sky instead of the earth, teach obedience to the wrong powers, [and] work to keep men boys."

This is really bad news that continues to stay news, and like the murderous shootings we have been assaulted with (remember the schools, malls, clubs, grocery stores, (remember Lincoln, Garfield, McKinley, remember Martin Luther King, Jr., remember Trayvon Martin, remember Tamir Rice, Jack Kennedy, Bobby Kennedy, remember Sam DuBose, Timothy Thomas...) As a nation, our failure to do something effective about it while preserving rightful liberties is more than frustrating, more than damning. In its lack of responsible governance, political courage, moral responsibility, and humane concern for the common good, to this witness it seems fundamentally and literally unmanning.

Richard Hague, 2020-2021 President of the Literary Club of Cincinnati, is author or editor of 22 collections of prose and poetry. He has been teaching, giving readings, and conducting workshops around the country since 1969. He has studied at Northwestern University, Xavier University, The Ohio State University, Bread Loaf Writers Conference, and Manchester College, Oxford on a National Endowment for the Humanities scholarship.

10 | *Out of Sight*

THADDEUS S. JAROSZEWICZ

WHEN I need to pray, I like to go to a small, old church. An intimate sacred space where I can whisper to God, and have a prayer answered. My favorite sacred space sits on Fourth Street, between Sycamore and Broadway — the Centennial Chapel of Christ Church Cathedral.

The Centennial Chapel is a sublime Gothic jewel box that is virtually invisible from Fourth Street or Sycamore. At night, from Broadway, across a parking lot, one can catch a glimpse of the stained-glass window depicting the Resurrection of Christ, but only if the chapel is lit. The chapel is sandwiched between Christ Church Cathedral on Fourth Street, the Episcopal Diocesan House on Sycamore, and various buildings on Fifth Street. Even from a satellite photo, it takes a few seconds to recognize the chapel's distinct, narrow rectangular shape in the middle of the block.

Christ Church was founded on Sunday, May 18, 1817. The first church building was completed in 1835. It took up about a quarter of the block between Sycamore and Broadway. The main entrance was on Fourth Street.

Christ Church was the spiritual home of many of Cincinnati's prominent Episcopalian families, including several members of our Club and the University Club, which is still the case to this day. The

The Chapel treasure by Peter Paul Rubens

Parish House, the tall clock and bell tower, made of dark brick, was built in 1909. The church building we see today, that stretches for three-fourths of the block east of Sycamore, was completed in 1957, blocking the view of the chapel forever. Christ Church became a cathedral in 1993, when the Right Reverend Herbert Thompson, a Literarian, was the bishop of the Episcopal Diocese of Southern Ohio.

In early 1917, the congregation wanted to commemorate the 100th anniversary of the founding of Christ Church. They decided to build a chapel. The initial cost estimate was $25,000. Literarian Charles Phelps Taft committed $10,000 to the effort, subject to the parish being able to raise the balance of $15,000. Thanks to the enthusiasm and significant wealth of the congregation, an additional $35,000 was raised. For perspective, $45,000 in 1917 had the same value as $1.1 million today.

Mrs. Thomas Emery, whom most of us know as Mary Emery, donated the land on which the chapel sits. Her sister Isabella Hopkins donated funds for a stained-glass window in memory of Mary's sons, Sheldon and Albert. Sheldon, a Literarian, died of pneumonia when he was only 24. Albert died at age 13 in a sledding accident. Their father and Mary's husband, Thomas, also a Literarian, had died in 1906, leaving her with a fortune that she used to improve Christ Church and countless other organizations that were getting started in Cincinnati at that time.

The architectural firm of Garber & Woodward was retained to design the new chapel. Frederick Garber and Clifford Woodward, Cincinnati natives, were best known for their design work on our neighbors — the Anna Louise Inn, the Guilford School, the Phelps Apartment House; and more notably for Withrow, Walnut Hills and Western Hills High Schools. Garber's son Woodward (Woodie) Garber joined our Club in 1957.

The parish had raised $45,000 for the project, almost twice the initial estimated cost for building and outfitting the new chapel. But in April 1917, the United States officially entered World War I. The inflation rate exploded to 18% and ran in the high teens until the brief depression that began in 1921. The cost of construction materials skyrocketed. Ultimately, the total cost of the chapel was $68,347, or about $1.7 million in today's money. The parish had no problem raising the additional funds needed to complete the project.

After a week of social and liturgical celebration, the chapel's cornerstone was set on Friday, May 18, 1917, Christ Church's 100th anniversary. Among the items placed in the cornerstone were the list of all of the Church's rectors, assistants, sextons, and superintendents who had served the parish for the prior 100 years; copies of recent newspapers; the 1916 Parish Yearbook, and a paper written in 1909 by Literarian Charles J. Livingston describing the design and construction of the Parish House and Bell Tower.

Even though a war was raging in Europe, construction was completed in about 18 months. Initially, only the large stained-glass windows at the front and back of the chapel, and two stained-glass windows on the upper walls were installed. The rest arrived over the next few years.

The official consecration took place on November 24, 1918, two weeks after the Great War had ended. A memorial service was held that afternoon in honor of the men of the parish who had died in the war.

The Centennial Chapel includes the essential elements of English Gothic church design, but on a much smaller, human scale. The chapel is only 34 feet wide and 73 feet long, an area of less that 2,500 square feet. There are four pointed archways along each of the north and south walls, and a tall central archway at the front, above the altar. Stained-glass windows line the upper level of the north and south walls. The coffered ceiling is paneled with wood and rises 40 feet above the chapel floor. The interior walls are made of Indiana limestone. The original altar was made of Vermont marble. The entrance was on Fourth Street, via a long path and gate.

The stained-glass windows are dazzling works of art that were made in London, England by the firm of Heaton, Butler & Bayne. Dennis Harrell, the cathedral archivist, wrote the following description of the windows for a pamphlet about the chapel:

> "Above the entrance door to the chapel is a window showing four angels representing the four elements of creation: air (blue), earth (green), fire (red), and water (purple). The large window on the west end of the chapel shows scenes from the birth of Christ, while the window above the altar on the east wall shows the Resurrection. In between, the clerestory windows illustrate scenes from the life of Christ from his teaching in the temple at age 12 to his agony in the Garden of Gethsemane. Two small windows on the sides of the sanctuary relate to events after the Resurrection: the supper at Emmaus and Jesus' commission to the Apostles." One window portrays the Transfiguration of Christ, and another the Crucifixion.

All of the furnishings and decorative pieces in the chapel and the stained-glass windows were funded with memorial gifts. In 1927, Mary Emery passed away and bequeathed a stunning painting of the Holy Family, portraying Joseph, Mary, an infant Jesus, Mary's cousin Elizabeth, and Elizabeth's infant son John, who went on to become known as John the Baptist. This work by Flemish painter Peter Paul Rubens and his students is one of several known versions that he did of this scene. One of them sold in 2019 at a Sotheby's auction for $6 million, plus a buyer's premium of $1 million. This Rubens painting was used for more than 70 years as the main prop of the Christ Church Boar's Head Yule Log Festival. Every year, it was removed from the chapel and hung above the altar of the main church for the Christmas season. An art consultant advised the church that it was a bad idea to move a 400-year-old Rubens painting on such a regular basis. Today, a copy of the Rubens is used for the festival and Christmas season, while the original remains in its permanent home in the chapel, protected by an infra-red burglar alarm.

The baptismal font that sits in front of the chapel entrance came from the original main church, which was torn down in 1955 to make way for the new church building we see today.

The chapel was originally intended to serve as an intimate space for daily and Lenten services, weddings and funerals. During the Second World War, the chapel was designated a Community War Shrine, and was open to the public 24 hours a day, seven days a week. In 1942, a Prayer Corner was established beneath the Rubens painting. A Book of Remembrance was donated as a place to record the names of soldiers from the parish who had died in battle. Flags of the Allied countries were hung from flag poles along the north and south walls. After the war, several flags were added to represent the countries of the United Nations. These flags hung in the chapel until the mid-2000's. Thanks to the indomitable efforts of fellow Literarian Ed Burdell, the flags were removed, cleaned and carefully preserved. By removing the flags, the beauty of the stained-glass windows was once again revealed.

The chapel has a finished basement, called an undercroft, with multiple meeting and storage rooms. Over the years, one of the rooms was used to house the Baby's Milk Fund, a clinic that provided free medical care, initially for the poor Appalachian community that lived along the river. The service was expanded over time to include the West End and Over-the-Rhine communities, which were mostly black. James Essex, and a 65-year-old executive at Western Southern, recounted his Baby's Milk Fund story to me as follows:

> "I grew up in the most underprivileged neighborhoods in Cincinnati. My mother and father worked hard but had no health benefits for eight children. I was second to the oldest and Dr. Louise Rauh serviced me and my sisters and brothers. We would come to the clinic for our baby shots and whenever we were sick. But it was special for me because I had a bad case of chronic bronchitis and required long-term care. I spent a lot of time at the clinic; at times, I remember not being able to breathe and Dr. Rauh would spend so much time making sure I was alright, she even made house calls in a neighborhood where she might not have felt safe. As a child I loved her and never forgot her and the clinic. The Christ Church Baby's Milk Fund Clinic was a special place where Cincinnati's children were valued and protected. The church and its staff back then were models of love and support for Black families that needed help to see their children safely to adulthood. Now as a 65-year-old man, I sit in an office directly across from the church. Every day its clock chimes the beginning and end to my day. I have a feeling of gratitude, warmth and fond memories of special years long ago."

The Centennial Chapel had its 100th birthday in 2017. In 2012, Ed Burdell and his colleagues on the Building & Grounds committee initiated an extensive renovation program that took five years to complete. Ed said the first job was cleaning up 100 years of dust and soot that had settled in spots that had never seen a vacuum cleaner or broom. The basics had to be addressed — electrical work, HVAC, roof, and tuck-pointing. And a small, vocal group in the cathedral parish wanted the chapel organ replaced. The chapel renovation cost about $1 million, and the new chapel organ, which required alterations to the building, cost $1.5 million.

Today, regular services are still conducted in the chapel, including a quiet, traditional service every Sunday at 8 a.m., and a non-traditional service at noon. A weekly musical performance takes place as part of a series called Music Live at Lunch. The chapel plays host to numerous local musical arts performance groups.

I encourage you to visit the chapel. Take in a concert. Say a prayer. Meditate on the wonders of the world, the incredible history of our city and our club. Enjoy the artwork, the chapel's elegant design, the vivid scenes depicted on the stained-glass windows, and the majesty of the Rubens painting. You can get there by entering the red doors of the cathedral on Fourth Street and proceeding to an interior stairway or elevator.

The chapel sits next to a beautiful interior urban garden and columbarium. My wife Anne and I plan to have our ashes interred there. We will be contemplating the beauty and wonder of the Centennial Chapel for ever and ever, AMEN.

Ted Jaroszewicz was born in Cleveland, Ohio, the oldest of six children whose parents were World War II refugees from Poland. He graduated from Yale in 1979, where he rowed and majored in Russian and Economics. Ted has been married to his wife Anne since 1985, and they have three adult sons. Ted joined the Literary Club in 2012.

11 Out of the Smoke

RICHARD R. KESTERMAN

THERE is, perhaps, no greater tool to mankind's communication than fire. From prehistoric man's first efforts, to fireplaces and tenement stoves, to modern fire pits and campfires, fire not only gives off the comforts of warmth and light, it also provides those gathered around it with a forum for discussion, be it for entertainment or instruction. There is, however, a byproduct of the fire that actually provided the most effective method of preserving and handing down our traditions. As the fire consumes its fuel, smoke rises from the flames, and ashes and charred remains of the material fall to the ground. From these fallen remains come such pigments as charcoal, bone black, and ivory black, all of which have been in use since prehistoric man painted images in caves.

Less tangible than these remains is the material that is carried away in the smoke, namely the soot. Defined by Samuel Johnson as "condensed or embodied smoke," the soot gives some of the smoke its darker color, and when captured by some means, produces a pigment that is variously known as smoke black, soot black, or lamp black. Although not a rare or particularly valuable pigment, lamp black makes up for its humble beginnings by being the basis for the earliest known ink, and as such, can be considered the foundation of one of the most common and lasting methods of preserving the written word.

A seventeenth century book entitled *The Gentleman's Exercise* provides a description of making lamp black which is likely timeless in its methods. The manufacturer, according to the book, is to "take a torch or linke, and hold it under the bottom of a latten basen, and as it groweth to be furd and blacke within, strike it with a feather into some shell or other, and grinde it with gumme water." This grinding together of the pigment into the gum water not only serves to break down the structure of the pigment, it also thoroughly combines the two materials to make a more consistent mixture needed for writing. Over time, various means have been used to trap the soot, some more successful or efficient than others. One early technique for obtaining the pigment used an elongated vessel that was suspended above the burning fuel to capture the soot. Although soot would be deposited along its length, that which was obtained farthest from the flame was deemed to be of the finest quality, as it would likely be the freest of impurities also trapped in the smoke.

Some of the earliest known examples of ink being used are found in ancient Egyptian hieroglyphic and hieratic writings. Dating from around the fourth millennium BCE, traces of ink have been identified as containing carbon, from either wood or oil, and gum from the acacia tree, known as gum arabic. This ink was formed into small, dry cakes that were held on the scribe's wooden pallet. With the addition of water, this dry ink would be reconstituted into the proper consistency prior to being applied to the writing surface. The tools used for writing were, at first, thin brushes formed from reeds, and later, pens, also made from reeds. These brushes and pens easily broke down with use, and frequently needed to be replaced by the scribe.

Concurrent to this ink was the development of an early writing material known as papyrus. Made from a wetland sedge of the same name, papyrus was formed by first weaving together strips of the inner pith of the plant, then flattening the interwoven mat into a thinner sheet with a mallet. Papyrus could be formed into sheets or even long scrolls. Since both the ink and papyrus were handmade and of uncertain quality, it is possible that the original development of both may have occurred considerably earlier than is presently known.

Egyptian writing also included a form of red ink that was used to emphasize headings along with other key words or phrases. This ink contained, among other things, iron oxide, which was most likely found in ochre, or simply put, the red earth found locally. This use of black and red ink together, commonly known as rubrication, is a convention still in use when there is a need to emphasize certain words in written or printed texts.

Through merchants and other forms of commerce, these inks and papyrus — or at least the knowledge of how they were produced — became available to other cultures in the Mediterranean world. As clay or wax tablets had been used in some cultures for preserving the written word, papyrus, being lightweight and flexible, was a highly desirable alternative. The writers of the Dead Sea Scrolls, for example, used a similar carbon soot ink that also included a plant-based gum as the binder. However, even though a few of the scrolls were made of an Egyptian-like papyrus, the majority of the scrolls were made of a newer writing material: parchment. Usually made from either sheep or goat skins, parchment provided a smooth writing surface that was both durable and readily available. Its main disadvantages were the expense of producing it, along with flaws on the animals' skin that remained on the finished sheet. Additionally, unlike papyrus that could be woven to almost any length, each section of parchment had to be stitched together lengthwise in order to produce a continuous scroll.

Reed pens, similar to those used in Egypt, continued to be the writing instrument of choice. The point, or rather, the nib of the pen, would be trimmed in the direction required for whatever script was being produced. For example, for Arabic and Hebrew scripts that were written and read from right to left, the nib would be trimmed obliquely to the left, while for Greek and Roman scripts that read from left to right, the nib would be trimmed obliquely to the right. In addition, the metal stylus that was used for writing on tablets was also adapted to writing with ink.

Although the development of ink in the Far East may have occurred independently to that of the west, it, too, relied on carbon soot as the preferred black pigment. The one major difference between the eastern and western inks was the eastern use of animal-based glue instead of gum as a binder. In China, for instance, both animal hides and deer antlers were boiled down into glue, while in Japan, with its natural abundance of seafood, fish skins were used.

Some of the earliest examples of the use of carbon soot ink in China are found on the Oracle bones of the Shang Dynasty, which date from around 1766 to 1122 BCE. Used as part of divination rituals, questions, answers, and other details were either scratched or written on the surface of the bones. Traces of both black and red ink can be found in the grooves of some of the incised letters and also on the surface of the bone. Additionally, ink appears to have been rubbed into some of the cracks found on the bones to make the patterns appear more prominent. The red ink found on these bones, and on later Chinese writings and seals, is made with vermillion which is the pigment formed from the mineral cinnabar. Cinnabar, also known as mercuric sulfide, is found in locations associated with either hot springs or volcanic activity.

Even though refinements have been made to the manufacturing of black Asian inks through the centuries, the two main ingredients of lamp black and glue have, for the most part, remained pretty much the same. First and foremost is the lamp black. For the best quality ink, only the best and purest soot should be used. The fuel for the lamp black varies and may be from pine knots, vegetable oil, fat, or literally anything that will create smoke. That being said, certain fuels will produce different types of black and can potentially bear an oily residue. Likewise, the glue should be the best available, the preparation of which might be even more important than the pigment. Glues of the purest and highest quality produce a more efficient dispersing agent for the pigment than a low quality can, resulting in an ink stick that contains a higher concentration of pigment.

Along with these two ingredients, other substances were sometimes added to the mixture as a means to add a pleasant scent or to aid in the prevention of deterioration or mold. These items were then blended into a mass with a similar feel to pottery clay. This mass was then pounded, kneaded, rolled, and hydrated until it reached what the ink maker knew was the proper consistency for it to be pressed into wooden molds to create sticks or any number of shapes. These shaped sticks and cakes then had to be dried slowly to prevent cracking. The time for curing these ink sticks of course varied, with some sources requiring as much as two years.

Once it was fully cured, the dry ink stick would then need to be ground and mixed with water to make a liquid medium to write with. To answer this need, an inkstone would be utilized. Traditionally carved from stone, "inkstones" can also be manufactured from clay, bronze, iron, or porcelain. The stone has a rough, flat surface on which the ink stick is ground using a slow circular motion, as well as a reservoir to hold water and catch the ink as it is ground. During this process, "The slow, thoughtful rubbing of ink on the stone should produce a calm feeling and release from tension. This is excellent preparation for the mind before the student begins to draw...As the artist rubs the ink, his mind is considering the painting—where to start, where to end. No outside noises distract him. Then he picks up his brush and begins".

In addition to the oracle bones mentioned before, other ancient Chinese writing surfaces included bamboo, tortoise shells and stones. These, along with possibly other even more perishable items, became obsolete as writing surfaces around the year 105 when Cai Lun, a court official in the Han dynasty, is credited with the invention of paper, which was made from a pulp of rag and other plant fibers.

Along with the ink, inkstone, and paper, the brush was the final tool in what would later become known as the "four treasures of the study," with the word "study" referring to the location being used to write in. Similar to those still made today, these early brushes were made from soft hairs gathered from various mammals that were then usually attached to a bamboo stick. This construction produced a rounded brush and helped give the bristles a pointed shape that was necessary for the proper creation of Chinese characters. The more common hairs for these brushes came from domesticated animals such as sheep, oxen, goats, and horses, along with wild animals like rabbits, martens, badgers, deer, and wolves. These hairs might be gathered from a single animal or from a combination of animals in order to obtain a desired texture, such as combining the hairs from both a weasel and a goat. Similar brushes to these were made in Japan and other Asian countries where the script lent itself more to a brush than a pen.

Chinese ink was also carried to other countries, with the formula being adapted to their resources. Making its way to India around 400 BCE, this ink was called Masi and contained carbon black from burnt bones, pitch, tar, and other substances. Applied to a variety of surfaces including palm leaves, birch bark, and paper, India scripts were written using a variety of tools such as sharpened needles and metal pens. In the mid 17th century, European merchants began importing ink from India, at which time the name "Indian ink" was used. Later, in America, the name was shortened to "India ink" to eliminate confusion.

While most of these Asian inks are still in use today, beginning in the fourth century, a different type of ink was being developed in the western world that substituted a chemical reaction for the lamp black and was to become known as iron gall ink. Unlike inks made with carbon that lie atop the writing surface, iron gall ink etches into the writing surface, creating an ink that is more or less permanent. This ink was prepared from four ingredients, namely oak galls, copperas, gum arabic, and either water or wine.

Oak galls are formed on oak trees as a protective reaction to eggs laid beneath the bark by a member of the wasp family. By soaking these galls in water, wine, or even beer, a mold forms, which then produces gallic acid. This, combined with copperas — also known as ferrous sulfate or green vitriol — produces a blue-black liquid. The final ingredient, gum arabic, helps with ink flow, along with stabilizing the materials in the fluid.

When first applied, iron gall ink appears as a light brown to sepia color. As the ink oxidizes, it becomes a darker brown-black to purple-black color. While the permanence of this ink is an asset, the acidic nature of its ingredients is potentially a liability, as it can cause the ink to slowly destroy the writing surface, leaving only the outline of where a letter once was. However, in spite of this disadvantage, iron gall ink was responsible for many important written works still with us today, including the 9th century *Book of Kells.*

According to Trinity College, "the *Book of Kells* was created around the year 800 AD... in a monastery on the island of Iona off the coast of Scotland. It appears to have been created by three artists and four scribes." When this island was attacked by Vikings, the monks moved to a sister monastery in Kells, where it is believed they finished the manuscript. The Book of Kells was produced on sheets of vellum, which was prepared from the skins of calves rather than sheep or goats like parchment. These sheets of vellum produced a smoother page that served as the perfect writing surface for the quill pens used by the monks.

Although they are first mentioned in a sixth century text, quill pens lend themselves so well to gall ink that it is possible that their first use was, in fact, of a much earlier date. The strongest quills were said to be obtained from live birds in the spring when new growth occurs. Only the five outer wing feathers were considered useful for writing, with those from the left wing being the best suited for right-handed writers since they would naturally curve away from the hand. Being both strong and flexible, quills were able to be trimmed into precise writing instruments that could produce detailed work that would have been difficult, if not impossible, with a reed pen, including the serifs and flourishes of the medieval monastic scripts.

In addition to the inked text, each of the manuscript pages in the Book of Kells contain intricately painted illuminations in the forms of initials, borders, and miniatures. The pigments found in these paints were either found locally or were purchased from merchants. Given the fact that the writings were the four Gospels, it is probable that quality was a major concern in choice. It is interesting to note that what is often thought of as gold leaf in the illuminations is actually orpiment, a highly toxic arsenic sulfide.

The binder that was used with these pigments often came from eggs. Egg whites were used to produce egg glair, which is a very flexible binder that lends itself to the vellum page. Egg yolk is used to produce egg tempera, which, although versatile, is liable to crack if laid on too thick. Other binders for these paints could include either gum or some type of animal gelatin.

While illuminated manuscripts were repositories of knowledge as well as works of art, they were both time-consuming to make and costly to own. Likewise, since each copy had to be done by hand, only a few could enjoy the writing. This would begin to change in the mid-1400s with Johann Gutenberg's invention of printing using movable type, along with the development of an oil-based printing ink. Neither the Chinese nor iron gall inks, both being water-based, would hold to the movable type being used for printing. Taking his cue from the oil paint used by artists, Gutenberg developed an ink which used lamp-black as the primary pigment along with graphite. For the binder, he used a mixture of linseed oil, walnut oil, turpentine oil, and pine resin. Also present in this ink were traces of cinnabar, sulfur, copper, lead, and titanium, the last three being responsible for the glittering surface found on the dried ink. This mixture was then boiled down until it had thickened to the proper viscosity needed for printing.

Gutenberg produced an edition of less than 200 sets of his Bible. While this might seem small by later standards, it was enough to spark the imagination of others, and soon, a printing revolution in the western world had begun. Hundreds of cities throughout Europe had printing presses, and by the year 1501, it has been estimated that collectively, over 10 million items had been printed, from nearly 40 thousand titles.

Not long after, an important innovation in writing ink occurred with the creation of what was known as portable ink. A description of how to make it was included in Hugh Plat's Jewell House, printed in 1594. In this description, Plat recommends heating copperas until it calcifies into whitish powder. Taking this from the heat, one should then "weigh out of this calcined copperas one part, one part of the best galls well powdered, and half a part of the clearest gum Arabeck well powdered." When needed, the mixed powder should have water, wine, beer or vinegar added and mixed together to make a liquid ink.

The commercial marketing of portable ink was begun in the late seventeenth century in London. As early as 1690, an advertisement by haberdasher Charles Holman advertised that under his "majesties pattent," he was entitled to make what he called the "London ink powder." In a later advertisement, the Holmans gave this description for preparing it:

> Take one pint of water (whereof rain or river is the best) to one paper of powder, and in proportion for a smaller quantity, shake or stir it well together, and it is presently useful; and though it seems pale when made new, it changes blacker and blacker as it dissolves, and grows better and better, by daily stirring, till it is a most beautiful black.

The manufacturing of Holman's ink powder was continued by himself and his family for at least three generations. The previous description dates from the time his daughter Alice had taken over in making the ink, and sometime later, the grandson, William Barnard, was in charge. This ink powder proved popular, and by the mid-eighteenth century, Holman's ink powder was available in New York City, Boston, Charlestown, and likely other places.

Like the Holman family, other manufacturers began producing powdered ink. In the Virginia Gazette, for example, powdered ink was advertised at various times in the 18th century, listed as black, red, Japan, or without any indication of type or color. Since the ink powder could be prepared in any quantity, it was very popular with soldiers and travelers who lacked adequate storage space for a corked bottle containing anything liquid.

By the beginning of the 19th century, the best instrument to write with was still the quill pen. Contrary to the impression many have from old illustrations, for most writing, the barbs of the feather would be removed, leaving only the shaft with the nib cut into one end. This would soon change with the invention of the steel pen nib. While metal had been used as a material for making pens for many years, the first patent for a metal pen point was by inventor Bryan Donkin in 1803. When Donkin's patent lapsed in 1822, John Mitchell of Birmingham, England introduced his own steel pen nibs to the public. Being machine-made, Mitchell was able to mass-produce them to a receptive public. Having an advantage over quills of lasting longer, not requiring sharpening, being able to be made in a wide variety of shapes and sizes, and generally being more reliable, these steel nibs helped bring writing into the industrial age.

Improvements in manufacture of these pen nibs also led to the development of new types of writing instruments, namely dip pens and fountain pens. Dip pens — so named because the nib was dipped into an ink bottle or ink well to charge it with ink — consisted of a metal nib that was secured in some manner to a handle. These handles were made in a wide variety of materials that ranged from the plain and inexpensive to the ornate and costly. With the variety of nibs available, the dip pen was practical and versatile as well.

The concept of the fountain pen began as early as the 10th century and continued through the years, yet most, if not all, of those built amounted to little more than isolated experiments. A renewed interest appears to have been inspired by these new metal nibs, and so by the middle of the 19th century, many workable fountain pens were produced, yet they all shared a similar problem in that the ink could leak out if the pen was stored or carried in the wrong position. This problem was solved in the mid-1880s with the pens developed and sold by Lewis Edson Waterman through the use of capillary action. Simply put, the ink was forced to flow through narrow areas built into the pen's chamber that allowed gravity to move the ink, but not so fast as to cause it to leak.

These pens were marketed to the public using advertisements that stressed the dignity and satisfaction that came from owning and using a Waterman pen. One particular advertisement depicted a pristine landscape with a winged sprite delivering a fountain pen, with the caption "Wherever the Vacation Spirit Calls." Under the main image were four vignettes that further defined the vacation as being, "At the Lake, In the Mountains, In Camp, At the Seashore." In each vignette, a person was depicted either writing in a journal or composing a letter, with the apparent ease of not having to replenish ink while enjoying their secluded and pristine spot in nature. The message was clear: with this fountain pen, you have the ability to write your thoughts when and where you have them.

Among the obstacles faced with creating a successful fountain pen, the one whose solution possibly had the farthest reaching impact was in the selection of what ink should be used. While dip pens could still use iron gall ink successfully, the acid in the ink could corrode the delicate insides of the fountain pen. Likewise, india ink contained both pigment and gum, either of which could clog the narrow capillaries of the pen. The answer was found through the development of dye-based inks which used solvents and dryers to produce a formula that not only solved the problem for the fountain pen, but also opened the door for the other types of pens that followed.

In 1895, John J. Loud of Weymouth, Massachusetts secured a patent for a pen designed to write on irregular surfaces, particularly leather, that would have been difficult, if not impossible, to write on with the common dip pen. This pen was not a commercial success, and in time, the patent was allowed to lapse, only to be picked up some years later by a young Hungarian named Laszio Biro. Laszio and his brother Gyorgy developed a pen that used a combination of a ball-socket tip along with a viscous ink to make a writing instrument that produced a constant, even flow of ink. First displayed at the International Fair in Budapest in 1931, the pen was later patented in 1938. In 1941, the Biro brothers fled from Hungary to Argentina, where, in 1943, they filed a new patent and formed their company, Biro Pens of Argentina. In 1945, the patent was sold to Marcel Bich, and the pen became the main product of the BIC company. The ball point pen proved so successful that by the late 1950s, it had replaced the dip pen as the preferred writing tool in most schools and businesses, relegating the metal nib to limited use in calligraphy and artist tools. Other pens and inks created in the late 20th century included the soft tip and rollerball pens of the 60s and the gel pens of the 80s, all of which, with their dye-based inks, seem to take us further and further from the fire that started it all.

Or have they? At first glance, it might appear that our ties to the past have been lost forever due to change, when in reality, the innovations of writing and ink were in themselves change. Prehistoric man had to face changing ways of life, and so do we. When we gather at the Club and listen to a story being told, we are participating in a tradition that extends back through the centuries. Whether the tools we use are pen and ink or touch screen and inkjet, we are carrying on the progression of communication, which defines our society for future ages.

Rick Kesterman is a lifelong resident of the west side of Cincinnati, and has been a member of the Literary Club since 2006. His experiences have spanned a variety of fields since he received a Bachelor of Fine Arts from the Art Academy of Cincinnati in 1983, including time teaching elementary school art and working with libraries and archives. His interests include travel, nature, and history.

12 The Phantom Runner

WILLIAM KILLEN

THE phone rang, and within a few minutes the whole world changed.

"It's back, Charlie's cancer is back! It's been over five years and it's not supposed to come back, but today it has." Diane could not shake the words from her mind.

Five years earlier Charlie had been stricken with Non-Hodgkins Lymphoma and underwent chemo and radiation treatments for this dreadful disease. This was the first serious illness Charlie and Diane had faced in their lives together. The stress was hard on them and on their elementary, middle, and high school aged children. It was frightening for the kids to see how the disease impacted their father. Charlie had always been fit and athletic, but within weeks he had changed before their eyes. Luckily the treatments were successful; his checkups showed no signs of cancer. All seemed well.

There is a school of thought that exercise is beneficial in keeping cancer at bay. The couple embraced this idea and continued their active lifestyle, adding more running to the regimen. Diane was more interested in endurance and trained for half marathon and full marathon distances. Charlie found the 5K and 10K runs and some of the novelty races more to his liking.

Just a few months before he got this new diagnosis, Charlie signed up for the annual three-race beer run series that took place throughout the

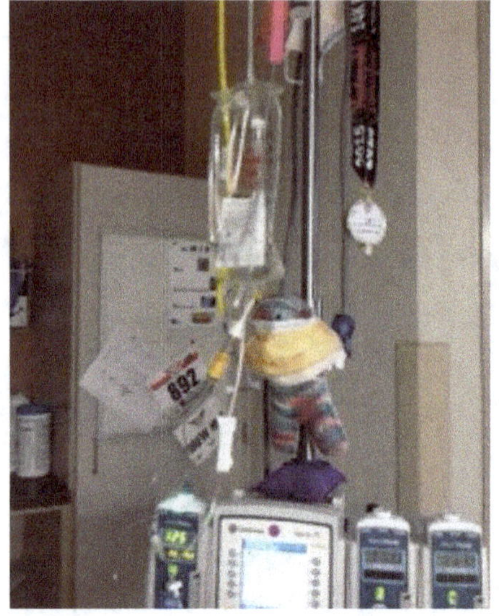

year. Those completing all three races would get the coveted title of Brew Hog. Charlie finished two of the three races that year before feeling the need to go into the oncology center for another checkup, which led to the shocking news. Finishing the third race, the 14K, now seemed in doubt, or even lost.

The appointment with the oncologist to discuss treatment options was anxious and tense. Charlie and Diane sat in the office, hand in hand, experiencing again the somber mood of the place, the smells, the fish tank, the hushed tones of the staff, and the cheap commercial art on the walls. The minutes ticked by slowly until the doctor opened the door.

He told them that this time a stem cell transplant was the only treatment left to eradicate this stubborn, deadly disease. "Yes, it is the most extreme treatment available, but it has a very positive success rate for long term health," the doctor said.

Over the next week, Diane and Charlie had long, serious conversations between themselves and with the doctor. At the next appointment, Diane looked at Charlie, took his hand, Charlie looked at the doctor and said, "What do I have to do?"

There was a lot to do. The time demands on Charlie over the ensuing weeks would be enormous, and continuing his normal department chair and teaching responsibilities at the college would not be possible. By moving his non-teaching semester forward and rescheduling the teaching load to his faculty, he was able to have the time required for treatment.

For Diane it was more difficult to carry on with her job and have time for the family, hospital visits, and caring for Charlie. She was a member of a creative team with an advertising agency working on a new ad campaign just weeks away from the launch date. And there was Senior Year. An "all hands on deck" meeting brought the family and grandparents together to organize coverage for those things that would need to be managed during the treatment period.

The first step in the treatment process was to determine if Charlie's cells were healthy enough to transplant, or if a donor would be needed. His cells proved to be usable. The next thing was to start the harvest of these cells to hold for transplant in a frozen state at the local blood bank.

This took weeks to complete. Diane was thankful that Charlie's mom could take him to these appointments and stay with him during those long, boring hours.

With chemo underway, Charlie and Diane accompanied their son to mid-field on Senior Night at the last soccer game of the season. It was evident that Charlie was weak, but he would not miss it. He was determined to be there at the graduation ceremony in the spring to see their boy receive his honors and diploma.

"It's time," Diane said to Charlie as she picked up the last few things he would take to the hospital. The drive was quiet and anxious. She went over in her mind the regimen of the oncology ICU, something she thought she would never face again. Go to the wash station just inside the door, scrub your hands, hit the Purell bottle, put on your mask, walk down the hall to the nurses' station to check in, dodge the gaggle of residents making their daily rounds, hit the Purell bottle, a coffee and snack cart, avoid a room full of family who was losing a loved one, gown up, go into Charlie's room, hit the Purell bottle one more time.

Charlie entered his room with a CD player, audio books, and a drum practice pad ready for an extended stay. During the first six days he was scheduled for very intense chemo treatments. Early in that week he was able to get out of bed, walk the halls, and even make coffee for the nurses coming in on their morning shift. Maybe all that running had helped after all. But that ended soon.

The day after the last chemo treatment, the team from the blood bank wheeled in the cryogenic tank containing Charlie's stem cells and the treatment process began. Since he was prone to getting out of bed, the nurses installed a bed alarm to prevent a fall. As the infusion process wore on into the seventh and eighth day, Charlie felt weaker and noticed pain more intensely. He told his dad, who was a frequent visitor, "I feel like I have been hit by a train and run over by a truck. I don't know if I will ever feel normal again."

In the midst of this, Diane received notice that it was time for the final 14K segment of the Brewery Run. "Oh, for Heaven's sake! What am I supposed to do with this?" she thought. This was the last thing on her mind right now. Charlie could not possibly run because he would hit the zero mark in the transplant protocol just two days before the race. He had told her when all of this started that he would not be able to run the third race. No Brew Hog for him, maybe ever. Then a thought occurred to her.

Late in the morning of the race Diane walked into the hospital and went to the nurses' station.

"Is my husband here?' she asked.

"Well yes." replied the nurse.

"Is he still on bed alarm?"

"Yes," said the nurse.

"Did he at any time this morning leave the hospital?"

"NO!" replied the nurse. "Where is all of this going?"

Diane smiled. "Then how do you explain that I have a medal, a bib number, and a timesheet with my husband's name on it claiming that he just ran the 14K Brewery Run this morning, turning in his best time by the way?"

Diane produced the items to the nurse's amazement. "Let's go tell him," said Diane with a wink.

Charlie was groggy when they entered his room. Diane hung the medal on his IV stand while the nurse put the bib number and time sheet on his bulletin board. Charlie and his visitors that day got a much-needed good laugh about his "accomplishment." He wanted to know how she had pulled this off. "Simple, I just ran with your bib number. Let's see if you can beat your time next year."

As the days passed, Charlie felt his strength returning. Those stem cells figured out what they were supposed to do and went to work. And one morning he greeted the morning shift with fresh brewed coffee, and a race medal around his neck.

Bill Killen, widower, father, grandfather, great grandfather, and retired from corporate life. Currently a resident of Covington, KY and a Literary Club member for the past nine years.

13 The Man of the House

MICHAEL H. KREMZAR

STANDING beside my mother's white coffin, the military headstones of the Jefferson Barracks National Cemetery stretch in geometric patterns in every direction. I remembered this open grave 39 years earlier, when my father, Lt. Col. Stanley J. Kremzar, was buried. After spending 33 years in the Army Air Corps and then the Air Force, he died of lung cancer in 1967 at age 61. Our life, like many career military families, was nomadic and, during WWII and Korea, filled with long periods of separation and worry. Although this is a personal story, it is simply an example of the unseen pressures on the spouses and children of military families.

Living with the separation anxiety caused by the absence for months and years of the soldier, sailor, or airman during times of war causes unique family pressures. In my family, Dad was overseas for more than two years during World War II between my ages of 7-9 and again during the Korean War during my ages of 13-16. Whenever he was gone, as the only child, I was given the ill-defined responsibility of "the man of the house." Mother never complained about the military lifestyle. However, she had to deal with her own angst about the safety of her husband while raising a son in a series of short-term living situations.

When World War II started, Dad had already been in the Army Air Corps for 17 years as an enlisted man. We were living in comfortable quarters on the 'Enlisted' side of the Army Air Corps Scott Field in Illinois, and our first move occurred when we relocated to the 'Officer' side as he was promoted to 1st. Lieutenant. He was given his overseas orders in 1942 for the middle of China as Maintenance Officer of an airbase flying transports over the Himalayas to India. Since we no longer had official connection to a base in the U.S., the Army gave us 30 days to vacate our housing. All our furniture and possessions except for two footlockers and assorted luggage were placed into long-term storage.

The three of us drove from Illinois to Utah where Dad was to report to his assembly location near Salt Lake City. As we said goodbye at the gate of a vast area of tents surrounded by barbed wire, Dad turned to me with his hand on my shoulder and said: "Mikey, you are now the man of the house, take care of your mother while I am gone." My 7-year-old instincts were to hug him, but I stood at attention and gave a slightly teary response of: "Yes sir!"

Since we were now homeless, Mother decided to drive on to California since she might be able to see Dad again on his way out of the country. We arrived in a Los Angeles experiencing an economic boom. The presence of several military bases, many defense contractors, and the major shipping ports made for an overcrowded, bustling city. The search for any kind of housing for the two of us started in Venice with a two-car garage. This small space was equipped with bed, chair, hot plate, but no plumbing — knock on the kitchen door and ask to use the bathroom. After a couple of months, she found a small cottage in Santa Monica with one-bedroom, adequate kitchen, and a real bathroom. This meant two different schools for me. The first was an old, overcrowded building where the educational focus was standing in line. I completed 2nd grade without any memory of classroom work. However, the second school was a nice, suburban school focused on arts and crafts. The 3rd and 4th grades were fun without the ordeal of learning reading, writing, or arithmetic.

Typical of many other families, we lived with the constant angst of not knowing if your husband and father was alive. Dad's letters informed us that his base was bombed routinely by the Japanese, so the threat of being part of a casualty report was real. Any cars that parked near our cottage caused mother to look for the obvious military detail that might bring the worst possible news. Dad was a faithful writer, but his letters took a month to arrive. With all of this, I was a real nuisance trying to do my duty to protect my mother as commanded by my father. Mother certainly did not need any help and had to deal with a son who was rude to guests that might seem to be too friendly. I had a secret plan that, if my dad was killed, I would drop out of school, get a job, and provide family support. A laughable idea from a child trying to find a way to deal with the wartime uncertainties.

After the war ended, we met at the top of an escalator in the LA train station. My parents embraced like every other re-uniting couple. He had lost 20 pounds and, with my nearly three years of growth, didn't seem as big as I remembered. Dad grabbed me by my shoulders and exclaimed about how big I was before I could give a little homecoming speech about doing my duty. However, I can still recall my overwhelming sense of relief and freedom that I was no longer man of the house.

Finding housing is a typical challenge for military families, and we were no exception. Dad's postwar assignment was back at Scott Field. All the housing on the base was filled so we lived for a few months with my grandmother and her husband in their two-bedroom cottage — parents on a rollway and me on a cot in the dining room. Mother's frantic search led to a two-bedroom, furnished flat on the second floor of a house with kitchen downstairs. After about six months, a nice rental house with one bedroom and an attic room was found, and all our furniture came out of storage. This presented me with three new Illinois schools from 4th to 5th grade with varying degrees of educational interest. The first was the hardest since my California sojourn had left me a full year behind in math. Fortunately, the third school starting mid-way in 5th grade was quite good and our house was adequate.

In early 1950, Dad was assigned to Japan with the expectation that

Mother and I, then 13, would join him promptly. We said goodbye in Union Station in St. Louis. Once again, even with the expected shorter separation, Dad admonished me: "Mike, you are the man of the house. Take good care of your mother." This time with no teary feelings I responded as programed with a snappy: "Yes sir!" However, those nasty North Koreans invaded South Korea in June 1950, and all relocations of dependents to Japan were canceled. The only advantage for this separation was that Mother and I stayed in the same rented house, and my schooling followed the normal path through Freshman in high school. The disadvantage for her was that I became a teen — ages 13 to 16 - with all the trappings and traps accorded thereto. Although I had a somewhat more balanced view of my role as "man of the house," I kept track of where she was, and how safe the house was every night.

After two years of the Korean War blocking travel to Japan, Dad worked out a transfer to Clark Air Force Base in the Philippines where we could join him. I learned this in the only voice contact available to us — a phone call patched through to a local amateur radio operator. Dad announced the transfer and the good news that we could join him soon. My immediate response was that I understood that he and mom wanted to be together, but my freshman year in high school had been great with sports, grades, and girlfriend. Without any forethought, I proposed that I could live with my friend Chuck until they rotated back to the states. With remarkable restraint, Dad said: "We thought you might feel this way. We really don't want to be separated but understand your feelings."

Once again, all our furniture and most of our possessions went into storage. Mom got me so involved with the packing and arrangements that I forgot about my plan to stay behind. She and I drove to California again — this time with me sharing some driving to San Francisco.

The trip to Manila was 21 days onboard a troop ship with a few cabins and stops at Hawaii, Guam, and Kwajalein. I shared a cabin with a Navy doctor and dozens of vials of mosquito larvae destined for Kwajalein, and mom was in a cabin with two other wives joining husbands.

Meeting Dad at the dock was just like meeting him in 1945 except that it was mother running down the gangplank to meet him. I trailed along, but this time, Dad looked up at his 3" taller son, shook my hand and said: "I guess we can't call you Little Mike anymore." My homecoming speech about delivering my mother to him was swallowed in the crush of other arriving passengers and general melee at the dock. It became obvious from the beginning that Dad and I did not know how to talk to each other. My self-image as a 16-year-old was closer to 21, and his view of me was closer to 12. The metaphor for our revived father-son relationship came after only a week in our nice three-bedroom Florida style home on Clark Air Force Base. Dad came into my room after dinner and closed the door. His countenance was serious, and my mind raced about what I could have done in such a short time to be in trouble. He reached into his pocket and took out a half dozen condoms in various shapes and colors and laid them on my desk. He said: "Do you know what these are for?"

If I said "No'" I would get an extremely embarrassing sex education lecture. If I said "Yes" I would get a morals and behavior lecture. There was no good answer here for Mike. So, I stammered the safest response I could think of: "...umm... sure, the guys have talked about them." He looked a little relieved, and then with the same stern countenance said: "Then you know two things. One is that these will keep you from getting a disease, and two, it keeps you from getting a girl in trouble. Do you understand that?" As quickly as I could to end the conversation, I said: "Yes sir." He finished by saying: "Then we know that if either of these two things ever happen, you were too dumb to be my son. Got that?" My mind exclaimed: "Oh shit," But I responded in my most manly way: "Yes sir!"

High school at Clark Air Force Base was great. We had 24 students in the high school grades with 6 highly qualified teachers — better than most private schools. Because of the heat, we went to school only until noon and had the rest of the day for swimming, golf, basketball, and fun times. Life was good.

About the close of my sophomore school year, Dad announced that he was being reassigned back to Scott Air Force Base. Again, my spontaneous answer was that I knew that he wanted to go back and Mom certainly with him, but I was getting a great education here and life was a lot of fun for me. I could stay with my friend Bill for another year. Dad promptly informed me that this was not a discussion agenda. He said: "Cut the shit soldier, we are all going home."

We did go back to Scott Air Force Base but the decision was to find housing in town so I could go back to the same high school as my freshman year. A two-bedroom rental house became our last home for my final two years of high school and college years. Dad retired following 33 years of active-duty military service as I graduated from college. Mom and Dad moved to Florida and Dad helped build the only house he and Mom ever owned — a nice two-bedroom Florida ranch with big sun porch.

Sadly, the Air Force physical exam did not detect a spot on his lung, and Dad died of metastasized lung cancer just nine years later. As he was dying, I flew from Cincinnati to be with him and mom at the hospital on MacDill AFB. Holding his hand and leaning close, I told him: "Dad, don't worry, I will take care of Mom." He squeezed my hand and died moments later.

Little did I know that when Dad died, his very nice retirement salary died with him. Mother at age 58 was left with only his $10,000 GI Life Insurance and the house — not even Social Security. So, for the next 39 years I was, again, "man of the house" making sure Mother was physically and financially comfortable. The other separations and anxieties about watching after her were simply training for that challenge. Fortunately, I was able to visit her several times a year and guide her from house to apartment, assisted living, and finally nursing care in a lovely retirement community. Fortunately, my career had done well, and the financial burden was manageable — with a wife that supported me at every step.

This brings the story back to the beginning. As I watched my mother's coffin being lowered into permanent rest with my father, our family history of separations raced through my mind. Although my beliefs do not include ghosts or spirits circling around cemeteries, I experienced a strong sense of presence. Standing at the foot of the open grave I was compelled to speak out loud: "Dad, I've taken care of Mom and brought her back to you. My duty is done — God bless you both." For the first and last time, I had said my little speech of homecoming. The feeling of relief was as palpable as it had been when I was a child. The reward was a distinct feeling that Dad was saying "Job well done."

Mike Kremzar is an engineering graduate of Princeton University and saw Army duty before his career at Procter & Gamble, finishing as a Vice President — Global Product Supply. After his retirement, he co-authored a book titled "ERP: Making It Happen" (John Wiley & Sons). His recent focus has been serving on several boards of non-profit organizations that focus on helping people in need to build self-sufficiency, as well as writing fiction and non-fiction short stories.

14 A Sheep Story: What the Flock?

BILL LAWARRE

For my dear friend and mentor G.G. Carey IV,
who was fond of saying, "In the fullness of time...
Gibby, in the fullness of time I am here with a paper.

IT was 7 a.m. Saturday the tenth of November 1976. It was colder than normal. As I walked out of my office and into the dark hallway on my way to the men's room, I was alone, or so I thought. Around the corner I heard voices and saw Alex talking on the phone and motioning for me to come into his office. Alex Stolley: President, CEO, and Chairman of the Board of Northlich Stolley Advertising Agency where I was Creative Director.

"Alex, you're in early."

"Been here since 5:30. I want you to know there's still time to call this whole thing off." He was perfectly serious.

It was unusual for Alex to become involved in any of the productions at the agency, especially at this late date. He clearly saw this spot as a more serious risk because it had the potential to create havoc in the streets.

So, I was stunned when he said there's still time to cancel the shoot. Little did he know that down in front of our building there were four truckloads of sheep fresh off the grass soon to be unloaded onto the streets of the Cincinnati Central Business District. They

were going to spend their day downtown along with a full camera crew from Minneapolis, numerous sheep herders, several semi-trucks blocking downtown streets and a client waiting for his commercial to be completed. Not to mention that our agency had invested $4,000 buying the sheep. Just for a second all my fears of coming down on the wrong side of the risk-reward equation surfaced, but I could not stop. I don't remember the rest of our conversation, but I left the office and headed for the street.

I stepped into the street and saw the first few sheep jump out of one of the trucks. I wanted to yell stop! But at this point another truck started dumping his load into 4th street and sure enough, as soon they saw the other ones they hastily trotted over. Before I knew it, I was knee deep in sheep. There were enough sheep on the ground that it was clear to us that not only did they have minds of their own but with little warning they were eating all the new landscaping on Fountain Square.

Back in the conference room when we were preparing the idea, we might laugh about the thought of the sheep devouring the landscaping on Fountain Square. But there was no laughing when you are staring a sheep straight in her eye and she is chewing on a small pine tree. Planted just a week ago.

Just about that time, I noticed out of the corner of my eye a sheep headed out of bounds up Elm Street to 6th where we had an 18-wheeler blocking the road. The minute I took off to catch her she hit a different gear. At the last second, I made a desperate dive and grabbed her hind legs at the expense of my knees and elbows. Behind me and around the corner I saw 60 or 70 more sheep coming toward me. At that moment I thought it was over, all the cameras were at the other end of the square and there was no one around. If those sheep came toward me, the whole group would follow. It was very frightening. And I thought, what the hell have I done? I had similar thoughts especially during my teenage years when everything seemed larger than life. This one felt bigger, maybe like this is the end of the world. It certainly could be the end of my world.

Down 5th street, I saw the sheep stop. The herders had turned them, and they had suddenly discovered the floor to ceiling windows on the building at 5th & Vine. Not only did they stop, but now we had two flocks of sheep separated and as much as they wanted to get back together, they couldn't resist squeezing up to their own reflections in the Mabley & Carew window. I started looking for help, but none was available. I tried to pull the sheep away from the window, but they were heavier than I had anticipated, and as soon as I pulled one away, there were two or more waiting to take its place. It was beginning to look like I was coming down on the wrong side of the risk-reward equation.

The sheep began to move down the street and for a moment I was overwhelmed as to how to proceed. My confusion didn't last long because they were proceeding without me. Just as I was trying to get some help, one of Cincinnati's finest beckoned me over to his cruiser.

He opened the back door and in an authoritative tone asked, "Does she belong to you?" The sheep was sitting on her tuffet, seat belted, four legs straight out & looking out the window of the cruiser.

"Where did you find her?" I asked.

"On the 8th street viaduct," the officer replied.

A few minutes later, one of the herders motioned me over to where he was standing. A pair of lambs had just been born in a side alley in the back of Jorge's Restaurant. The flock is increasing; do I have any grandparenting responsibilities here?

As the day wore on, it got colder and colder and the odd flake of snow was beginning to fall. I kept one eye on the sky and the other on the woollies. This was a one-take shoot. Most of the corrections, if any, were going to be done in the editing suite and half of the commercial had been shot without snow. We had to finish, and no way could we finish with snow on the ground. Especially since we had four blocks to clean up.

The clean-up people we hired were sure they could simply sweep up the droppings. But mass amounts of sheep droppings tend to roll around like marbles, so cleanup was stopped before it got started. We finally brought the fire department in to wash down the sidewalks and streets.

Unfortunately, a businessman had just purchased a new pair of wingtips at Nettleton Shoes, a high-end shoe store on 5th Street. When he stepped out of the store it resulted in a lawsuit aimed at Northlich and our 200 friends.

Three weeks earlier the creative team and I were racking our brains about how to market a new concept tacked on an old, well-known, slowly fading bus company. The Green Line had served Cincinnati for as long as anyone could remember. The city had purchased the bus company and was hell bent on changing the image based on the strategy of competing with the automobile.

When I first heard this, I almost laughed out loud. The whole idea seemed preposterous and impossible, not to mention expensive.

So, it was no surprise that I was, I guess the best way to say it is, I was not interested in the fact that Cincinnati had purchased the bus company. Well, the city needed to announce that it was now the Queen City Metro. Bus was not really a word they wanted to use at all. Metro wanted buses to be coaches. The word coaches was drilled into my head very quickly. We were doing coaches.

I remember there was some talk in the agency about, "we may get a shot at this." Well, I always think that "getting a shot" at something means that other people are also getting a shot. We made a presentation of our credentials. We didn't do any creative work. A guy named Peter Weiglin had come to town and was the new General Manager of Queen City Metro. Pete was a jolly good fellow, and he quickly made the decision to hire our agency.

The creative department was in the back of the agency where your typical client really wasn't allowed to roam around, for good reason. You don't want your clients to see Proctor & Gamble or Kroger or any possible competitor's work there. I was thinking we must produce a TV spot for Metro. It's a bus. What the hell am I going do with that? So, as we moved along in the process, there was Craig Jackson, Cliff Schwander, Mark Serrianne and me.

We were all in the same room one afternoon and I knew we had to do this spot. What are we going to do? There was this thing we developed as an internal tool called the Northlich stare, which meant you could throw any idea you wanted out there. If nobody said anything, you looked around to see who's staring at you. They were thinking, what a dumb ass, without saying it. We were kind to one another, but some of these ideas about the bus and Metro were getting the stare both from me and from other people.

I'd like to be able to remember how it came up. I know I came up with it, but I don't know why. I guess it came up because I thought sheep was a good metaphor for traffic running bumper to bumper. But I didn't think there was any chance of it ever happening. I certainly didn't have Cincinnati in mind as a place where the sheep were going to be. I didn't have anything in any detail. It's just that sheep reminded me of traffic.

So that went by the wayside, and I got the stare from everybody. The thought was sitting there like a bump on a log. I kept looking at the bump and did not hear anything from anybody else. I tried again in a different form. I said, "I don't know if we can do this. Can you imagine a bunch of sheep running down the street, in the middle of Downtown Cincinnati?" The stare came back again, but not as intensely and the idea was beginning to gain acceptance. The more we talked about it, the more it seemed possible. Now we had something to tie to their strategy, which was to replace the car with the bus as a basic mode of travel. We all knew that was ridiculous, but there it was. Our client wanted excitement and creativity, and this became our raison d'etre for the rest of the shoot. When we left the room, the sheep idea was the one we took with us, and we went to work to create a storyboard.

Pete Weiglin, who as I said was the General Manager of Metro seemed to be a pretty good guy. A slap on the back kind of fellow. He was a very upbeat and enthusiastic person. When he saw our storyboard, he did a double take, like what is this? And then he got all rah rah about it. He loved it. He wanted something that was different and creative. And I thought, oh shit, this is going to happen. Even though we didn't know him very well, it was clear he was immediately committed to the concept. Very few clients are that way. Pete took the storyboard back to his office for final approval from Will Scott who was Metro's Vice President of Marketing.

When Pete called to report Metro's approval of the commercial, I can't remember whether I was nervous or not. I probably was, given the radical nature of this idea. I walked out of the room thinking this was too easy, something's going to go wrong. I'm prone to finding the downside of anything anyway. I didn't know what we needed. Just then I saw one of our producers, showed her the storyboards, and asked, "What do you think?"

She said, "I think we need some sheep."

"Yes," I said, "I think we do."

It's always good to see what a fresh perspective can provide.

Our producer went to the stockyards in Lebanon, Ohio, and paid $4,000 for the sheep. They wouldn't rent them, and we couldn't borrow them.

We started talking about how to produce the spot. Well, there wasn't much more that I knew about that because I had a people doing the work, buying the sheep, getting trucks to transport them and so forth. I knew the film production company we were going to hire. We had used this company and many others over the years. We knew the players well and who would be best for which chore. We chose a group called Wilson Griak out of Minneapolis.

Minneapolis in those days was a booming town. They had a new IDS center downtown, twice the size of Fountain Square. Big building. The town was really moving. The way we learned about Wilson Griak was through a guy at Kellogg's. They were shooting for Kellogg's. We thought, well, if they can shoot for Kellogg's, they can shoot for us. They had a couple guys, Jim Hinton and Steve Griak. Griak was chosen to direct the spot. They came to town for a pre- production meeting. We talked about everything, including where the cameras were going to be located and the amount of film we would require.

Wilson Griak was a big fan of ours. Not many agencies come to production companies with storyboards as interesting as some of ours. Most of what they shoot are moms standing in the kitchen with a product insert. Yeah. We love it. The kids are smiling. Bye. We didn't have any of that on our reel. We had people like Charlie Daniels, Liberace and James Earl Jones and now we were going to have a commercial starring sheep and they wanted some of that on their reel. It was a big deal for them. Of course, nobody knew what this shoot was going to be like. But we all figured it was going to be better than mom and the kids with a product insert.

I'm sure we went through this because somebody brought it up: How are we going to know that this is a bus company? What do you mean? This is where in my experience ideas are going to die and this one looked like it was on the way to the graveyard. How are we going to know that?

Well, you got a bunch of sheep on the ground and we're talking about moving people around town. Nobody knew that Metro was a bus. Everything was new. The signage was new, and the fare pricing was also new, up 25%. Buses were now coaches, and we were promising that Metro was a lot less hassle than driving your car.

With a couple of print ads in the newspaper the announcement had been made, but there was no strong media behind it. So how are we going to have a bus in the spot? I didn't think we needed one. I said, look, we have this idea. It's clean and it's pure. It's either going to work or it isn't going to work. Why do we want to put a bus in there? Well, the final shot, the ending frame is the new logo on the back of the Queen City Metro bus/coach.

We had that discussion over and over, and these were well qualified, smart people. Our strategy was to get people out of their cars and onto the bus, which I could never get straight in my head because I knew it was impossible in America to take a guy out of his car. I was driving a Porsche at the time, and I thought, you think you can get me out of a 911? No chance in Hell.

I, however, had as much history of bus riding in my early life as anyone I knew. Everything from flagging down a Greyhound to go fishing a few miles away to taking it on my first date. It was the only dependable way to travel and was much better than hitchhiking. The bus had the biggest impact on my life when I was in the fourth grade.

School for me was a series of events that seemed to have no connection to one another. The things I thought I was good at often fell flat leaving me wondering if I would ever get out of school. When you are addicted to the adrenaline that comes with success, it can seem a narrow bumpy road to get there. Such was my case. Art and sports were the two things that interested me more than anything else. Most of the coaches already had their favorites, and art class was not offered at my school.

Art had produced the rush I lived on from an early age. In first grade I won best watercolor artist in The Covington School System. In third grade, I won best poster for fire prevention two years in a row. But the biggest impact on my future was when my fourth-grade teacher announced that I was the only student in my school chosen to attend Baker Hunt Art Academy in Covington. It was a great feeling to stand up in class at 2:00 in the afternoon, leave school early and hop on the bus. The bus for all its social stigma was the only way for me to get to Baker Hunt from Erlanger. It was a once-a-week 45-minute bus ride to the academy and when you add that to the trip home it solidified my relationship to the bus company. It wasn't long before I got to know the drivers and greet them by name.

For a while it seemed that things were getting better: less homework, and fewer embarrassing in- class questions, for which I was not prepared. As a recalcitrant student who seemed to be continuously in some kind of trouble, this greased the wheels of redemption in the eyes of the adults in my life. It seemed to be a smoother trip and coupled with a small degree of plausible deniability and my mother working in the school lunchroom, a feeling of self-importance took over. Being excused from class once a week and riding the bus by myself gave this 9-year-old a feeling of confidence. I was being recognized for my artwork. When I was a senior in high school, I ran into a student from Central Academy of Commercial Art in Cincinnati. This was on the same day as the high school career fair where I was unmoved and uninterested in any of the offerings from five branches of the military to a selection of expensive colleges. At that time, I didn't know what "commercial art" was except that it promised you could make money as an artist and that sealed the deal. So off I went to art school, but my training had in no way prepared me for a day spent with 200 sheep in downtown Cincinnati.

We had booked time in Minneapolis to edit the spot. They had it all set up on KEM tables for splicing. Editing then was a physical activity unlike today. They turned on the machine and the sheep were moving along on the screen when suddenly they were moving slower and slower and slower. I said, "What?" We put the music on. It wasn't even close; the sheep were out of step.

Which ones were fast enough? Well, the very first ones, because they're the "first off the grass." We didn't know what that meant. We didn't even know the phrase "first off the grass." We just found out the hard way that sheep slow down quickly when they're living on concrete and not grazing. Well, we had covered the spot with four cameras and enough angles both high and low that we had enough footage to make it work. We had to change a few things in the edit. It was not an A, then B, then C, kind of edit.

The other bit in the spot was an actor we had hired to look like some nefarious character collecting money at a parking lot. In the voiceover we were talking about the problems of getting downtown in your car. Part of the voiceover said, "or maybe you'll find a nice man to watch your car for you." Everything else for the whole 30 or 60 whatever we shot, had sheep in it. The voiceover was excellent; and done by none other than Pete Weiglin, who was, in addition to everything else, a voice talent. I remember it coming together in such a way to make me think that nobody can confuse us with some other product. We've got enough going on here, and we certainly had the footage to put it on the air. Which we did.

The sheep spot became the standard of craziness that we had to have for an idea to be approved by Metro. Here's one example: The spot opens with a woman driving her car through the Shillito's Department Store while shopping. She was driving her car in the store because she couldn't find a place to park downtown. Finally, the store security guard came up and said, "Get out!" She got flustered and drove right through one of those big plate glass windows onto 7th Street. That was tricky because it was dangerous. Quarter-inch plate glass. We had put Hollywood glass in one of the windows and that was an issue as well. The pressure inside the store bowed the window outward. We had a stunt driver in the car, dressed up so much, I think he could have stopped a knife blade let alone actual glass.

We produced another television commercial along with several print ads. The sheep spot ran with heavy media dollars. The music that was behind all this really moved along. It was an old fiddle tune from down south, called "Lee Highway Blues." This song was chosen because it was the right cadence. My friend Buddy Griffin played the fiddle for the spot. He went up two octaves and did a slide down into the key of D to create a raucous sound. That was the hallmark of the commercial. You could hear it all over the house and I was told every kid in Cincinnati would run to the TV when they heard it. Well, I hope that's true, but who knows? It was very compelling, no doubt about it.

The client was thrilled, and we were pleased. For Metro, it meant 42 consecutive months of increased ridership. For Northlich Stolley, the spot won awards among them; the Best National Spot by the Transit Association in Washington, D.C., honorable mention at the Clio Awards in New York City, and here it was Best of Show at the Cincinnati Ad Club.

The commercial has become a legend in advertising. It is taught to students on how to recognize, create, and nurture a breakthrough idea along with the value of thinking outside the box. I didn't realize at the time that we were about to produce a spot that was to become iconic starring 200 of our wooliest friends and it all happened right here in good old "cutting edge" Cincinnati.

And the Woolies? We tried to sell them back for what we paid for them, but they had lost $1700 of weight — an expensive detour through downtown on their way to the stockyards.

The lessons to be learned from this experience? Plant more foliage on Fountain Square. What the flock!

Bill Lawarre, who started selling newspaper ads in Covington as a teenager, became the owner/operator of the largest advertising agency in Cincinnati. He was an aficionado of Bluegrass music, played a mean mandolin, and among his outside interests served as president of the Yellowstone Foundation. His wife shared that when he passed away on July 4, 2024, the sound of fireworks echoed in the background.

15 The Cow That Stole Christmas

EDGAR E. LOYD

TWENTY years ago, on December 9, 2003, a 6½-year-old black and white Holstein cow born in Canada, was slaughtered by Vern's Meats in rural Moses Lake, Washington—geographically speaking somewhere around the midpoint between Yakima and Spokane.

As the United States routinely slaughters about 35 million head of cattle per year, that event would hardly qualify our notice. Yet, something here proved unique. The veterinary medical officer noted that one of the cows presented for inspection that day was unable to walk off the trailer. It was, in the parlance, "a downer," an animal that remained in a recumbent position, unable to walk. A routine tissue sample was taken and submitted to the U. S. Department of Agriculture's National Veterinary Services Laboratories in Ames, Iowa. Meanwhile, the carcass was processed into the food supply.

Two weeks later on December 23, 2003 during the noon lunch hour at USDA's Washington, D.C. headquarters on the National Mall, Deputy Secretary of Agriculture Jim Moseley and Undersecretary Bill Hawks came in quick succession into the office of Chief of Staff Dale W. Moore with news they had received a phone call from Ames. Within a few moments, Moore was calling Secretary of Agriculture Ann M. Veneman, who was in the White House mess having a Christmas

Ed Loyd, left, with his boss, U.S. Agriculture Secretary Mike Johanns

lunch with her family visiting from California. "Ma'am, I hate to do this, but we need you to come back to the Department. We got a call from Ames and have an issue on the livestock front. I can't say more over the phone."

Within a few hours, the presumptive test result they had received would be heard around the world: the United States had its first case of Bovine Spongiform Encephalopathy, better known as BSE or colloquially as "mad cow" disease. That's a term we worked vigorously to avoid repeating yet perhaps an apt one. In general, a cow with BSE has trouble walking and getting up and may also act in a nervous or even violent manner, which is the origin of the "mad cow" term.

Beef consumers domestically and abroad were suddenly bombarded by images from the late-1980s where the bucolic country idyll of rural England had been shattered by this new disease that seemed to emerge spontaneously to disastrous consequences for animal and human health. There, more than four million head of cattle were eventually slaughtered, and 178 people died from the human variant of the disease years after eating infected beef.

My previous paper could be summarized as bananas, a story of Chiquita and Cincinnati. In some regards, tonight I bring its companion paper. For among the two most litigated items in world trade are bananas and beef and even more remarkably—or only in Cincinnati—I have played with both.

In early 2003, I arrived in Washington to take up my post as Deputy Press Secretary of USDA. Over the course of the following four years, I circumnavigated the globe on trade missions, toured disaster areas, participated in Farm Bill listening sessions and sat in front of the Agriculture Committees of the U.S. House and Senate. There were days with farmers and ranchers, visiting feedlots, experiencing the way the scent of meatpacking facilities sticks to you, contrasted with being in ministerial meetings at the WTO in Geneva and other capitals.

WHERE'S THE BEEF?

The U.S. is simultaneously the world's largest producer, the largest consumer, the third-largest exporter and the largest importer of beef in the world. Considering Americans represent less than 5 percent of global consumers that is an astounding statement. Even more pointedly, some studies have found just 12 percent of the U.S. population eats 50 percent of the beef consumed in a day. As this sub-set that so exceeds USDA's recommended Dietary Guidelines for eating beef was identified as being primarily men, aged 50 or older, I would suggest to our Board of Management that for the good of the order it be recommended to Nico to offer more beef than fish options for our post-paper repasts.

We have built our national and cultural identity around beef. The Western frontier—the cowboy. No potato famines here. We had endless miles of cattle country from the old Northwest Territory to the Great Plains, and then there's Texas. Where incomes rose, so did the consumption of red meat. How can you celebrate the Fourth of July without hamburgers and firecrackers or binge-watching "Yellowstone?" As the railroads expanded and refrigerated railcars arrived in meatpacking centers, like Chicago and Cincinnati, a powerful industry took shape by the 1880s.

One of many complexities that make the beef industry so challenging is that the animals processed into meat result in a vast array of different products of different qualities that, in general, don't exactly match the preferences of consumers. For instance, U.S. beef demand largely revolves around ground beef and steaks. Ground beef can, of course, be made from a lean meat of widely varying qualities, but steak is mostly oriented toward high-quality middle meat cuts.

We'll eat what we produce, yet if we don't produce exactly what we prefer, the total value that consumers offer the industry will be adjusted down as prices are reduced in order to entice consumers to purchase what we have, as opposed to what they really want. This makes the role of exports, particularly exports of lower valued products, especially important to enable the industry to adjust the product mix to reflect the need of the domestic market, while realizing a monetary value for products otherwise nearly worthless. Thus, the export of items like select chucks and rounds to Asia and Mexico is complementary to the U.S. market and supports a vital portion of U.S. farm income and jobs. In 2003, U.S. beef exports totaled $7.5 billion.

The import side, by contrast relates mostly to hamburgers and the extremely competitive fast-food market. Ground beef production requires additional lean to mix with the trim. It's not very efficient to fatten cattle at feedlots and then grind the meat back into hamburger. Even at a relatively low value as a muscle cut, these products have a higher value for export than grinding. I'll only mention in passing that the economics get more intense as beef competes vigorously with poultry and pork—the short leggers. Even a fraction of a cent per pound change in cost affects industry competitiveness.

My crash course in BSE began May 20, 2003, when a case was confirmed in Alberta, Canada. The U.S. promptly banned imports of Canadian beef and cattle, much to the ire of our Canadian friends. This was only the second case in North America, some 10 years after the first in a cow that had been imported to Canada from the United Kingdom.

The intervening decade had brought significant advancements in the science of understanding BSE as a progressive neurological disease, its origins and effective mitigation measures to limit its spread. The UK outbreak originated in the practice of supplementing protein in cattle feed with meat-and-bone meal. In plain English, the spinal cord and other leftover remains could be rendered down like compost that would make cows grow bigger and grow faster. So who would have thought that such a cannibalistic practice, especially in the first year of life, would produce such dire, unintended consequences?

BSE involves infectious misfolded proteins known as prions in the nervous system. For reasons not completely understood, the normal prion protein folds abnormally, enabling other prions to do the same and latch together in chains that begin killing cells and leaving sponge-like holes in the brain. As the proteins are a natural part of the anatomy, the immune system doesn't identify them as a threat and mounts no defense. There is no treatment. The cow gets sicker and sicker until it dies, usually within six months.

By incorporating the remains of an infected animal in cattle feed with meat and bone meal the disease can spread to animals that eat it. It usually takes four to six years from the time of infection to first showing symptoms. During this incubation period, there is no way to tell that a cow has BSE and no way to test for it until the animal is dead.

For nearly two decades, one scientist at the University of California, San Francisco championed research into these infectious particles of protein that that contain no genes or genetic material—a detail that distinguishes them from other infectious agents such as viruses, bacteria, fungi and parasites. He named prions. While he endured derision, eventually the scientific community began to find merit in his work. The Nobel committee in 1997 provided further validation when it named Dr. Stanley Prusiner a rare single winner of the Nobel Prize in medicine. The committee cited his "pioneering discovery of an entirely new genre of disease-causing agents and the elucidation of the underlying principles of their mode of action."

When Dr. Prusiner was asked whether he harbored any ill will toward his doubters he replied to the contrary: "I think that science should be very reticent to accept new ideas. Ninety-nine percent of new ideas are wrong. We have to be very tough on our colleagues." For all his accolades, this sounds about what you'd expect from a fellow Eagle, for Prusiner is perhaps best known within our Club as a member of the Walnut Hills High School Class of 1960.

A VERY BRITISH SCANDAL

The United Kingdom's outbreak of BSE first became publicly reported around Christmas of 1984, perhaps not precisely what George Orwell had envisioned. A political and public health crisis resulted, and British beef imports were banned by numerous countries around the world. Some bans remained in place as recently as 2019. During the height of the crisis, the UK government came under criticism particularly for how slow it was to acknowledge the problem, to inform the public and to take steps to deal with the outbreak.

The Brits had seen a similar neurological disease first documented in 1732 in sheep. Scrapie had never presented a risk to human health or been known to cross to other species. This was an unfortunate precedent, because when the first cattle began to exhibit BSE symptoms and government veterinarians investigated and found the tell-tale spongy holes in cow brains, a governmental memo from the time read, "If the disease turned out to be bovine scrapie it would have severe repercussions to the export trade. At present I would recommend playing it low key."

The government kept silent as the number of cases increased. By 1988, 200 cases of BSE were being reported every week and the government began to act. Agriculture Minister John Gummer, who seems to have been aptly named, took up the message that beef was safe. "There is no need for people to be worried and I can say perfectly honestly that I will go on eating beef." He went on to accuse scientists of scare mongering. Researchers were even removed from their positions. As the evidence mounted, even cats were contracting BSE and finally people—a full, utter panic ensued. By then, BSE cases were being detected across many European nations. It wasn't until the mid-1990s that the practice of feeding animal remains to other animals was banned, followed by the use of mechanically recovered meat in human foods.

AN ABUNDANCE OF CAUTION

By the early afternoon of December 23, 2003, the USDA had the advantage of knowing precisely how not to proceed with the public. Preparations were underway for an announcement within hours. Our chief of staff continued to make calls to the team, effectively cancelling their Christmas. Mike Torrey, a senior congressional relations leader answered a call while getting off a plane in Kansas City. "Get on a plane and come back," he was told. "All hell is going to break loose today." Alisa Harrison, the Communications Director and my boss received a call and promptly left the staff lunch she was hosting at the Willard Hotel, after which many of us were planning to travel home.

A press conference was arranged for 5:30 p.m. Eastern time. The White House communications shop sent a note to all the networks saying the Department of Agriculture had an announcement and that they would want to have their reporters and satellite trucks on site. The incoming calls exploded to an unprecedented level—the reporters knew enough to get their B-roll shots of ailing livestock cut and prepared. Droves of reporters arrived and were ushered into the press briefing room. As the hour drew near and the press was settling in, I went up to "The Cage," as the Secretary's office is known after the clear glass windowpane wall and doors that formed the entrance to the reception area and executive suite. There I saw Secretary Veneman seated at the desk of one of her aides putting her final edits to the remarks she would soon deliver. Speechwriter Matt Raymond had worked swiftly through numerous stakeholders but even his final draft still had placeholders and phrasing options. Yet the core of the message was clear and concise. It included the following points:

- The safety of our food supply and public health are very high priorities.
- Even though the risk to human health is minimal based on current evidence, we will initiate a product recall out of an abundance of caution.
- Since 1990, USDA has had an aggressive surveillance program to ensure detection and a swift response. We developed a BSE response plan and it has been activated today.
- In October, we announced findings from the Harvard Center for Risk Analysis that found that even if an infected animal were introduced to the U.S. animal agriculture system the risk of the disease spreading is low based on the safeguards and controls we have already put in place.
- We will provide daily briefings to the public, providing you with all the information we can as quickly as possible.
- At this time of year, many Americans are making plans for holidays and for their food. We see no need for people to alter those plans or their eating habits.
- I plan to serve beef for my Christmas dinner, and no one in this nation should hesitate to do the same.

The next 24-hours was a somewhat chaotic blur of media triage. Our export markets were shuttered. There was a lot of effort educating reporters on food safety, animal health and generally how farm-to-fork agriculture operates. I learned it was never an easy day's work trying to explain ag issues to *The New York Times*. As the skies began to glisten on Christmas Eve, Alisa came around to send us all home—even offering to purchase flights so we could be with loved ones. On the nearly nine-hour drive to Cincinnati into the early hours of Christmas morning, I began to form my own version of lyrics to the holiday classic, "I'll Be Home for Christmas."

> Christmas Eve will find me at USDA.
> Please let all reporters know
> I've got some things to say.
> There's a cow in Washington,
> A downer, now it's known.
> BSE, it's all the rage,
> Our markets gone away.
> Now an abundance of caution we'll take
> To bring them back again.

While government and business normally shut down between Christmas and New Year's Day, USDA was taking proactive steps to further strengthen our food safeguards. Secretary Veneman announced on December 30, that the United States was:

- Banning meat from "downer" animals for human consumption. This was commonly referred to as the 4D cattle rule as it barred dead, dying, disabled or diseased meat.
- Expanding surveillance testing and holding meat from animals tested until there was a confirmation it did not have BSE.
- Strengthening meat processing safeguards by expanding controls on advanced meat recovery systems and prohibiting mechanically separated beef from the food supply.

- Clearly prohibiting SRMs — specified risk materials — central nervous tissues that could contain prions such as the brain, spinal cord, and lower intestines from being used as food for human consumption.

The public response to all this was more sanguine than that of the reporters. There was a two-week dip in the amount of beef consumed in the U.S. before it normalized. Regrettably, that was not the case in some East Asian nations. There the media frenzy was so strong that in South Korea beef consumption fell by 30 to 40 percent and remained depressed. Yet, as the days and weeks led into months and years, the focus was on a diplomatic crisis rather than food safety concerns.

USDA PRIME

Protecting the food supply and figuring out how to reopen our markets wasn't just a USDA priority. It was a frequent conversation at the White House. After all, President George W. Bush's neighbors in Texas were among the largest ranching families. The President made his priorities clear to the senior staff this way: "Here's the thing I'm looking at, my neighbors in Crawford and Cheney's in Wyoming are calling us and looking to us to fix this now. The inside of cows talk may not be pleasant, but please act accordingly." With that, the request for varying status reports to the White House surged. It compelled our Chief of Staff to reach out to Secretary Card with a plea for relief. Andy Card, one of the most effective and personable White House Chiefs of Staff, shared one of his threshold principles in response to receiving such requests: "Who in the White House is asking for this?" He had Judge Alberto Gonzales cleanly and efficiently clear up the confusion at the next morning's senior staff meeting.

In 2003, the United States exported beef and beef products to nearly 120 countries (counting the European Union member states individually). Many of these countries announced bans on U.S. beef accounting for $4.8 billion of the $7.5 billion annual trade. Much of the excess that remained was for by-products, such as hides, skin and embryos.

For countries already impacted by BSE, having the U.S. join them in trade purgatory was a welcomed development. Not so much for the pleasures of *schadenfreude*, but because, as the Irish attaché expressed it, "you've got the resources to figure out how to get out of this mess we are all stuck in." Indeed, even before our first case, the agriculture ministers of Mexico, Canada and the U.S. had come together and requested that the OIE — the World Animal Health Organization — implement a practical, risk-based approach that would enable countries to trade confidently in beef in spite of isolated cases of BSE. By December 2004, that work had progressed into a final rule in the Federal Register that established minimal risk regions for BSE. This marked the United States' leadership role in fostering trade of low-risk products and adherence to strong risk mitigation measures, with ruminant-to-ruminant feed bans and surveillance. Thus, the U.S. reopened trade with Canada and looked to expand on that example.

Based on these principles, over the course of 2004, with painstaking effort, markets slowly reopened. The Philippines was first, followed by Mexico, Indonesia and others. Each was heralded as a victory even if the sales there were small. Along the road came some surprises. Vietnam was an early win and they seemed to be doing a brisk business with us, more so than prior to 2003. Careful market observers discovered why: The Vietnamese were purchasing U.S. certified angus beef and repackaging it under its own country of origin for sale to China where U.S. beef was still banned but in high demand.

By the summer of 2004, it was clear where the largest pockets of resistance were going to be. Japan by then accounted for 50 percent of the total market value not reopened to U.S. beef and represented more than a third of all U.S. exports of beef products. Japan's position was that all 35 million cattle slaughtered in the U.S. be tested for BSE. Their demands were based on marketing rather than science and, candidly, the initial mishandling of their own cases of BSE in 2001. To appease consumer fears, Japanese officials opted to test all cattle for BSE. Of course, theirs was a much smaller herd and the test results essentially a given as this disease almost exclusively affects animals older than 32 months, while most cattle are slaughtered at 24 months. They weren't really looking for substance from their program. Meanwhile, this eventually spawned one industry player, Creekstone Farms, to say that they would test 100 percent of their cattle and proceeded to sue USDA to do so. Tensions were running high.

A working group of technical experts was established between our nations and one of my assignments was to accompany them to Ft. Collins, Colorado for three days of discussions and tours of a slaughter facility, feed lot and feed mill to see our safeguards in action. At this point I need to note that, from the outset, any appearance by the Secretary around Washington would be swarmed by a gaggle of twenty or more Japanese correspondents and cameras all jockeying to thrust microphones and recorders at close range. All of them wanted to travel to Colorado so we arranged tours and photo opportunities for them that resulted in praise and condemnation of me by reporters. The experts, however, loved it. We shielded them from the most pernicious questions, and they got to be filmed in their white lab coats and hats marching past the flags of trading partners as if they were astronauts headed to the moon. Eventually, the experts determined 100 percent BSE testing wasn't necessary, but they continued to debate at what age would that be acceptable.

As the calendar reached 2005 there was a lot of motion but minimal momentum. Then a new Secretary of Agriculture arrived for the second Bush term. Mike Johanns, the Governor of Nebraska, grew up on a dairy farm in Iowa and knew the industry well. As Senator Pat Roberts of Kansas remarked, "he was the kind of fellow you could talk awhile with on the wagon tongue."

Johanns quickly lifted the morale of the USDA team and brought a new vigor, focus and determination to the mission. He also made several astute personnel changes among his sub-cabinet — and in Washington personnel is policy. Though of little note, at this time I was promoted to Press Secretary of USDA. This was quite an achievement for one who had no prior experience in agriculture, and it may have at first seemed to some a befuddling choice. However, I had early on realized that my lack of background was a strength. It never troubled me to ask officials to explain an issue or answer why is this program significant to farmers and ranchers? If I could translate that answer from beltway jargon into English, I could help educate reporters and ensure our message resonated with more constituents.

The process with Japan was Byzantine, and each tentative step was greeted with suspicion. My team was the cause of one such example when we issued a news release one Friday that announced the upcoming dates of another technical working group meeting. Later that night, Secretary Johanns departed for a weekend of WTO negotiations in Geneva, which Communications Director Terri Teuber was covering since I had just returned from a 14-day international tour and was desirous of rest.

In the days before it was possible to select a personalized ringtone, I recall being awakened early the next morning by a shrill, metallic urgency from my mobile phone that I had never heard. It was the National Security Council who had Ambassador Nancy Kassebaum Baker on the line from Tokyo and with the Secretary still in the air, they had worked their way down to me. It seemed that our release had lit a firestorm because one of the meeting dates was different from what the Japanese had agreed, and they were threatening to cancel the whole meeting suspecting a U.S. ambush where we had made a typo. The rest of the day was spent coordinating an agreement and statement between Geneva, Washington and Tokyo that enabled us to arrive back at our starting position. This was a trivial episode but a representative example of the ongoing efforts and the game of chutes and ladders the Japanese excelled in playing.

In one White House meeting, after hearing Secretary Johanns review the latest machinations, an exasperated President Bush asked, "what do we need to do?" Ambassador Zoellick, the U.S. Trade Representative, uncharacteristically noted, "I am at a loss for words." This prompted Karl Rove to chime in to memorialize, "At this time and date Ambassador Zoellick is at a loss for words." Levity aside, beef was one of the key topics Bush raised each time he spoke with Japanese Prime Minister Koizumi. It was becoming an irritant in our relationship and even Congressional members began to agitate for the imposition of retaliatory sanctions, which would not have assisted our cause.

Complicating matters at the outset was the uncanny ability certain industry players had to mine the contents of secret diplomatic cables on beef issues. In one instance, a detailed cable of our position and instructions was sent to our Embassy in Tokyo at 4 p.m. By 9 a.m. the next morning, an industry player called to quote portions of the cable verbatim to add their perspective on our work. The National Security Agency was called in and was able to determine what sources had been hired in Japan to relay information back to U.S. industry. Needless to say, it became standard operating procedure that such meetings would be held only in person, and no one was permitted to bring a mobile phone into the secured meeting room.

Secretary Johanns would go on to detail a credible offer to the Japanese which was immediately rebuffed. Undersecretary J.B. Penn handed Johanns a note with follow-up discussion points, but the Secretary demurred looking at it and launched into his own response. "I am disappointed and frankly I'm embarrassed for you," Johanns began. "I thought I was meeting with someone with the authority to get this done and I'm embarrassed. I'm sorry to have taken your time," he said as he began to leave the room. The Japanese pleaded with him to stay, then stepped out to have a conversation amongst themselves before coming back to the table for a more productive conversation. Penn came home saying he was scared of this Secretary. He was effective. He knew what needed to be done.

By December 2005, when the WTO Ministerial was held in Hong Kong, we had reached a conservative agreement with Japan for the resumption of boneless beef from animals up to 20 months of age. It was a major breakthrough and was one of the few items that U.S. Trade Representative Rob Portman and Secretary Johanns could return with, as otherwise the Doha round of WTO negotiations was floundering.

We celebrated the beginning of beef shipments in January 2006. Within a matter of days, Chief of Staff Dale Moore placed an early morning call to Secretary Johanns. He started out by congratulating Johanns on his first-year anniversary on the job. "Dale, I've been around long enough to know there's another reason for why you're calling me this early," was the gist of the response. And there was. A facility in New Jersey had sent a shipment of bone-in beef to Japan. Johanns called Japan's U.S. Ambassador Kato to apologize personally and he publicly de-listed the processing plant from further shipments, required all USDA beef inspectors undergo additional training and dispatched a team to Japan. While nothing that was done represented a food safety risk, it had violated our Japanese agreement. These actions notwithstanding, trade was halted as quickly as it had begun, and it would be another eight months before shipments would resume.

Meanwhile, our negotiations with South Korea, which represented our third largest export market worth $815 million, were at the final stages during this period preparing for a March 2006 trade resumption. A message then arrived from the Japanese that they thought best to send through an industry emissary rather than governmental channels. It was to make sure that the U.S. didn't make a better deal with South Korea than with Japan! At the end of such a day, the Chief of Staff queried, "Boss what would make tomorrow better?" "A good night's rest," was Johanns' quick response before adding, "but can you figure out what I need to do to be Secretary of something other than mad cows?"

In all, it took years for Japanese consumers to regain trust in American beef, and it wasn't until 2011 that our exports had eclipsed 2003 levels. By 2021, the United States was the top beef exporting country in the world, with global sales of beef and beef products valued at more than $10 billion, with exports of U.S. beef to Japan accounting for $2.4 billion. In 2023, cattle production is forecast to represent about 17 percent of the $520 billion in total cash receipts for agricultural commodities.

EPILOGUE

Now a score of Christmases have come and gone since that lone cow in Washington State upended our markets. Our faith and trust in government institutions have probably never been lower. Yet, if you can impart a little measure of grace, this season of the year, to acknowledge we are often too hard upon one another; and to assign good intent to those with whom we may disagree, and if you seek an example that could inspire, remember "The People's Department," as President Lincoln named USDA in his final message to Congress. It was the cabinet department he proudly created to serve the people even in the midst of war—and it continues to fulfill that mission today.

Ed Loyd has more than 20 years' experience leading external affairs programs for corporate, governmental and non-profit organizations. During the George W. Bush Administration, he served as press secretary of the U.S. Department of Agriculture, traveling to more than 20 nations with Agriculture Secretary Mike Johanns. Ed has been a frequent speaker on local history and agriculture in the tropics.

16 The Sobering Power of Witness

EDWARD LYON

A witness can change the world. Witness 17-year-old Darnella Frazier, who captured a video of four Minneapolis police officers casually snuffing out the life of George Floyd. Her 10-minute video, uploaded to Facebook, revealed those officers to be common thugs. It sparked the biggest social protests in American history. And it shone an unflinching light on a casual face of brutality that still threatens millions of citizens and stains our American character.

But witnesses don't have to change the world to flex their power. Witnesses play an important part in life's everyday occasions, too. Graduations, weddings, and christenings are celebrations, to be sure. But those celebrations all start by assembling a group of people to witness the event being celebrated.

And sometimes we harness the power of witness to motivate us to become better versions of ourselves. A public commitment, witnessed by friends or family or colleagues, can help hold us to the sorts of ordinary promises we make to ourselves and the people around us. Which is how I found myself in the basement of the Church of the Redeemer on a cold February night in 2001.

I was born in August of 1964, at the very tail end of the baby boom, and grew up in a WASPy family in a WASPy Cincinnati suburb. My father was a character straight out of a John Cheever story, or maybe a *Mad Men* episode. There was always a drink at his side. My mother drank, too. And the rest of the family. And their friends. And our neighbors. Alcohol was a constant, a given, as omnipresent as the cigarettes every adult seemed to smoke. One of my earliest childhood memories involved seeing my father "napping" on the living room floor after a day of "work" (on the golf course) and wondering why he smelled so funny.

I'm not going to try and describe the siren song of alcohol, or the uneasy *pas de deux* it dances with madness. Better writers than I have wrestled with that challenge. The best of them — the Hemingways, the Fitzgeralds, and the Bukowskis of the world — chose to show us in addition to telling us. They didn't just pour their words out onto a page. They poured out their lives like the amber splash of scotch hitting a rocks glass, neat.

I started drinking on weekends when I was 15 and had my first hangover before I got my driver's license. In college, I discovered I could get drunk every night of the week if I avoided (or simply skipped) early morning classes. My fraternity gave me their "getting drunk and puking" award so many years in a row that they renamed it for me. (Somehow that honor never made it to my LinkedIn page.) I kept it up through two years of work on Capitol Hill, where I was shocked at how much legislation starts out scrawled on the back of cocktail napkins. (Katie Couric, who was just starting her career as a local reporter, interviewed me after a Presidential speech after several pitchers of Natty Bo in my favorite booth at the Tune Inn, a Pennsylvania Avenue institution.) And because quitters never win, and winners never quit, I kept it up through law school and what I now laughingly refer to as "the early years of my career." I picked up an arrest for drunk driving just a month after my first daughter was born. The court sentenced me to a three-day "driver intervention program" in lieu of actual jail, where I discovered

I had the highest blood-alcohol content of anyone in the group. (Also not part of my LinkedIn profile.)

Eventually, though, I got tired of calling my hangovers "mornings." I was married, with children, a mortgage on a house I shouldn't have bought, and a business I had started when my former bosses attracted some unwelcome attention from the SEC. It was time to grow up, and my gradual sense that I was drinking too much morphed into resolve. I took some unlikely inspiration from our then-President "Dubya" who had quit at 40. And while I was just 36 at the time, I knew I shouldn't wait out those extra four years.

Looking back, I can't remember why I picked February 17 to be my last day drinking. (Drunk. Who am I trying to kid?) I just knew I had to set a date. I didn't even go out that night . . . I stayed at home with my family, started drinking at lunch, and savored that last alcoholic glow descending over my brain as I contemplated what it was that I was giving up, and how life might be better if I did.

I had already announced my decision to my wife. But I wanted a bigger commitment. I wanted *witnesses*. So I went online, found a nearby AA meeting at the Redeemer, and showed up for the 8 p.m. start. When the chair asked if there was anyone attending their first meeting, I stood up and said, "My name is Ed, and I'm an alcoholic." I needed to say those cliched words out loud, to a room full of people, in hopes that their witness would hold me to my promise. I knew that bidding alcohol farewell meant crossing a bridge, that many people return back over. Declaring my intention in front of those sympathetic witnesses was my very explicit attempt to burn that bridge so I could never go back again — or at least to make it difficult and embarrassing to do so.

Reader, it worked. The day after I planted my flag, Anheuser-Busch stock went down. (Did I mention I drank a *lot* of Budweiser?)

I attended three more meetings the next three days in a row, where I learned that "one day a time" would be my route to success. Then after the fourth meeting, my wife asked if maybe I wasn't taking it all a little *too* seriously. Was AA going to become my cult, the way it had for her brother when he quit drinking? So that was it for the meetings. I became a "dry drunk" — AA lingo for someone who quits drinking without addressing the "defects of character" that made them dipsomaniacs in the first place. But at least I was dry. (And svelte, too — I lost 15 pounds in the first couple of months after I quit!)

Eight years later, the marriage finally stalled out for keeps. My sobriety kept chugging along. By then, I was simply someone who didn't drink. I had no problem going out to bars and restaurants and other places where other people were drinking. I had a fully stocked bar in my house for entertaining. I just didn't drink, myself, not anymore. I'm happily sober for 22 years now, which is longer than I was drunk. My sobriety is even old enough to buy a beer!

(In fairness, I've become a connoisseur of nonalcoholic beers, which are enjoying a moment right now. I've even gotten to try an IPA or two, which wasn't popular before I quit. Truly disgusting, btw.)

And I've finally addressed those "defects of character," with the help of a great therapist. She even says I'm "self-actualized." And while I'm not sure I can define that term, it makes me (almost) happier than an extra zero at the end of my net worth. I do still attend meetings. Every year, on or near February 17, I find a meeting where I can stand up and say, "My name is Ed, and I'm an alcoholic, and thanks to this program I'm celebrating X years of sobriety." I take the chip home and set it on my dresser next to my watches where I can see it every day. And I've "twelfth-stepped" a time or two, introducing friends to the program when they decided for themselves that they were ready for witnesses to help them get better.

It all comes down to those witnesses — that group of men and women in the basement of that Hyde Park church that long-ago chilly night. I'm sure that none of them knew what a powerful role they would play in my life as I stood to speak those cliched words: *"My name is Ed and I'm an alcoholic."* I'm sure that none of them remember what they saw and heard. But the fact that they *did* see it and hear it made all the difference to me. All of the graduations, weddings, and christenings I've witnessed since then have been happier and healthier celebrations because of it.

Ed Lyon is a tax attorney by training who focuses his career on helping accounting and financial advisors to sell proactive planning services. He's a downtown Cincinnati resident and father of two daughters and a son. He joined the Literary Club in 2023 and is looking forward to learn the club's diverse members and perspectives.

17 | *High Crosby Alert*

JOE MORAN

DURING the Great Depression, American horse racing was at its peak, likely the most followed sport of its time. It was dominated by the East Coast establishment, but virtually unheard of on the West Coast. During the 1930s, however, interest on the West Coast slowly picked up due to the efforts of one individual born in the state of Washington, far from the hub of East Coast racing. He was Bing Crosby, who was to become the leading force in creating the best years in American horse racing.

Although Crosby is best known as a talented singer, actor, avid sportsman and World War II patriot, few today are aware that he was also the best benefactor of horse racing, investing large amounts of his personal money, talent, time and celebrity status to popularize the sport.

Over the years, a number of random events has pulled me into an abiding interest in Crosby, whom I have come to believe might be America's biggest all-around sportsman of the 20th Century.

My interest was first sparked when, 20 years ago at the Rosemary Clooney festival in Maysville, Kentucky, I met Bing's widow, Katherine. Then in a series of coincidental encounters, the Crosby legacy kept cropping up. For example, I learned from Kenny, my carpet installer, that he had more than a thousand Bing Crosby recordings in his collection in Northern Kentucky. Another time, visiting a client in Cincinnati, I glimpsed a box frame of Bing Crosby's racing silks hanging in his office. Last year at the Southern Side-By-Side Sporting Clays event

Bing is off to the races

in Sanford NC, a representative at Griffin and Howe firearms relayed the story of creating a special sporting gun he made for Bing Crosby with "White Christmas" musical notes inlaid in gold on the barrel of the firearm. Then I learned from fellow Literary Club member Bill LaWarre that the 4K ranch he owned in Montana also had Crosby connections. Such stars as Crosby, Marilyn Monroe and Babe Ruth all had visited the historic ranch.

With such evidence piling up, I realized it was time to assemble a Literary Club paper on Crosby.

Going on-line, I found excerpts from a diary he kept, a day-to-day summary encompassing several decades of his life, published in a 96-page book entitled *A Diary of a Lifetime*, by Malcolm MacFarlane, the editor of Bing Magazine. In 2001 Scarecrow Press published an 800-page detailed edition of his life, *Bing Crosby Day-by-Day*, documenting virtually every day he was performing concerts or hosting charity events for the war effort, particularly for the U.S. armed forces. In the rare time that he had for his own interests, he was either hunting, fishing, golfing or attending the races. With his multiple talents and energy, he became the highest paid performer of his era.

Bing Crosby was born in 1903 in Tacoma, Washington, far removed from the world of horse racing. He was the son of a hardware store owner, a child from humble origins. He went to Gonzaga University in Spokane but left during his senior year to pursue a singing career. At the same time, he began playing golf, realizing that the sport gave him a chance to communicate with associates as well as to conduct business while playing. He took to hunting and fishing for similar reasons—chances to communicate and conduct business. Horse racing offered the same social opportunities, and it became his number one pastime.

Since Bing had Sundays and Mondays off from his singing responsibilities with the Paul Whiteman Orchestra, he and his bandmates often made the 260-mile round trip from Los Angeles to Agua Caliente racetrack in Tijuana, Mexico. There he was alongside 23,000 other fans on March 20, 1932 to watch Australian champion Phar Lap, one of history's all-time great thoroughbreds, make his North American debut and win the biggest race of the year by setting a record for the 1 ¼ mile. Unfortunately, it was but a month before the chestnut gelding was suddenly stricken in his stall and died a mysterious death.

Bing's first investment in racing was $10,000 with the Santa Anita Race Course in Los Angeles to guarantee him a lifetime box on the finish line. He was at Santa Anita for its inaugural race on Christmas Day in 1934 and spent most of the winter at the track entertaining people who stopped by his box to say hello. While at Santa Anita, Bing met East Coast racing titan John Hay 'Jock' Whitney, proprietor of Greentree Stables, who sold him his first horse; he named it 'Zombie.' Bing registered his personal racing colors with the Jockey Club -- blue with gold polka dots, blue sleeves with gold chevrons and blue and gold quartered cap. The colors were inspired by Bing's first hit, "Where the Blue of the Night Meets the Gold of the Day."

The same year Bing and his first wife Dixie Lee purchased a breeding farm in Rancho Santa Fe, California, naming the operation "Binglin" stables. The second part of that name was for a partner, Lindsay Howard, the polo playing son of Charles Howard, owner of the legendary Seabiscuit. With Lindsay's powerful Argentinean polo friends, the partnership began purchasing horses in Argentina and racing them under the auspices of the Argentine Jockey Club. Lindsay and Bing's ranch in Argentina was called "Caballeriza." Bing went further and bought still another breeding farm, this one in Ventura, California. The acquisition put Crosby with an impressive three horse ranches to his name. As if owning the three for his own horses was not enough, Bing became financially involved with another new racetrack in California. On May 6, 1936 the Del Mar Turf Club had its first board meeting and Bing was unanimously elected its first president. Bing's close actor friend Pat O'Brien was elected vice president and Bing's older brother the secretary-treasurer. Hollywood actor Oliver Hardy became a board member. Even though it was during the Depression, Bing and Pat O'Brien raised virtually all of the capital for Del Mar by pledging a combined $600,000 in interest-free loans against their personal life insurance policies.

Opening day at Del Mar was July 3, 1937 with Crosby himself manning the main admission gate in a race track attendant's uniform. About 15,000 people showed up and Bing's horse, High Strike, won the first race of the day. Hollywood stars in the crowd that day included Bette Davis, Robert Taylor and Barbara Stanwyck, who awarded the winner's trophy for one of the races. Bing himself did most of the track announcements that afternoon, broadcasting the fourth race over the NBC radio network.

The party Bing staged after the day of racing attracted Jimmie Durante, Bob Hope and Red Skelton among the guests. Bing even performed the Del Mar signature song which he co-wrote, "Where the Surf Meets the Turf." To this day the song is part of Del Mar's soundscape and played before the first and last races each day.

The following year Bing invited Bob Hope to Del Mar on August 6, 1938, a day before the track's high profile "Motion Picture Day." After the races that evening Bing hosted a clambake in Del Mar's backstretch for the stable hands and some selected guests. After a few drinks, Hope and Crosby began exchanging witty barbs. The crowd was enjoying the banter and Paramount Film's producers William Le Baron and Harlan Thompson took notice and came up with the idea for the movie, "Road to Singapore," starring the pair. That led to these two entertainers adding "Zanzibar," "Morocco," "Utopia," "Rio," "Bali" and "Hong Kong" in a successful series.

Two years after Del Mar Racetrack was conceived, the Hollywood Racetrack opened with Crosby and several other Hollywood stars as shareholders and box holders. Cary Grant was such a regular attendee that when he died track executives renamed the clubhouse the "Cary Grant Pavilion."

Crosby was also a shareholder and box holder at Los Angeles' Santa Anita track, making him the film industry's most visible face in the racing world. By now Bing was heavily involved with three major California racing venues.

The highlight of Bing's racing career came on August 12, 1938 when the famous Seabiscuit was pitted against Ligaroti in a $25,000 "winner take all" match race at Del Mar. Ligorati was Bing Crosby and Lindsay Howard's six year-old Argentinian import to Binglin Stables. Bing recognized the powerful promotional value the race would mean for the new track. Seabiscuit was the hottest horse in the country and every track was trying to get him to race at their venue. He was the grandson of legendary Man 0' War and was the five-year-old king of the U.S. handicap circuits. For the match, it was decided Seabiscuit would carry 130 pounds and Ligaroti only 115 pounds — exactly what Bing and Lindsay had hoped. However, the race raised several potential conflicts challenging what was seen as the purity of racing. Among these was the fact that Seabiscuit was trained by Tommy Smith while his son Jimmy trained Ligaroti for Binglin Stables. There was also an Argentina-U.S. conflict within the Howard family ownership. So the California Horse Racing Board, in a rare motion, forbade the public from any wagering on the race.

The match took place before a record Del Mar crowd of 22,000, far greater than the track's usual attendance that seldom exceeded 5,000. Crosby himself joined Pat O'Brien in a national broadcast from the roof of the grandstand. Bing brought in a bevy of Hollywood stars including Clark Gable, Carole Lombard and Spencer Tracy.

The race itself was so competitive that the two jockeys, George "The Iceman" Woolf and Noel "Spec" Richardson, were both banned for the rest of the year for their mutual vicious fouls, although the action was later rescinded since the race had been a no-betting exhibition.

Oscar Otis, Del Mar's track announcer, gives an account of the race in the book, *Del Mar: Its Life and Good Times:* "That was as rough a race as I've seen in my whole life. They were hitting each other over the head with their whips, and Richardson had Woolf in a leg lock. I've never seen so much trouble in one race, and there was a hell of a stink about it." At the finish line, Seabiscuit won by a nose in 1 minute 49 seconds—a full 4 seconds off the track record.

Looking back, the race proved beneficial to the fledgling Del Mar track. Soon afterwards it became a major force in the horse racing industry, drawing in prime talent, larger purses, bigger crowds and higher mutuel handle. Soon Del Mar was known as "The Saratoga of the West" — all to Bing Crosby's credit.

The race was also a prelude to a following match race between Seabiscuit and War Admiral on November 1, 1938, at Pimlico Racetrack in Baltimore, a moment still considered to be the pinnacle of American horse racing history. War Admiral was admired for his speed and Seabiscuit was known for his slow pace and skill of holding with the pack, then approaching the finish line with late acceleration. War Admiral was the fourth winner of the coveted Triple Crown (the Kentucky Derby, the Preakness Stakes and the Belmont Stakes). The race took place on a Tuesday with a standing room only crowd of 40,000. Uncounted millions tuned in on the radio.

Again, like the race at Del Mar three months prior, there were some unusual nuances with the family connections of the parties involved. Alfred G. Vanderbilt had just married the niece of Charles Howard's second wife Marcella, herself the sister of Lindsay Howard's wife Anita. Lindsay Howard and Anita divorced soon after and she then married Alfred G. Vanderbilt's brother!

Horse racing's legendary Alfred G. Vanderbilt had personally landed this "match of the century" by chasing War Admiral's owner Samuel Riddle through Pennsylvania Station in mid-town Manhattan and preventing him from boarding his train until he had signed the contract. Seabiscuit won the race by four lengths, proving himself the better horse.

Bing used his celebrity status to promote horse racing through paid endorsements for products with horse racing backdrops. He was one of Hollywood's most coveted commercial endorsers and the highest paid entertainer in America. There was an expression "Attach the name 'Bing Crosby' to a product and the company was halfway to heaven." Among those firms, Bing was a spokesperson for Minute Maid orange juice, Royal Crown Cola, Chesterfield cigarettes and Stetson hats. To many of the ads he included background scenes of his racehorses or of Del Mar.

After a dozen years of active participation, a tragedy struck a blow to the Crosby racing interests. On November 1, 1952, his wife, Dixie Lee, died of ovarian cancer. Because of large inheritance taxes that built up with their common business partnerships, Bing was forced to sell all of his racehorses, even though he eventually was able to return to the sport.

Bing used his singing talents to promote horse racing, at times crooning in the winner's circle or at events for his fans. Once, when a horse he owned named Meadow Court, who on June 13, 1965, won the Irish Derby on June 13, 1965 at the Curragh with legendary jockey Lester Piggott wearing his racing silks, Bing did an impromptu singing of "When Irish Eyes are Smiling" at the trophy presentation. He joked, "Wait until [Bob] Hope finds out."

Bing's impromptu singing became an expected occurrence. When he purchased Khayyam and promised to enter it in the 1936 Kentucky Derby, he promised the seller he would serenade the horse just before the big race.

Bing used his singing talents to pay tribute to fellow entertainers. While spending some free time at the races in Saratoga Springs, New York, he was relaxing the evening of August 16, 1935, at the Arrowhead Club when he learned of Will Rogers' death. He promptly sang an impromptu version of "Home on the Range" to mourn the passing of his entertainer friend.

Crosby's singing talents eventually made their way into his other two hobbies, fishing and golf. He was an avid angler and would sometime surprise guests with an impromptu song at the fishing camps. It was a rule that at private clubs in Canada whenever celebrities of his caliber visited, the staff was expected to be professional to a "T," but this did not necessarily prevent emotions taking over. Indeed, who could remain indifferent to the man who had captivated the world with "Stardust" and "White Christmas"? Bing came to the Montbello Club of Canada as a guest of J.P.E. Colette of Montreal. He fished for trout, sampled caribou, and got in 18 holes of golf. After dinner one night, someone asked him to sing. He agreed, but only if was a way of thanking the staff who had taken such good care of him. From the stage, Crosby noticed a shy, young smiling waitress. He made his way to where she stood, took her hand, and led her up to the front of the orchestra, and, as though just for her, sang "Stardust." His kiss kept her awake a long time that night, and the next morning she went to the fishing club's maître d' with a request that she remain on duty full time for the whole Crosby visit. Bing Crosby could certainly croon and cast.

One of the finest salmon fishing destinations in the world is the Grand Cascapedia river in New Brunswick. In the 1940s and 1950s Bing visited New Dereen camp on the Cascapedia at the invitation of Mr. & Mrs. Raymond Guest. He had met Mr. Guest, then a Virginia state senator, at a party at Yale. Eventually his host would become the U.S. ambassador to Ireland. On the first day during the 1949 fishing season when he went to the club, he was put into one of the better New Dereen pools called "Jack the Sailor." He promptly landed a 33-pound salmon. Over the next 10 days, he netted five more averaging 24 pounds. Up and down the river natives knew of his visit and went on "High Crosby-Alert." One evening he sang to the enchantment of Guest, who later maintained that Crosby's famous song, "Cruising Down the River," had been inspired by his trip to Camp Dereen.

In the early 1970s Bing sang the praises of Scottish salmon for the ABC program, "The American Sportsman," a TV show co-hosted by comedian Phil Harris which enjoyed a wide audience on Sunday afternoons from 1965 to 1986. Bing joined the Atlantic Salmon Association in 1970 and supported it for the rest of his days; his membership card has been given a place of honor in the association's museum in New Brunswick.

In addition to horse racing and fishing, Crosby became well known for his golf talents as well as his ownership of a major league baseball team. Following the Second World War, Crosby talked with his horse racing friend, John Galbreath, owner of Darby Dan Farm in Columbus, about becoming a part owner in Galbreath's baseball team, the Pittsburgh Pirates. Since Major League Baseball rules prevented a racetrack owner from owning a baseball franchise, Crosby sold his 35 per cent stake in the Del Mar track on November 3, 1945, so that he could be granted the Pirates ownership. His pal Bob Hope was a part owner of the Cleveland Indians, so another friendly rivalry arose. With Bing as a part-owner, the Pirates went on to win the World Series in 1960 and 1971.

On the links, Crosby made golf look easy. He enjoyed a two handicap and competed in both British and U.S. Amateur championships. Both he and Bob Hope are enshrined in the World Golf Hall of Fame. In their day they did as much to popularize the sport as Ben Hogan, Jack Nicklaus and Arnold Palmer. They made it cool to play golf, just as Crosby had made it cool to go to the races.

In 1937 Crosby hosted the first Pro-Am Golf Championship, known as the "Crosby Clambake," at the Rancho Santa Fe Golf Club. He threw lavish parties at his nearby home. The "Clambake" eventually became the AT&T Pebble Beach National Pro-Am.

Two of Cincinnati's premiere golf clubs played host to Crosby during his career. According to Malcolm McFarlane's diaries, while playing at Kenwood Country Club on September 15, 1942, on a visit to promote U.S. War bonds, he sang for his onlookers both on the course and afterward in the clubhouse. Five years later on June 7, 1947, he visited the Hyde Park Country Club and again, as hoped, he sang for an audience in the clubhouse.

Golf was with him to the end. On October 14, 1977, at age 74, he played on a course in Madrid, Spain and shot a remarkable 85. Walking off the green, he suffered a heart attack and died.

World War II had cast a shadow on the racetracks of California. Del Mar was taken over by the Marine Corps. Santa Anita became a relocation center for Japanese Americans. Hollywood Park served as a storage depot. But it was a time for Bing Crosby the patriot to contribute to the war effort as an entertainer. At rallies across the states, he raised money for war bonds and he traveled to military bases throughout the U.S. and in both the European and Pacific theaters to entertain the troops. On the lips of servicemen and women, along with the folks back home, it seemed everyone could hum Bing's renditions of "The Army Air Corps Song" (better known as "Off We Go into the Wild Blue Yonder"), "Yankee Doodle Dandy" and "The White Cliffs of Dover." After the war, *Yank* Magazine hailed him as the "man who had done the most to boost the morale of American servicemen."

Today, 80 years later, horse racing at many racetracks is just a numbers game. The growth of slot machines, casinos and lotteries have made gambling smoother and more manageable. Casinos, once only found in Las Vegas and New Jersey, now exist in at least 38 states. Control over horse racing has shrunk into the hands of just a few large gaming corporations, which would be happy to get rid of the tracks altogether if they could be replaced with more lucrative gaming options.

Chris McGrath, a journalist writing in the *Thoroughbred Daily News* on July 30, 2021, lamented: *"But if horseracing becomes merely an incidental adjunct to the soulless stimulations plied to the casino addicts, then the only "match of the century" we'll ever know will be the one lighting the bonfire of our heritage."*

Will the upcoming Kentucky Derby become kitsch? A spectacle of hats devoid of any larger meaning or purpose? Today we need another Bing Crosby to get involved in horse racing. He brought pageantry and glamour to the sport amid the Great Depression. Now we need to jumpstart his favorite sport the way he and Frank Sinatra did in the movie *High Society* by announcing, "What a swellegant, elegant party this is" as we head for to the races.

Joe Moran has had an interest in equestrian sports and has traveled extensively to many sporting destinations. He has an appreciation for sportsmen like Bing Crosby who have made significant contributions to the sport of horse racing. He enjoys collecting period information about sporting figures from the nineteenth and early twentieth century.

18 | *Witness for the Paw-secution*

SEAN OWENS

IN May of 2015, police in Ensley Township, Michigan, arrived to a grisly scene at the home of Martin and Glenna Duram. According to news reports, the house had been ransacked and Martin, 45, was dead. He'd been shot five times and was found lying in nothing but underwear and a pool of his own blood. His wife, Glenna, was nearby, clinging to life with two gunshot wounds, one to the head. Though unconscious and seriously wounded, she would ultimately survive.

At first, authorities believed the Durams had been victims of a burglary gone terribly wrong. But later, suspicions turned towards Glenna. Martin had been unable to work after a debilitating car accident and Glenna struggled with her role as both wife and caretaker. She also struggled with a gambling addiction that had left the couple deeply in debt, and police found what read like suicide notes in Glenna's handwriting hidden in the house. Glenna adamantly denied shooting Martin, but also claimed that she remembered little else from that terrible night.

Had they both been innocent victims of a dangerous criminal? Or had Glenna murdered her husband in a rage and then attempted suicide to end it all? The investigation was at a standstill.

The only other witness? The couple's African grey parrot, Bud.

Shortly after the crime, Bud started obsessively repeating what seemed to be an argument between a man and woman. In two different voices, he would screech:

"No, no."

"Shut up!"

"Don't fucking shoot!"

The last voice, relatives insisted, was Martin's. Glenna would eventually be convicted of murder and sentenced to life in prison.

I thought about Bud the parrot as I stood in my kitchen, eating a chicken sandwich. My cat, Scruffy, was staring at me the way cats do when you are holding a chicken sandwich. Scruffy is the sort of animal that could eat a Las Vegas casino's entire buffet and still act like he hadn't eaten in days.

I stared back.

"What has he seen that I would rather he hadn't?" I wondered. "And what would it take for him to turn on me?"

Because animals are always watching, always listening...and Bud the parrot wasn't the first pet to spill the bird seed.

Sometimes, pets have been called to testify on their own behalf. Like in 1886, when the *Cincinnati Enquirer* reported on a dog settling a dispute over its ownership. The plaintiff claimed he had purchased the "fine-looking Newfoundland" years prior and named him "Rover." The defendant argued he too had purchased the dog, whose actual name was "Jack." The presiding judge instructed each man to call the dog. After watching as the animal "wagged its tail most graciously, and leaped upon the plaintiff, seemingly delighted to see him," the jury awarded him his pet.

A decade later, the *New York Herald* reported a Mrs. Fanny Henning and her dachshund Claude were accused of disturbing the peace due to Claude's incessant barking. It was her word against the complaining neighbor's until Claude dramatically took the stand. The neighbor and others "did their best to force him to bark. They tickled him in the ribs, rubbed his head roughly, pinched his hide and pulled his ears." But after Claude "just yawned and blinked," the case was dismissed. Whether Claude's silence constituted an invocation of his Fifth Amendment right against self-incrimination, or whether he and Mrs. Henning engaged in a nefarious conspiracy to torment their neighbor and escape prosecution, remains an open debate.

Other cases are like an episode of *Scooby-Doo*, where a meddling pet cracks the mystery like a sunflower seed from a birdfeeder. *The Milwaukee Sentinel* reported that the victim of a burglary arrived home to discover not only the theft, but also that her pet parrot had learned a surprising new welcome message: “Hullo, big feet!” The bird repeated the greeting as the police arrived and, when shushed, responded with “Oh, hurry up, big feet!” In a flash, the inspector remembered “Big Feet” was the nickname of a known local burglar, who was promptly arrested along with an accomplice. “[T]he bird,” the paper reported, was “to be produced as a witness against them at the trial.”

But as I stood in my kitchen holding my sandwich under the unblinking gaze of my cat, I was more unsettled by cases like Bud the parrot, where a pet’s testimony led to the ruination of its owner. Think I’m paranoid? In the 1990s, after a member of the New Orleans mafia was arrested on federal charges, he was reportedly convinced that his pet parrot, Echo, had seen too much and would turn into a stool pigeon. Authorities were so concerned for the bird’s safety that they placed it in avian witness protection at an undisclosed bird sanctuary elsewhere in the state.

And it’s not just parrots who’ve squawked. A hundred years earlier, in San Francisco, a man was accused of using a trained monkey as a pickpocket. At trial, the prosecutor called a single witness: the capuchin monkey, Miss Mono. As soon as she was led into the courtroom, she reportedly leapt on the judge, snatched his watch and chain, and went “scampering over to the accused, [who knew] that San Quentin stared him in the face.” A few years later, the same scene played out in a New York courtroom after a burglar accidentally left his lookout, a fox terrier, in a victim’s apartment. If these news reports add up to anything, it’s that the loyalties of pets only go so far. And if I had something to hide, who’s to say Scruffy wouldn’t let the cat out the bag? There had to be a way to make sure he would stay as loyal and quiet as Claude the dachshund, who refused to rollover and speak.

I’ve yet to find reports of cats being called to testify against their owners, which is perhaps not surprising if you’ve ever tried to compel a cat to do...well...anything. But cats are sly and treacherous. They are vindictive. If my cat decides I've slept too late in the morning, or that I should be paying attention to him rather than a book, he will begin to systematically destroy the room around me until I capitulate. Newspaper on the side table? Shredded. Mail on the desk? It looks better on the floor. Framed pictures on the mantel? "SCRUFFY! GET DOWN!"

Edgar Allan Poe knew what felines were capable of when he penned "The Black Cat." Written from the perspective of an alcoholic descending into madness, the fictitious narrator recounts how he abused and killed one pet cat, then attempted to kill another, and finally brought the axe down on his own wife's skull. Concealing her body behind the basement wall, he smugly believed the crime would never be discovered. But his wife's corpse wasn't the only thing hidden in the basement, because when police arrived several days later to search the house, "a cry, at first muffled and broken, like the sobbing of a child, and then quickly swelling into one long, loud, and continuous scream, utterly anomalous and inhuman -- a howl -- a wailing shriek" emanated from behind the wall! Breaking through the masonry, the police found the wife's decaying corpse with the vengeful and screeching cat sitting on her head.

Have you ever heard a cat scream?

I have.

Scruffy does not trill or daintily meow. He barks and growls. He bays with a smoker's rasp like the mascot of a pirate ship.

He would be heard through the basement wall.

Of course, most of us aren't thieves and fewer still have murdered their spouses. But pets hear our hidden whispers. They reside with us behind closed doors. They see our secret selves. Which is why Marty and Glenna shouldn't have argued in front of Bud, why that mobster shouldn't have conducted business in front of Echo, and why monkeys make terrible accomplices. At a minimum, Poe's narrator shouldn't have crossed those cats. And Scruffy was still staring at my sandwich.

He barked.

I looked down at my cat and sighed. Resigned, I ripped a piece of chicken off and dropped it on the floor. He pounced, immediately purring, and devoured the morsel. Then he looked up at me, licked his chops, and contentedly walked away.

"Better safe than sorry," I thought.

Silence has its price.

Sean Owens is an intellectual property attorney in private practice and an adjunct professor at the University of Cincinnati College of Law. He writes primarily in memoir, whatever nonfiction rabbit holes grab his attention, and (theoretically) humor. A native Cincinnatian, Sean lives in Prospect Hill and has been a member of The Literary Club since 2023.

19 Choice Words

RICK PENDER

I'VE been writing about theater — especially musical theater — for a long time, nearly 40 years. Strangely enough, I'm not personally musical, and I'm certainly not a singer. By popular request, I don't even try. Nevertheless, I'm fascinated with words sung by performers of musical theater.

Perhaps the greatest source of those words in the latter third of the 20th century was the composer and lyricist Stephen Sondheim. He started, at age 26, working with composer Leonard Bernstein and writing lyrics for *West Side Story* in 1956. It was an auspicious beginning. Here are some words he wrote for "Something's Coming," sung by Tony, a romantic young man (modeled on Romeo from Shakespeare's *Romeo and Juliet*). These were his breathless thoughts:

> Could be, who knows?
> There's something due any day —
> I will know right away,
> Soon as it shows.
>
> It may come cannonballing down through the sky,
> Gleam in its eye,
> Bright as a rose.
> Who knows?

Stephen Sondheim

It's only just out of reach,
Down the block, on a beach,
Under a tree
I got a feeling there's a miracle due,
Gonna come true,
Coming to me!

Could it be? Yes, it could.
Something's coming, something good,
If I can wait.

Something's coming,
I don't know what it is,
But it is gonna be great!

I had the good fortune to edit a magazine about Mr. Sondheim for a dozen years and then to write an extensive reference book about him and his many Broadway shows, published in 2021. Here's a quick sketch of his life.

He passed away in November 2021 at the age of 91 after a prolific 65-year career that included 18 full-fledged musicals. It would be impossible to overestimate his influence on American musical theater. He began his Broadway career writing lyrics for *West Side Story* in 1956. Two years later he produced lyrics for *Gypsy* with composer Jule Styne in a production that featured the legendary Ethel Merman as a self-centered, domineering stage mother. He finally achieved his career dream of writing lyrics and music for *A Funny Thing Happened on the Way to the Forum* in 1962. That opened the floodgates for many more now legendary and award-winning shows: *Company* (1970), *Follies* (1971), *A Little Night Music* (1973), *Pacific Overtures* (1976), *Sweeney Todd* (1979), *Sunday in the Park with George* (1984, winner of the Pulitzer Prize for Drama), *Into the Woods* (1987) and *Passion* (1994).

Sondheim was a product of classic Broadway. As a teenager he met and was mentored by Oscar Hammerstein II, the most successful lyricist of the Broadway's Golden Era in the 1940s and 1950s. But Sondheim went on to open the door to something totally new to Broadway. His subjects were wide-ranging and often unexpected. Some of his songs had inventive structures that did not adhere to familiar song forms. Many were built on harmonies that resembled avant-garde classical music. Some of his shows, such as *Sweeney Todd* and *Passion* were sung through like operas, even though he steadfastly refused to categorize them that way.

Most theatergoers today have seen or at least heard of some of Sondheim's shows. But his fame is also rooted in the fact that many subsequent Broadway composers emulated him, including Jonathan Larson, who created *Rent*, and Lin-Manuel Miranda, whose *Hamilton* has been the greatest Broadway hit of the 21st century.

Sondheim won Tonys, an Oscar, Grammys and a Pulitzer Prize. He was appointed to the "Cameron Mackintosh Chair in Musical Theatre" at England's Oxford University, and he received honors from the Kennedy Center. He was awarded a Presidential Medal of Freedom by Barack Obama. Despite his eventual fame, some of his shows were flops when they opened, such as *Merrily We Roll Along* (1981) which closed after just 16 performances. It was revived as an Off-Broadway production in 2022 and became standing room only hit on Broadway in 2023.

A 2022 concert staging of his fairytale musical *Into the Woods* featuring singer-songwriter Sara Bareilles later became an unexpected and more fully staged Broadway hit. Movie star Jake Gyllenhaal played artist Georges Seurat in *Sunday in the Park with George* in 2017. Pop star Josh Groban played Sweeney Todd, the "Demon Barber of Fleet Street," in a Tony Award-winning revival in 2023. Sondheim's impact on the world of theater is quite remarkable, and his shows continue to be revived.

If you've seen one Sondheim show, you've seen **ONE** Sondheim show. Each of his works is unique in terms of music and story. "I like to change styles," Sondheim once told an interviewer. "One of the things that appeals to me about stories is if I've never done anything like it before. It has to be some unknown territory. It's got to make you nervous. If it doesn't make you nervous, then you're going to write the same thing you wrote before." He once wrote a song called, "I Never Do Anything Twice," a sentiment he clearly embraced.

At age 15 Sondheim shared with Oscar Hammerstein the script and score for a musical he had written for his boarding school. He was certain his mentor would be bowled over and option it for Broadway that afternoon. Of course, that didn't happen. Young Steve asked for honest feedback, and Hammerstein gave it to him: "I have to say that it's the worst thing that ever crossed my desk. It's the worst thing I've ever seen. It's the most unproducible. It makes no sense." That judgment was surely deflating. But Hammerstein then offered to tutor the aspiring and precocious teenager in what he needed to do to become successful as a creator of musical theater. He suggested four lessons:

First, Hammerstein had Sondheim adapt a good play as a musical. He chose George S. Kaufman and Marc Connelly's *Beggar on Horseback*, a 1924 play that had a successful two-year run on Broadway. Sondheim turned it into *All That Glitters*, which had three performances at Williams College in 1949, his junior year at that renowned Massachusetts liberal arts school.

The second exercise was to adapt a flawed play as a musical: Maxwell Anderson's *High Tor*, the 1936 Pulitzer Prize winner, was Sondheim's choice. He sought permission to stage his rendition at Williams, but Anderson planned to adapt it himself and turned down the request. (It never happened.)

Hammerstein's third exercise was to adapt another form — a novel or a short story — into a musical. Sondheim put in time on P. L. Travers's "Mary Poppins" stories, but he abandoned them, saying, "I couldn't figure out how to make the disparate episodes hang together."

Hammerstein's final task for Sondheim was to write a musical that was entirely his own. It was titled *Climb High*, written just after his 1950 graduation from Williams. In retrospect he described it as "a four-hour summation of my views on life, ambition, morality, theater, and art with a passing swipe at love." The first act was 99 pages, to which Hammerstein simply said, "Wow." It was never produced.

Sondheim said Hammerstein trained him "to think of songs as one-act plays, to move a song from point A to point B dramatically." Years later Sondheim said his afternoon with Hammerstein offered more than he might have garnered from a lifetime of study. From another teacher, a professor of music at Williams, he learned the lesson that, "Art is craft, not inspiration." That means it takes work.

My own admiration of Sondheim began when I was 13. My first LP purchase was not the Beatles or the Beach Boys — although I loved them. Instead it was the cast recording of the Academy Award-winning movie of *West Side Story*. I was captivated by those lyrics such as the ones I cited at the beginning of this essay. They certainly lit the spark. "Could it be? Yes, it could. Something's coming, something good."

Back then I didn't know who Stephen Sondheim was. But his lyrics infected me. Sometimes they were romantic, as in "Maria" and "Tonight." Sometimes they were cleverly funny — "Gee, Officer Krupke," and it's cleverly masked final-line obscenity, "Gee, Officer Krupke, **krup** you!" Sondheim had dreamed of being the first person to insert the F-word into a Broadway show. But a female producer's blanched reaction convinced him that the time was not yet right.

At a family gathering in 1973 my Aunt Margaret, an inveterate community theater performer, belted for the assembled relatives the song

"Broadway Baby" from Sondheim's 1971 show *Follies*. Even though I didn't know half of the topical references in that song, I thought it was a great number. A few years later I saw a very polished amateur production of *A Little Night Music*, full of clever witty songs in waltz time about a trio of confused love affairs. It was the words that really drew me in.

In 1979 I heard that Sondheim was creating a musical about Sweeney Todd, a fictitious Victorian serial killer who cut throats and provided filling for meat pies. I thought, "This guy's gone off the deep end." It was hard to imagine audiences warming to the tale of the *Demon Barber of Fleet Street*. But over time it's been impossible to deny this show's power. Many consider it Sondheim's masterpiece. Director Tim Burton's 2007 cinematic rendition of the Demon Barber's story featured actor Johnny Depp.

In the mid-1980s, Sondheim's *Sunday in the Park with George*, inspired by Impressionist painter Georges Seurat and his famous painting, won the Pulitzer Prize for drama, a recognition generally reserved for plays, not musicals. In 1987 Sondheim headed in yet another new direction with *Into the Woods*, a show using fairy tales to convey a message about community. That one too became a film, Rob Marshall's 2014 production starring Meryl Streep as a Witch, and James Corden and Emily Blunt as a Baker and his Wife.

But what deepened my appreciation happened back in 1990. I was recovering from some surgery and, to pass the time, I picked up some CDs from the public library. One was "A Collector's Sondheim," a three-disk set of original cast performances from more than a dozen of his shows. I listened repeatedly, fascinated by Sondheim's elaborate, ornate and yet seemingly inevitable lyric writing.

When the Cincinnati Playhouse produced *Sweeney Todd* in 1997, I offered to write a review for a recently established quarterly magazine, *The Sondheim Review*. One thing led to another, and by 2004 I was its managing editor, a part-time job I had for a dozen years until it ceased publication. During that time I became modestly acquainted with Sondheim personally.

In 2006 when the Playhouse produced his new version of his 1970 Tony Award winner Company with actors playing their own musical instruments. Sondheim came to Cincinnati for previews, and I invited him to sit down for an interview at WVXU-FM, where I was a regular contributor to a weekly show about the arts, *Around Cincinnati*. He agreed, and we recorded an hour-long conversation. He complimented me on my preparation for our session.

In 2010 and 2011 Sondheim published two volumes of lyric studies, digging in depth into the words he'd written for his 18 major shows and beyond. I had the singular opportunity to interview him about *Finishing the Hat*, covering lyrics from 1954 to 1981 and *Look, I Made a Hat*, annotating lyrics from 1981 to 2011. Our conversations were unbelievably illuminating — and often terrifying.

In 2017 I was enlisted by a publisher to write a reference book, *The Stephen Sondheim Encyclopedia*. My 650-page volume took two years to complete. It was delayed a year by the COVID-19 pandemic and finally published in April 2021.

If anything, my attention to Sondheim's lyrics over the past three decades has deepened my appreciation of his work. His singular genius was combining lyrics and music, but for me it was the words he chose that attracted me so many years ago. I love to share his brilliance with people who appreciate the selection of "choice words."

Sondheim followed three overarching principles during his career. The first was that **CONTENT DICTATES FORM**. In other words, a show's story must shape the music and words — be they archaically Victorian as in *Sweeney Todd*, delicately Asian for *Pacific Overtures*, or rooted in various eras of American history and music in *Assassins*. His second principle was **LESS IS MORE**, a reminder to be as concise and direct as possible. Third was **GOD IS IN THE DETAILS**. He slaved slowly and meticulously over both the words and the melodies that he crafted for his many shows. All of these, he summarized, "in the service of **CLARITY**."

Sondheim explained that "One difference between poetry and lyrics is that lyrics sort of fade into the background. They fade on the page and live on the stage when set to music." A singular skill at rhyming was one of Sondheim's greatest tools in writing lyrics that defined characters and told stories. His very first professional foray was actually *Saturday Night*, a show he worked on even before *West Side Story*. He was 24 when he wrote songs for this story of an ambitious young man trying to make a killing on the stock market. But it stalled on its way to Broadway when its young producer passed away unexpectedly. (It was finally produced 50 years later!)

For a young couple in *Saturday Night* who were falling in love he wrote "What More Do I Need?" It's full of clever rhyming and the ironic twists of imagery.

> Once I hated this **city**,
> Now it can't get me **down**.
> Slushy, humid and **gritty**,
> What a pretty **town**.
>
> What, thought I, could be duller,
> More depressing, less **gay**?
> Now my favorite color is **gray**!
>
> A wall of rain as it turns to **sleet**
> The lack of **sun** on a **one**-way **street**
> I love the **grime**
> All the **time**,
> And what more do I need?
>
> My windowpane has a lovely **view**:
> An inch of **sky** and a **fly** or **two**.
> Why, I can **see** half a **tree**,
> And what more do I **need**?
>
> The dusk is thick and it's **galling**.
> It simply can't be exc**used**,
> In winter, even the **falling** snow
> Looks **used**.

My windowpane may not give much **light**,
But I see **you**, so the **view** is **bright**.
If I can love you, I'll pay the dirt no **heed**.
With your love, what more do I **need**?

Some**one** shouting for **quiet**.
Some**one** starting a **brawl**.
Down the block there's a **riot** —
And I'll **buy it all.**

Listen now, I'm **ecstatic**.
Hold me close and keep **still**.
Hear the lovely **pneumatic drill**!

A subway train thunders through the **Bronx**.
A taxi horn on the corner **honks**.
But I **adore** every **roar**,
And what more do I need?

I hear a crane making street **repairs**.
A two-**ton** child **run**ning wild **upstairs**.
Steam pipes **bang** —
Sirens **clang** —
And what more do I need?

The neighbors yell in the **summer**.
The landlord yells in the **fall**.
So loud I can't hear the **plumber**
Pound the **wall**.

An aeroplane roars across the **bay**.
But I can **hear** you as **clear** as **day**.
You said you loved me,
Above the sound and **speed**?
With your love what more do I **need**?

After *Saturday Night* failed to be produced, Sondheim took some career advice from Oscar Hammerstein and moved on to *West Side Story* in 1956 and then *Gypsy* in 1958. With both shows he grudgingly stepped into the role of lyricist, not composer. In 1962 he finally got to fire both barrels of his creative gun with *A Funny Thing Happened on the Way to the Forum*.

That show's famous opening number, "Comedy Tonight," was added at the last minute, during the show's pre-Broadway tryout in Washington, D.C., in 1962. Out-of-town audiences seemed not to understand that the show, inspired by comedies by Plautus, an ancient Roman playwright, was going to be a farce. Sondheim's initial opening song was a sweetly romantic number, "Love Is in the Air." Among the many lessons that Oscar Hammerstein taught him was that an opening number could make or break a show, and that one was not working. When the curtain came up on "Comedy Tonight," there was no doubt what was to follow:

> Something familiar,
> Something peculiar,
> Something for everyone:
> A comedy tonight!
>
> Something appealing,
> Something appalling,
> Something for everyone:
> A comedy tonight!
>
> Nothing with kings, Nothing with crowns;
> Bring on the lovers, liars and clowns!
>
> Old situations,
> New complications,
> Nothing portentous or polite;
> Tragedy tomorrow,
> Comedy tonight!

Something convulsive,
Something repulsive,
Something for everyone:
A comedy tonight!

Something aesthetic,
Something frenetic,
Something for everyone:
A comedy tonight!
Nothing with gods, Nothing with fate;
Weighty affairs will just have to wait!
...

Nothing that's grim.
Nothing that's Greek.
She plays Medea later this week.

Stunning surprises!
Cunning disguises!
Hundreds of actors out of sight!

Pantaloons and tunics!
Courtesans and eunuchs!
Funerals and chases!
Baritones and basses!
Panderers!
Philanderers!
Cupidity!
Timidity!
Mistakes!
Fakes!
Rhymes!
Crimes!

Tumblers!
Grumblers!
Bumblers!
Fumblers!

No royal curse,
No Trojan horse,
And a happy ending,
Of course!
Goodness and badness,
Panic is madness—
This time it all turns out all right!
Tragedy tomorrow,
Comedy tonight!

It's a breathtaking array of rhymes. With that final list and its sense of acceleration — starting with six syllables and working down to four, three, two and one syllable before the rhyming set of four: "Tumblers, Grumblers, Bumblers, Fumblers" — so the audience clearly saw what was coming. It's a deliriously clever opener with an avalanche of witty words that firmly established *Forum* as a world-class comedy, one that continues to work flawlessly six decades later.

For *Finishing the Hat*, Sondheim's first volume of lyric studies, he wrote an essay, "Rhyme and Its Reasons." In it he declared the importance of true (or "perfect") rhymes: That is, two words or phrases whose final accented syllables sound alike except for the consonant sounds that precede them. Such rhymes are "masculine" if the accent falls is on the final syllable – for example, *convey* and *dismay* — or "feminine," when the accent is on the next-to-last syllable – such as *never* and *forever*.

In his lyric writing, Sondheim strove to use true rhymes. "Rhyming," he stated, "is the glue that holds a song together, it spotlights a line, a thought. It's also hard work." It's also a necessity in musical theater, helping listeners understand what has just been sung.

Sondheim used rhyme to underscore the message of his songs. "A good lyric," he wrote, "should not only have something to say, but a way of saying it as clearly and forcefully as possible, which involves rhyming cleanly. A perfect rhyme can make a mediocre line bright and a good one brilliant. Perfect rhymes reinforce the meaning of lyrics with greater clarity, and they 'resonate' better with the melody." He continued, "A near rhyme dampens the impact so it's less useful to the primary purpose of a theatrical lyric, which is to be heard. It causes your ear to listen less carefully or to disregard a lyric altogether and to simply let the music wash over you."

Sondheim's essay also explains how near or "false" rhymes rely on assonance, when vowel sounds are alike, and the following consonants are different – *home* and *alone* or *together* and *forever*. A "slant" rhyme relies on consonance, when consonant sounds are alike, but the accented vowels are different – *buddy/body*. If you're accustomed to pop and rock songs, you're used to hearing these "near" or "slant" rhymes.

Using such rhymes, according to Sondheim, is like juggling clumsily. "It can be fun to watch," he pointed out, "and it is juggling, but it's nowhere near as much pleasure for an audience as seeing all the balls — or in the case of the best lyricists, knives, torches and swords — being kept aloft with grace and precision."

For an example of the pleasure good rhyming can produce, I like to describe an experience Sondheim had with Cole Porter, the veteran musical theater composer and lyricist. In 1958 Sondheim and composer Jule Styne visited Porter at his Waldorf-Astoria apartment while they were writing lyrics for *Gypsy*. Porter was deeply depressed over his broken physical condition; his leg had been amputated recently, the ultimate result of a serious and painful horseback-riding accident two decades earlier.

Sondheim and Styne played and sang some of *Gypsy*'s songs, including "Together, Wherever We Go." This number is sung by Rose, the tyrannical stage mother and the show's central character, with her boyfriend Herbie and her daughter Louise, who Rose will soon push onstage to fill in for Louise's kid sister, the juvenile star of the vaudeville act that Rose aggressively promotes, who has eloped. Rose wants shy Louise to step into the spotlight — where she will eventually become striptease artist Gypsy Rose Lee. Here are the opening lines of "Together, Wherever We Go""

Wherever we go,
Whatever we do,
We're gonna go through it together.
We may not go far.
But sure as a star,
Wherever we are, it's together!
Wherever we go, I know **he goes**,
Wherever we go, I know **she goes**.
Not fits, no fights, no feuds and **no egos** —
Amigos, together!

When they got to the word 'Amigos,' Sondheim heard a gasp of delight from the corner of the room. Porter had been surprised by the song's quadruple rhyme — **he goes/she goes/no egos/amigos.** It was a memorable moment for Sondheim. "Needless to say," he recalled, "surprising a pro is one of the greatest joys a writer can experience, and this pro [Porter] not only was a master of surprising rhymes, he also often sprinkled his lyrics with foreign words and phrases as markers of his cosmopolitan style. Any time I need an ego boost, I conjure up that gasp; it may well be the high point of my lyric-writing life."

For another quick example of how Sondheim's precise lyric rhyming could reinforce the message of a song, here is a passage from "Ah, But Underneath," a song from *Follies*, about a gorgeous showgirl with an inferiority complex:

In the depths of her **interior**
Were **fears** she was **inferior**
And something even **eerier**.
But no one dared to **query her superior exterior**.

I imagine those lines could well have evoked several sighs from Cole Porter. One more example, this one from *A Little Night Music*. It's called "Night Waltz," sung by a quintet of minor characters about Sweden's long summer night.

The vespers ring.
The nightingale's waiting to sing.
The rest of us wait on a string.
Perpetual sunset
Is rather an unset-
tling thing.

The sun won't set.
It's fruitless to hope or to fret.
It's dark as it's going to get.
The hands on the clock turn,
But don't sing a nocturne
Just yet.

Need I say more? Well, of course, I will.

How did Sondheim came up with all these remarkable rhymes? He often relied on a rhyming dictionary. He explained that the first thing he resolved was to understand what a character needed to say and then decide how to phrase that desire. Then he would improvise a rhyme scheme to match the melody he had in mind. After that he would begin to seek rhymes, which solidified meaning and helped listeners focus on important themes.

Sondheim used Clement Woods's *The Complete Rhyming Dictionary*, published in 1936, which lists rhymes vertically. He preferred this to rhyming dictionaries with traditional horizontal lines, which he felt could cause a user to skip over words. Using Woods's rhyming dictionary, a word might pop out, and he would list any words that seemed relevant to what he was trying to say. He said, "I might have a line that ends with **day**, and I want to say how she loves me. So I go to the rhyming dictionary. There are many rhyming words for **day**. They will somehow encompass or pinpoint what I want to say – perhaps ***may***, ***play***, ***say*** and ***way*** — or even 'Biscayne Bay.'"

Sondheim had delicious fun with the song "A Little Priest" in *Sweeney Todd*. The serial killer barber is ready to undertake a spree of throat-cutting, and Mrs. Lovett, his accomplice, suggests a novel solution to dispose of the bodies — her business is baking meat pies. Based on the show's underlying conceit that professions feed on one another, Sondheim developed a list of roughly 160 careers and types of people to consider. He began with Bishop, Priest, Earl, and Lord. He sometimes paired words and phrases: "Artist – smartest" or even, "We have shepherd's pie peppered/With actual shepherd/On top."

Sweeney sings:

> How gratifying for once to know –
> That those above will serve those down below."

And then he and Mrs. Lovett have the following competitive exchange:

> She says: It's priest. Have a little priest.
> Sweeney: Is it good?
> Mrs. Lovett: Sir, it's too good, at least.
> Then again, they don't commit sins of the flesh, so it's pretty fresh.
>
> Soon Sweeney asks: Haven't you got poet,
> Or something like that?
> Mrs. Lovett: No the trouble with poet
> Is how do you know it's
> Deceased? ...
> Try the priest.

Those verbal shenanigans lead to a sort of rhyming challenge:

> Mrs. Lovett: Now let's see ... We've got tinker ...
> Sweeney: Something pinker.
> Mrs. Lovett: Tailor?
> Sweeney: Paler.
> Mrs. Lovett: Butler?

Sweeney: Subtler.
Mrs. Lovett: Potter?
Sweeney: Hotter.
Mrs. Lovett: Locksmith?
[At that, Sweeney shrugs, defeated.]

All in all, the song includes about 40 jobs as potential pie fillings, a remarkable demonstration of inventive rhyming and storytelling that makes cannibalism almost palatable (please forgive that distasteful comparison). "A Little Priest" is great if gruesome fun.

I'll next explore some numbers from a tamer, more civilized tale, the Tony Award-winning *A Little Night Music*. Based on Ingmar Bergman's 1955 film, *Smiles of a Summer Night*, in Sondheim's creative hands it became a romantic farce with almost every song in waltz time. The story revolves around Desirée Armfeldt, an attractive middle-aged stage actress who yearns to rekindle a past romance with Fredrik Egerman, now a stodgy attorney. That's complicated by her current unfinished affair with Count Carl-Magnus, a pompous military officer who sees himself as God's gift to women.

The show opened on Broadway in February 1973 and became one Sondheim's most successful original works, winning many awards and becoming the longest running of his numerous collaborations with producer-director Hal Prince. It had 601 performances and fully paid off its investors. It's not as violent as *Sweeney Todd*, but Prince did once describe the show as "whipped cream with knives," so it certainly has an edge.

There's a song from *A Little Night Music* that I suspect you know: "Send in the Clowns." Sondheim jokingly called it "my hit." It had its first national exposure when Frank Sinatra performed it on an NBC-TV special in 1973. Frank breezily described it this way: "It's a story of two adult people who had a very nice life together and suddenly, in older age, one of them decides to split." That's actually not quite the story: In fact, *Night Music* is a tale of what might have been between a pair whose timing has *never* been in sync.

Pop singer Judy Collins included the song on her 1975 album *Judith*. Her poignant rendition won the Grammy for "Best Pop Vocal of the Year." Many of the songs in *A Little Night Music* are performed by multiple characters with complex counterpointing of voices and perspectives. But this song was a solo number.

"Send in the Clowns" was a late addition to *Night Music*'s original production, written under pressure in just two days. Rehearsals for the show's Broadway premiere began on Dec. 10, 1972, with several songs still missing. There had been doubts about the singing skills of Glynis Johns, who originated the role of Desirée. The production team determined that she could sing a solo number if it wasn't too vocally demanding.

Sondheim and director Hal Prince discussed a scene late in the show between Desirée and Fredrik, the pair whose past affair evaporated because of her busy stage career and his first marriage. Now, with both at middle age, she desires Fredrik. He, alas, has a sweet 18-year-old wife ... who remains a virgin.

The show's book writer Hugh Wheeler drafted an interior monologue for Desirée, which Sondheim shaped into an ironic, wistful number suitable for Glynis Johns's silvery, breathy voice, using short, clipped phrases, many ending in consonants. The result was the rare ballad that actually succeeds without sustained notes, a song with a precise rhythm and a thoughtful style.

Describing how he wrote "Send in the Clowns," Sondheim explained, "I decided to write a series of short musical lines so Glynis wouldn't have to sustain notes. That suggested questions, little phrases. And then I wanted not to have any open vowel sounds at the end of the opening line — 'Isn't it rich?' — so that it wouldn't seem like she couldn't sing." Here is how he phrased the lines and emphasized key words with rhyming.

Isn't it rich?
Are we a pair?
Me here at last on the ground

You in mid-air,
Send in the clowns.

Isn't it bliss?
Don't you approve?
One who keeps tearing around,
One who can't move.
Where are the clowns?
Send in the clowns.

Just when I stopped
Opening doors
Finally knowing the one that I wanted was yours
Making my entrance again with my usual flair
Sure of my lines ...
No one is there.

Desirée's life is in the theater, so her song is full of theatrical references. With simple phrasing, closed vowel sounds and consonants at the end of each line, the song continues.

Don't you love a farce?
My fault, I fear.
I thought that you'd want what I want
Sorry my dear.
But where are the clowns?
Send in the clowns
Don't bother
They're here.

Desirée is as honest and straightforward as she can be, but she realizes that honesty and baring one's soul can be manipulative. Her self-awareness adds to the layers and the bittersweet quality of the song: It's how she concludes that the "clowns are *here*."

Isn't it rich?
Isn't it queer?

Losing my timing this late
In my career.
Where are the clowns?
There ought to be clowns
Well, maybe next year.

By the way, Sondheim is credited with coining the phrase "send in the clowns," which has become a commonly understood (and occasionally misunderstood) phrase, appearing in cartoons, movies, TV shows, articles, editorials, ads and conversations.

A Little Night Music has another solo number that demonstrates Sondheim's remarkable rhyming skills. "The Miller's Son," performed by Petra, the Egermans' saucy maid, is a fantasy about lovers she might take on and what they would mean for her future. Listen for Sondheim's complex rhyming at the end and within the song's lines as well as the repeated phrase "In the meanwhile" as Petra's imagination becomes more and more vivid and expansive with a strong whiff of "carpe diem."

"The Miller's Son" is sung by this very secondary character after she's had a "roll in the hay" with Frid, a hunky manservant. The song was another very late addition to the score, a demanding vocal tour-de-force, full of rhetorical, tongue-twisting rhymes. It's designed to be belted by a lusty young woman. D'Jamin Bartlett who played Petra won several Broadway awards for her one-song performance.

Here's the first section of "The Miller's Son." Watch for the rhymes:

I shall marry the miller's son,
Pin my hat on a nice piece of property.
Fr**I**day nights, for a bit of fun,
We'll go dancing.
Meanwhile ...

It's a wink and a **wiggle**
And a **giggle** in the **grass**
And I'll trip the light fandango,
A pinch and a **diddle**
In the **middle** of what **passes by**.

It's a very short road
From the pinch and the punch
To the paunch and the pouch and the pension.
It's a very short road
To the ten-thousandth lunch
And the belch and the grouch and the **sigh**.
In the **meanwhile,**
There are mouths to be kissed
Before mouths to be fed,
And a lot in between
In the **meanwhile.**
And a girl ought to celebrate what **passes by**.

That **wiggle** and **giggle** have "assonance," a similar sound with **diddle** and **middle**. And the final words "**passes by**" link back to a few lines earlier with **grass** and **passes**, as well as **sigh** and **by**.

What follows the repeated adverb **"meanwhile"** in each verse is anything but a simple song. It features virtually every kind of rhyming in the English language — end rhyme, internal rhyme, interstitial rhyme, assonance, consonance and an array of rhetorical devices as Petra elevates her possible path to ever higher social strata. Check out the rhyming in the song's second section:

Or **I** shall marry the businessman,
Five fat babies and lots of security.
Friday n**i**ghts, if we think we can,
We'll go dancing.
Meanwhile...

It's a push and a **fumble**
And a **tumble** in the sheets
And I'll foot the H**I**ghland Fancy,
A dip in the butter
And a flutter with what meets my **eye**.

It's a very short fetch
From the push and the **whoop**
To the squint and the **stoop** and the **mumble**.
It's not much of a stretch
To the cribs and the **croup**
And the bosoms that **droop** and go **dry**.

In the meanwhile,
There are mouths to be kissed
Before mouths to be fed,
And there's many a tryst
And there's many a bed
To be sampled and **seen**
In the **mean**while.
And a girl has to celebrate what **passes by**.

The density of rhyming increases the song's pace — **fumble** and **tumble** (them **mumble**) as well as **whoop/stoop/croup/droop**. Petra's third fantasy is indeed fantastic. But it also reminds her that climbing up the social scale does not necessarily end with greater satisfaction.

Or **I** shall marry the Prince of Wales —
Pearls and servants and dressing for festivals.
Fr**I**day nights, with him all in tails,
We'll have dancing.
Meanwhile ...

It's a rip in the **bustle**
And a **rustle** in the hay
And I'll pitch the Quick Fantastic,
With flings of con**fetti**
And my **petti**coats away up **high**.
It's a very short **way**
From the fling that's for **fun**
To the thigh pressing **un**der the table.

It's a very short **day**
Till you're stuck with just **one**
Or it has to be done on the **sly**.
In the **meanwhile**,
There are mouths to be **kissed**
Before mouths to be **fed,**
And there's many a **tryst**
And there's many a **bed**.
There's a lot I'll have missed
But I'll not have been dead when I **DIE**!
And a person should celebrate everything
Passing by.
And **I** shall marry the miller's son ...

That big belted **"DIE"** in almost the last line is the song's highest note (a B-natural), putting the most extreme emphasis on the subsequent, slightly modified rhyme, **passing by**. There are, in fact, at least seven rhymes for the word **"by"** in the song, which emphasize "**what passes by.**"

I hope this closer look has provided some sense of Sondheim's careful choice of words, not just for sound but also for meaning. Such examples are to be found in every one of his shows.

To conclude, here are some self-deprecating lines he wrote for *Sondheim on Sondheim*, a 2010 Broadway production that used film of him in his workroom/study, talking about the craft of writing songs. For this show, he wrote a tongue-in-cheek number poking fun at his status, first suggested by a cover of *New York Magazine* in April 1994. It featured an image of him enhanced with a halo and a headline asking, "Is Stephen Sondheim God?" The number was sung by the cast of *Sondheim on Sondheim* looking up worshipfully at his image on a large video screen while he roamed around his studio clumsily dropping things and being decidedly "un-God-like." Nevertheless, the number is called "God."

God.

I mean the man's a god.

Wrote the score to "Sweeney Todd,"
With a nod
To de Sade —
Well, he's odd!
Well, he's God.

Smart!
The lyrics are so smart!
And the music has such heart!
It has *heart*?
Well, in part.
Let's not start —
Call it art.
No, call it —

God.

Well, you have to have
Something to believe in.
Something you can celebrate,
Elevate,
Venerate — Something like

Italian poetry ...
Old movies ...
Butterflies ...
Politics ...
Wine ...
Picasso ...
Skiing ...
Stamps ...
Musicals!
It might as well be musicals.

And does he know how to rhyme!
Sublime ...
He'll surprise you every time.

You're never sure just where the
Tune is going next,
Just like the lyrics —
No the "text."

Just when you think it's going up,
It's going down.
Just when you think it's going on,
It stops.

It doesn't finish, it just stops.

But you have to have
Something to believe in,
Something to appropriate,
Emulate,
Overrate—

Might as well be Stephen
Or to call him by his nickname:
God!

We've got God!
Look who's God!
He's still —

An exasperated cast member interrupts: Why don't we just sing the songs?
In harmony the cast sings: Amen!

Choice words, indeed.

Rick Pender, a lifelong fan of musical theater, has been an arts journalist, critic and historian as well as a public relations professional in his adopted hometown of Cincinnati for four decades. From 2004 to 2016 he edited a quarterly magazine, The Sondheim Review. With several books to his credit, he's a proud graduate of Oberlin College and received advanced degrees from Case Western Reserve University.

20 I Don't Know Much About Books

WILLIAM PRATT

IT is the fall of 1937. The country is still suffering from the depths of the Great Depression, and the misery index is high, especially in Oklahoma where the Dust Bowl has been turning the sky from blue to brown every summer for years. But for me, it is a time of great adventure. I am ten years old and have been invited by my Uncle Mac to come all by myself by train from Shawnee, Oklahoma (where I live) to Oxford, Mississippi (where he lives) to be his guest for the Ole Miss-Mississippi State football game, one of those fierce sectional rivalries that epitomizes American sports. I am thrilled at the prospect, and my mind is on football as I walk with my uncle to his drugstore on the town square, just a few blocks from his house on Lamar Street, the main street of town. It is named for its most famous native son, Lucius Quintus Cincinnatus (Yes, Cincinnatus) Lamar, a post-Civil War statesman who served as Senator from Mississippi, and later as Secretary of the Interior under Grover Cleveland, and still later, as an Associate Justice of the US Supreme Court. As we walk along, we pass a number of people who greet my uncle with a smile and a friendly "Good morning, Mac" Then, across the street, we notice a slight figure ambling along with his head in the air, paying attention to no one. He never even looks our way. My uncle bends down to me and says, in a low voice: "That's William Faulkner. He's a writer." It was the first time I'd seen a living writer. I wasn't even sure what it meant, but at that early age I was fascinated. I was too young to read anything he had written, but I knew that one day I wanted to find out for myself what kind of writer he was.

As I look back now on was what for me a lifechanging moment, it's my guess that Faulkner's mind was far away, probably working on his next novel, *The Unvanquished,* which he would publish in 1938. It turned out to be one of his best, but what he meant by "the unvanquished" was not what the reader might expect. They were not the Confederate soldiers who had fought and lost the Civil War. The unvanquished were the women who had stayed behind and had never given up. Many of the men never came back, or surrendered reluctantly after Appomattox, but the women refused to accept defeat. It was the women who remained defiantly unvanquished, and who preserved family integrity and honor despite the humiliation of defending what proved to be a lost cause. *The Unvanquished* was Faulkner's second novel about the Civil War. The first had been *Absalom, Absalom!,* which he published two years earlier, in 1936. Faulkner's name was nationally known by then, but it was not yet a household word. His two Civil War novels had come out just before and just after Margaret Mitchell's *Gone with the Wind,* the all-time bestseller that cleared the field for Civil War fiction long afterward.

Neither of Faulkner's novels ever rivaled hers in popularity, though they were a good deal better artistically. They did not become bestsellers until much later, when everything he wrote was a bestseller, nor were they made into Academy Award-winning movies, as hers was, but they did mark a major turning point in his career. Much later, when I was old enough to read both novels, I came to see that *Absalom, Absalom!* was tragic; it dramatized the Civil War as a tragedy that the South had brought on itself and that it deserved to lose, even if heroically. Faulkner was a realist who was both the South's greatest writer and its most severe critic. He believed that the American Civil War was caused by grave faults of which the South was guiltier than the North, though there was plenty of guilt to go around. He thought Americans in general, and Southerners in particular, had been guilty of exploiting man and nature: they exploited man by importing and enslaving African Negroes and driving out the native race of red men, and they exploited nature by destroying the wilderness for their own selfish use.

His first novel about the Civil War was a tragic vision of human ambition and greed, ending inevitably in death and defeat. But his second novel about the Civil War, *The Unvanquished,* was not tragic; it was broadly comic; it viewed the Civil War as proof of the loyalty and bravery and willing sacrifice of Southerners, even though they were clearly doomed to defeat, and it ended with the deliberate renunciation of revenge.

Though the two novels were published just two years apart, they reveal a seismic shift in Faulkner's viewpoint toward the South, toward America, toward the whole human race. I now think that when I first saw him, his mind must have been moving from his Tragic Phase to his Comic Phase. Katherine Anne Porter, a Southern writer who admired Faulkner more than any of her contemporaries, thought all his work was on a hairline between tragedy and comedy, with either outcome possible in any given work. Certainly there are comic moments in *Absalom, Absalom!*, and tragedy hangs over every chapter of *The Unvanquished.* Nevertheless, the first is definitely tragic, a great novel by any measure, and the other is ultimately comic, taking a more hopeful view of life in the mythical kingdom of Yoknapatawpha County, Mississippi, which Faulkner created and gave to the world. A few years later, in *Intruder in the Dust*, Faulkner would write that "For every Southern boy fourteen years old, not once but whenever he wants it, there is the instant when it's still not yet two o'clock on that July afternoon in 1863" — and he fights the Battle of Gettysburg over again in his imagination. When I first saw him, in 1937, I think Faulkner must have been re-enacting the Civil War in his mind, but making up his mind to laugh rather than weep at human folly. Shakespeare had written both tragedics and comedies in his poetic dramas; so did Faulkner in his fiction.

Of course, no such thoughts were in my mind when I first saw him on the main street of Oxford, Mississippi in 1937. But by the time I met him12 1/2 years later, in the spring of 1950, I had begun to understand what kind of writer he was.

I was 22 by then, and had graduated from the University of Oklahoma, forty miles west of my hometown, and then had gone a few hundred miles east to Vanderbilt University to do graduate work in English literature. I wanted to be an English professor some day, and Vanderbilt had been strongly recommended to my father by a Methodist bishop whose opinion he respected. Since my father had been born in Mississippi and my aunt and uncle still lived there, I had a natural interest in Faulkner. I was able to satisfy it most fully in the summer of 1948, before my senior year in college, when I landed a job with the US Forest Service in Yosemite National Park. Into my gear for the trip to California I packed a pocket-size dual edition of *The Sound and the Fury* and *As I Lay Dying.*

Yosemite was a perfect place to spend a summer, and Faulkner's two short, comp lex novels made for excellent reading underneath the giant sequoia trees. It proved to be a decisive choice. I found both novels mystifying and beautiful, like everything Faulkner wrote, and I began to think that if I studied him more closely I might understand him better. So in 1949 I chose to write a Master's thesis at Vanderbilt on *The Sound and the Fury.* My mentor was Donald Davidson, one of the Fugitive poets, who as a critic had written one of the earliest favorable reviews of Faulkner's work. I was working on the thesis when I went to visit my uncle again, during the Easter vacation of my first year at Vanderbilt. My Uncle Mac had graduated earlier from Ole Miss, and though he did not share my literary interests, he approved of them, and he set it up for me to meet his friend Bill Faulkner. He knew Faulkner was an important writer but he didn't fully understand why: "I'm not a deep student of his work," he told me, "I'm just an old friend who has known him for a long time." He said Faulkner had given him several autographed books over the years but he hadn't had time to read them. He didn't know, and neither did I, that Faulkner would receive the Nobel Prize for Literature later that same year.

And so, on Easter Sunday of 1950, Uncle Mac drove me in his comfortable Plymouth sedan out to Rowan Oak, a few blocks from his house, where his friend Bill Faulkner lived. We drove into his spacious domain in Bailey's Woods, through the entrance gate with its conspicuous "No Trespassing" sign, down the potholed gravel road leading to his fading white-columned mansion, the sort of house a Southern writer ought to live in. It had been called The Old Sheegog Place before he bought it, but he renamed it Rowan Oak—not for the Virginia town of that name but for a Scottish superstition that rowan trees ("mountain oaks" Americans call them) were lucky. He had bought the antebellum mansion in 1930, just before breaking into commercial success with his most sensational novel, *Sanctuary*, published in 1931, which he later said he wrote to make money. He succeeded so well that it embarrassed him, because in his view making money was not a worthy aim for a writer. He was not entirely honest in that view, because he did a lot of writing for money, especially when he willingly accepted jobs to write screenplays in Hollywood, but *Sanctuary* happened to be the first novel by Faulkner I had read, and, in spite of Faulkner's low opinion of it, I found it fatally attractive. It hooked me once and for all on Faulkner.

I had heard many anecdotes about Faulkner before I met him, because his eccentricities had become legend, along with his reputation as a writer. An early interviewer quoted him as saying matter-of-factly, "I was born male and single at an early age in Mississippi...of an Indian slave and an alligator..." Faulkner had a wicked sense of humor, and was fond of saying that writers were born liars; he was equally fond of proving it. As an undergraduate at Oklahoma, I had gone to a lecture by Hodding Carter, the widely known Editor of the *Delta Democrat-Times* in Greenville, Mississippi, who told some outrageous stories about Faulkner from his own experience. I remembered one of Hodding Carter's anecdotes in particular, as we drove up to Faulkner's house. He said that Faulkner was fiercely protective of his privacy, and hated intruders. Not only did he make a practice of digging holes in his gravel driveway to discourage casual visitors, but once, on the porch of Rowan Oak, he became so annoyed at the approach of an uninvited stranger that he stood up, opened his fly, and said, "Well, he's come to see me and I'll give him an eyeful," and calmly urinated into the bushes. I was half afraid he might welcome us in some equally shocking way, but my uncle was an old friend, and Faulkner was on his best behavior the whole time we were with him.

We parked in front of the house and walked through an alley of tall old cedar trees to the front door, where Faulkner courteously greeted us. I had seen him before but was surprised to find myself being introduced to a short, slight man with a high squeaky voice. From reading his books, I had imagined a tall, imposing figure with a deep voice. In a polite but diffident way he invited us to come in, and then walked us through the dark hall of his mansion to the back door. I noticed as we passed through the main hall that the rooms were sparsely furnished and minimally decorated, and I spotted a small niche in the wall for the telephone, next to which he had penciled some phone numbers, including one for Gathright-Reed, my uncle's drugstore. He took us all the way through the house and out to his back yard, where he offered us seats on the bench of a plain wooden picnic table and began talking to my uncle. I was an outsider, and took little part in the conversation between the two men, which mainly concerned people in town they both knew. Though he had lived there most of his life, Faulkner had always seemed oblivious to the daily life of the town, but I found he was aware of almost everyone, and everything that went on there, and took as much interest in it as my uncle did. They enjoyed gossiping about their neighbors as much as anyone in town, and I listened quietly as they talked about people who were strangers to me.

Faulkner took an interest in the natural world as well and was keenly aware of his surroundings in the Mississippi woods, being a farmer, a hunter, and a dedicated conservationist as well as a writer. As we sat there, he pointed to a pear tree which had fallen on its side near the picnic table, and which in April was loaded with blossoms. He explained that he had given his yard man strict instructions never to cut down a living tree. Then he went on talking with my uncle about Oxford citizens they knew, who meant little to me.

Once I made a clumsy attempt to enter the conversation by asking about a new book I had heard he was writing, called "Notes on a Horse Thief." It would become an episode of a longer novel called *A Fable*, which he published in 1953. The novel was about the First World War and was set in France, but the horse thief episode took place in his mythical Yoknapatawpha County and was better than the rest of the novel. His reply quickly cut me off. "I don't know much about books," he said. "A book's a book to me, and they're all too durned expensive." I knew it was a lie, and he knew it was a lie, but it was the sort of disingenuous answer an expert might give to a novice to keep him from asking further questions. I kept quiet after that. Later that year I would buy the book at my favorite bookstore in Nashville, after it had been published by Hodding Carter on his Greenville Press, in a run of a thousand copies numbered and signed by the author. I still have it in my library. I bought it for $15 in 1950; fifty years later, I had it appraised for $1,189.

Faulkner was a professional writer, and his income came almost entirely from his publications, yet he acted most of the time as if he were indifferent to them. In his early years, people regarded him as a ne'er-do-well, though the Falkners (the family spelled the name without the "u") were a prominent family in Mississippi. His great-grandfather, the first William Falkner, had been a Confederate colonel, a railroad builder, a state legislator, and a writer of popular novels, and Faulkner as a schoolboy said he wanted to be a writer like his great-grandpappy. But he was never a diligent student, and often played hookey. Later, he would call himself "the world's oldest living sixth grader." That was no lie; it was close to the truth. He never finished high school, and though he took a few courses at Ole Miss, where his father was the Business Manager of the university and the family lived on campus, he pledged a fraternity but failed English. As a young man he had no steady job, working for a time in his grandfather's bank but preferring to paint houses or shovel coal in the university power plant. He wrote one of his best novels while working at night in the power plant. It was *As I Lay Dying*, and he said it was the easiest novel he ever wrote, because the humming of the dynamo was soothing to his ears. Everyone in town knew that Bill Faulkner wanted to be a writer; but it took him a long time to make it a paying profession. Most of the people in town were in the habit of calling him "Count No 'Count" and expecting nothing serious ever to come from him.

Their disdain turned to awe in the fall of 1950, when Faulkner won the Nobel Prize for Literature. It stunned the town, and though it pleased Faulkner when he got the news, he went out hunting with some friends after he heard it, and he would have preferred to accept the honor in absentia.

It took his daughter Jill to persuade him to go to Stockholm and receive the award in person. She was the editor of the high school newspaper when the award was announced, and it was a golden opportunity for her to cover a news story of international significance. He doted on his daughter, who was his only child, and agreed to fly to Sweden with her. On the w ay, he took the time to write the acceptance speech that turned out to be the most famous ever given by a winner of the Nobel Prize. For fifty years Nobel Prizes for Literature had been given to writers of genius, from William Butler Yeats and George Bernard Shaw to T.S. Eliot and Winston Churchill, but their acceptance speeches were forgotten afterwards, while Faulkner's address was the only one to be widely quoted long after it was given. Sentences from it are carved today in stone on the wall of the Ole Miss library, which houses a Faulkner Collection that is its main claim to fame: "I decline to accept the end of man," he had said in Sweden, to an international audience; "I believe that man will not merely endure, he will prevail." These words astonished the world, which was trying to live in the shadow of the nuclear mushroom cloud that exploded over Japan in 1945. Many felt that it was just a matter of time until the human race obliterated itself. Faulkner felt otherwise and was openly optimistic about the future of man: "He is immortal, not because he alone among creatures has an inexhaustible voice, but because he has a soul, a spirit capable of compassion and sacrifice and endurance. The poet's, the writer's duty is to write about these things.8 0 He wrote those stirring words just a few months after I met him. They were not what he said to my uncle and me as we sat at his picnic table in the back yard of Rowan Oak on Easter Sunday of 1950. He talked informally and easily about the hunting trips he enjoyed with friends, in the deep woods of the Mississippi Delta, about farming a patch of land he owned near Pusskuss Creek, not far from Oxford, and about riding his favorite horse, Stonewall, which later threw him and precipitated his untimely death in 1962 at the age of 65. All he said to my uncle, as we got up to leave, was "Mac, you don't come out to see me often enough." Then he got up from the picnic table, led us back through the house to his front door and said goodbye with a courteous old-fashioned bow.

It was in the spring of 1950 that I had my first personal encounter with a great living writer, and it had a lasting effect on me. I had a second encounter five years later with a great writer very different from Faulkner, which proved even more consequential.

It happened by chance in the spring of 1955, when I was a young officer in the US Naval Reserve in Washington, stationed at the Pentagon, where my job, as Assistant Special Congressional Liaison Officer to the Judge Advocate General, was to attend the meetings of Congressional Committees that oversaw military spending and to report back in writing to the admiral in charge. I served as the eyes and ears of the Navy on Capitol Hill for two years, and my main charge was to let the Judge Advocate General know whether, when Senator Joe McCarthy finished disemboweling the Army by his investigations of Communists in government, he might turn his attention to another military service and begin looking for hidden traitors in the Navy. He headed what was called the Government Operations Committee, and under his electrifying leadership it had become a news-making blockbuster. There were headlines every day that showed how effectively Senator McCarthy had seized the attention of the media. McCarthy was the man of the hour in Washington, and I had the privilege of being close to the action, not as a journalist but as an observer, trusted to make confidential reports without creating a sensation. I did my best to deserve the assignment. It was pure luck that I had the job, and even luckier that it led to my encounter with another great writer.

The Navy had been generous enough to grant me a commission simply because I had earned a college degree following an earlier tour of duty as a naval air cadet at the end of the Second World War. When I was called back in 1953 for a second tour of duty during the Korean War, some obscure Navy administrator must have noticed that I was about to finish a doctorate in English literature at Vanderbilt, and he knew the Navy needed someone who could write. The Navy had appointed as its Special Congressional Liaison Officer a captain whose previous duty had been the command of one of the battleships sunk by the Japanese at Pearl Harbor. The Navy probably thought that since he had proved himself such an able wartime captain, an easy desk job would be his peacetime reward. I was happy to work under him, because he was an affable Tennessean of sterling character, and he and his wife were kind to me and my new bride. But he lacked one essential qualification for the job: he couldn't write. So, as his lowly lieutenant, I was given the job of going from the Pentagon to Capitol Hill every day in my uniform, attending the hearings of the McCarthy Committee and other Congressional committees concerned with the military, then returning to the Pentagon and writing the reports, which the captain dutifully signed and sent upstairs to the admiral. The admiral never complained about them, probably because I was able to write reassuringly about what was happening in Congress, causing him little worry about what Joe McCarthy might do to the Navy.

Together, Captain Gill and I had the pleasure of witnessing at close quarters the decline and fall of Joe McCarthy, which happened fairly precipitously under our watchful gaze, to the amazement of almost everyone else in the world, who had come to believe that McCarthy was an indestructible American demagogue. My first encounter with a great living writer came during the Great Depression in Mississippi; my second came during the McCarthy Era in Washington.

This second encounter was not directly connected with my job. I lived in Washington from the summer of 1953 to the summer of 1955, and when I first got there I shared a house in Georgetown with two other young bachelors, both graduates of Harvard Law School. One of them was a lawyer for the Department of Justice; the other was an economist in the Office of Management and Budget. Harvard had given them a good education and plenty of good connections in Washington. Later, after I married and moved out to Falls Church, they took me and my wife to dinner at the University Club, where we met some of their Harvard classmates. They introduced me to a young psychiatrist named

Michel Woodberry, who was on the staff of St. Elizabeths Hospital, the national mental asylum. When he heard that I was writing a doctoral dissertation on three American expatriate writers, Henry James, T.S. Eliot, and Ezra Pound, his interest picked up and he began to take me seriously. The most famous inmate of St. Elizabeths Hospital at that time was Ezra Pound. Everyone knew that Pound had been indicted for treason in 1945 but had never faced trial. Instead, he had been declared "incompetent to stand trial in his own behalf" by three court-appointed psychiatrists. Dr. Woodberry saw an opportunity waiting to be seized and told me that Ezra Pound was lonely and needed literary company. He insisted I should go out to see Pound, and he told me exactly how to do it. I was first to write him personally to ask if I could pay him a visit. Then I was to write to Dr. Winifred Overholser, one of the psychiatrists who had examined Pound, now the head of St. Elizabeths, for official approval of my visit. That was what I did. I screwed up my courage and wrote to Pound the very next day. His reply came a couple of days later. I still have his letter among my most valuable possessions, scrawled in his inimitable hand in his patented abbreviated style, and signed with a flourish that looked rather like a caricature of his own profile:

S. Eliz. 23 Ap. [the year was 1955]

Dear Mr. Pratt:

By all means. Write to Superintendent S.Liz. for permission. Thursdays are best. I like slow talk can't crowd into ¼ hour. Visiting hours 2-4 Sat. Sun. Tu. Th.

E. Pound

Dr. Overholser replied shortly afterward that if Mr. Pound agreed to my visit, so did he. Thus, on a sunny day in April 1955, I went to meet Ezra Pound in the insane asylum where he had been living for ten years, believed by most people in the country to be a traitor and a lunatic. He had built a daunting reputation for himself as a leading international poet in the 1910's and 1920's, when he was living in London and Paris, but in 1924 he moved to Rapallo, Italy, and became an outspoken admirer of Benito Mussolini, the Italian dictator, whom he began referring to as "The Boss." He even met Mussolini once and was flattered that Il Duce, as the Italians called him, seemed to listen seriously to what Pound had to say about economics. We don't know what Mussolini thought of Pound, but much later, in the 1940s, Pound was given the chance to make broadcasts over Rome Radio during the Second World War. In those broadcasts, which got him into so much trouble later, he said whatever he wanted to say in plain American English, using slang and dialects in the tried and true method of American humorists — reading poetry, including his own, talking about the writers he knew, expounding his pet ideas on economics and other subjects — but, unfortunately for him, often praising Mussolini and the Fascists, and urging Americans not to fight against Italy, which had become Pound's home though he never gave up his American passport. I knew a good deal about how Pound had come into the humiliating situation in which I found him, because though I was primarily interested in his literary work, I had looked up the transcripts of his speeches in the Library of Congress and knew there was good reason why he was arrested in Rapallo by Italian partisans in 1945, imprisoned in an American Army prison camp in Pisa, and then flown to Washington to be indicted for treason. But it was while he was a prisoner at Pisa that Pound wrote a series of poems called *The Pisan Cantos,* which became the most famous of all his voluminous writings, and when they were published in 1949 he was awarded the Bollingen Prize for Poetry, an American literary prize even more prestigious than a Pulitzer Prize. Pound was by that time an inmate of St. Elizabeths, and the award touched off a firestorm of protest by a host of American writers, which was countered by an equally spirited defense from the writers who had awarded him the prize, an eminent jury of his peers that included T.S. Eliot, Archibald MacLeish, Allen Tate, Robert Penn Warren, Katherine Anne Porter, and Robert Lowell.

So when I met Pound in 1955 he was the most controversial figure in American letters, and I went to see him with some trepidation, wondering what it would be like to meet him in person. It turned out to be easy.

I was careful to change out of my Navy uniform when I visited him so as not to put him on his guard. I found him seated in a canvas lawn chair on the spacious grounds of the hospital, with a small circle of admirers around him, including his wife Dorothy, a dignified English woman who visited him every day. Pound was no longer the dashing figure with red hair and beard, flashing the bohemian costume that had dazzled London literary circles in the period before the First World War. T.S. Eliot said that when he met Pound in London in 1914, Pound's clothing was so flamboyant that only his socks could be worn by anyone else. Eliot himself dressed like a banker, which he was for a time, but despite the difference in their dress, the two American expatriates hit it off immediately, and Pound was responsible for getting Eliot's first poems published and starting him on what became the most distinguished career in Anglo-American letters. Eliot would rise above Pound in public esteem, and would win a Nobel Prize for Literature which Pound never achieved, but when the two men met it was Pound who was the acknowledged leader of the Modern movement, and that was why Eliot sought him out. Pound at that time headed the *avant garde*, as a poet, translator, essayist, and editor, a man every aspiring writer, English or American, wanted to meet, including the yet unknown T.S.Eliot.

I knew about the dashing earlier Pound whom Eliot met in London in 1914, but when I met him at St. Elizabeths in 1955, forty years later, he was in disgrace, a prisoner in his own country, convicted in the minds of many of his fellow countrymen as a traitor and a lunatic. The charge of treason for which he had been indicted was clearly legal, but his offense had been entirely verbal: he had made broadcasts over Rome Radio during the Second World War, when Italy was our enemy, though he always claimed that he was only exercising his American right of free speech. That claim led to the second charge, that he was insane, a charge which was never proved, because though it was apparent to everyone who knew him that he lacked common sense in some of his opinions, chiefly political and economic, he was completely lucid when he talked about literature, and he never lost his sense of humor.

I remember once hearing him say, when he was asked whether a rather eccentric woman feeding squirrels on the grounds of St. Elizabeths might be an inmate of the asylum, "No, but I think she's responsible for someone's being here."

The Pound I met in the spring of 1955 was a grandfatherly figure: elderly, portly, clad in a flannel shirt gaping at the navel, with a fur-lined hunting cap on his head, and wearing shoes without socks. Meeting him was a greater shock than meeting Faulkner, but if it was Faulkner who had caused me to be seriously interested in modern literature; it was Pound who took my interests farther than they would ever have gone without him. His friend and fellow poet, William Carlos Williams, said that when he met Pound as a college student at the University of Pennsylvania, even before Eliot met him in London, his life had been changed by it. Before and after meeting Pound, he said, was like the difference between B.C. and A.D. I knew exactly what he meant. I didn't know it immediately, but it gradually dawned on me, while I continued studying and teaching Modern Literature for the next fifty years, that Ezra Pound was the Modern writer at the center of the action, or as Eliot himself testified, that "Mr. Pound is more responsible for the 20th century revolution in poetry than any other individual." Eliot was one of Pound's disciples, and another was the younger poet E.E. Cummings, who wrote that Pound was "the authentic 'innovator,' the true trailblazer of an epoch..." My awareness of Pound's central role in modern literature took a long time to sink in. What struck me on my first meeting with Pound, after I got over the shock of his appearance, was how gentlemanly he was. I was prepared for some angry raving and ranting from this flaming rebel who had so dramatically upset the world, but instead I was treated with old-fashioned courtesy the moment I shook hands with him He was eager to talk. He wanted to know what I was up to, and I told him I was studying "The European Tradition in American Literature." His eyes lighted up and he began telling me how he had to leave America for Europe to avoid being trapped in provincialism. He wanted to belong to the world tradition in literature, he said, and so he chose to live in a number of European cities, never settling for long in any of them: first in Venice, then in London, then in Paris, and then in Rapallo. He said other American writers had to do the same to avoid provincialism: Henry James went to Europe to get away from the shadow of Hawthorne; T.S. Eliot went to Europe to escape the heavy influence of Emerson; and Pound himself had gone to Europe to flee—of all people, from the ghost of Henry Wadsworth Longfellow! These were the three expatriate writers I had chosen as the subject of my dissertation, and I was fascinated by what I was hearing from one of them. I knew all three had become great world writers, who together revolutionized American literature in the twentieth century, transforming it from what was then a largely national audience to what is now an international audience. At first, I wasn't sure which of the three had been most influential, but after long study I came to the conclusion that it was Pound. Pound had been the central figure in Modernism, the major movement in intellectual history after Romanticism, and meeting him was the beginning of my lifelong pursuit of what Modernism meant. To me, Modernism meant a change for the better, creating and fostering a new international style of writing, and going deep into the inner workings of the human mind, deeper than anyone had ever gone before — so deep that modern literature still remains incomprehensible to many readers, particularly if it's the kind written by Ezra Pound or William Faulkner.

Pound could be as severe a critic of America as Faulkner, yet he remained a loyal American, even when he made those treasonable broadcasts over Rome Radio. He insisted he was only exercising his American right of free speech in an effort to keep his country out of the war. In his broadcasts as well as in his writings, he came down hardest against what he called Usury, the making of excessive profit, which to him was the cardinal sin. He thought it led inevitably to war, because those who had too much money would be constantly at odds with those who had too little. Americans, he believed, were especially guilty of an obsession with money. He argued that caring more about money than art was bad for society. But since economics was hardly his specialty, he persuaded few people that he was right about the cause of war, in particular the

Second World War that was then raging. Poetry was his real specialty, and there his influence was much more effectual.

Long before he was incarcerated, Pound had successfully shown, through his intellectual leadership both in poetry and in criticism, that a new period of literary greatness was possible. His motto was "Make it New," and his study of poetry in a variety of languages had convinced him that poetry was the key to making it new, because he took poetry to be the essential form of literature, and literature is, as he liked to say, "news that stays news." Faulkner would certainly have agreed, for he called himself a "failed poet" in spite of being a highly successful novelist, and it was Faulkner, not Pound, who said that in a poem every word must be perfect. To Faulkner, whose medium was fiction, the short story was second and the novel third in the careful use of words. Pound's medium was poetry, and language was the source of poetry.

Pound believed that a poet uses words as a painter uses color and line, or a composer uses rhythm and sound. He therefore began early in his life to study the major languages of the world, hoping to know more about world poetry than any living man. He studied Greek and Latin as a schoolboy in Philadelphia, and then, at Hamilton College in upstate New York , he studied Anglo-Saxon and French, Italian, Spanish, Provencal, Portuguese — capping it with the study of Romance Philology at the University of Pennsylvania, where he completed a Master's degree and nearly finished a doctorate. He learned languages not as a scholar but as an artist: he wanted to know the best poetry that had ever been written so that he could try to equal it himself.

At his best he did equal it, and I learned much about poetry from meeting and talking with Pound. I also learned from meeting and talking to his wife Dorothy. It was she who told me Ezra's best-kept secret: you didn't need to know all there was to know about a language to master it; you needed to know it well enough to recognize its best poetry. That's what he did, she said, and it made him first of all a great translator of poetry, in fact the greatest translator who has ever lived. Pound's best translations don't read like translations; they read like original poems. To anyone who asks me what to read first in Pound,

I say *Cathay*, a selection of some of the best ancient Chinese poems converted into modern American English. It is so readable that Eliot credited Pound with becoming "the inventor of Chinese poetry for our time." His own poetry is full of translations from poetry in other languages, often quoted in the original. That's what makes reading his poetry so difficult: you feel you must know every language Pound knew to understand him. It isn't really as necessary as it seems, however, because Pound at his best incorporated world poetry into his own very characteristic American poetry, no matter how strange the combination looks on the page. Reading Pound can be a liberal education in itself, as I should know. I have been reading Pound for over fifty years and I am still trying to understand him. He is the kind of writer whose meaning eludes you yet entices you to go on trying to grasp it. Trying to understand Pound can become a lifelong pursuit.

My meeting with Ezra Pound at St. Elizabeths in 1955 was the real beginning of my professional career. I realize that all my education up to that point had been haphazard, a matter of personal interest combined with dedicated study, but after meeting him I was on the track of something more specific: I was trying to understand how words could be used to express meanings that went beyond words. That was what Pound at his best could do. I believe he understood the true motive for writing better than any writer who ever lived, and he understood it as nothing less than a quest for immortality, a lifelong journey of the soul. "It is tremendously important that great poetry be written," he maintained, "but it makes no jot of difference who writes it."

Pound never claimed too much for himself. He probably expressed his artistic credo best in a line that is often quoted from the *Pisan Cantos*: "What thou lovest well is thy true heritage." He loved great poetry, and he helped renew its power in his own lifetime. Like his alter ego, a fictional poet he called *Hugh Selwyn Mauberley,* "he strove to resuscitate the dead art/ of poetry, to restore 'the sublime' in the old sense." Pound did restore the poetic quest for greatness in his lifetime, and he encouraged gifted friends and fellow writers like Yeats and Joyce and E liot and Hemingway to do the same. He was the champion of Modernism, a major epoch in world literature, and for that cause he will be remembered long after his political sins have faded into history. It was my good luck to meet him at a crucial point in my life, and I have been in his debt ever since.

I have an enduring souvenir of my visits to Ezra Pound. It is a copy of the book he published in 1954, the year before I went to see him at St. Elizabeths, his translation of *The Classical Anthology Defined by Confucius.* In those straitened circumstances, with few books around him to consult, he had translated a whole book of Chinese poetry. His wife Dorothy told me that sometimes he gave her Chinese characters to take down to the Library of Congress and check for him. I carried my copy of the book out to him on my last visit to St. Elizabeths in the hope he would sign it. He readily agreed. On the flyleaf of the book is this inscription: "Certified to hv been in the possession of Wm. Pratt. June 28 1955. Ezra Pound." I bought it in 1955 for $5. When I had it appraised fifty years later, it was valued at $1,975, proving how right Pound was: "literature is news that stays news."

William Crouch Pratt Jr. (1997-2024), professor emeritus of English at Miami University, was a scholar, teacher, writer, and Southern gentleman. He taught for four decades and was a world authority on Modernist poetry, principally the works of Ezra Pound. He possessed a contagious zest for life and boundless curiosity about the world around him. He loved birding, travel, grandchildren. Dearest to him in later life was his membership in The Literary Club, which he joined in 2006 and which he served as president in 2015-16. For the club he contributed memorable papers, including this one on his personal encounters with two of the towering figures in 20th Century literature.

21 Freedom:

Witnesses of an escape from death: A story of a family bound together through impossible challenges

DAVID C. RANDOLPH

"DR. Nguyen, your father is on the phone."

"Thanks. Excuse me for a minute." There would be a brief delay in the Cardiac angiogram. Lam Nguyen MD, an Internist and Interventional Cardiologist trained at LSU, Tulane and Duke on scholarship, would stop all activities when his father called. This was out of respect.

A thousand miles away, and several minutes later, the other Dr. Nguyen, Dr. Trang Nguyen, MD PhD, received a similar call. This Dr. Nguyen, also a medically trained physician at LSU, University of Texas Southwestern Medical School in Dallas, trained in Anesthesia, Internal Medicine, and boarded in Occupational and Family Medicine, with a PhD in Epidemiology would stop her activities to speak with her father whenever he called. Their father had called to make sure everything was going ok, and to see if they needed anything. Both adult children would smile at the thoughtfulness, then return to their work.

Naturally, many children would be happy to speak with their parents. But these physicians had a unique bond with their parents, forged through mutual respect after surviving a life threatening and prolonged escape from most certain suffering and likely death, associated with the collapse of the government of South Vietnam on April 30th, 1975.

At the time, Lam was ten years old. Trang was 8. There were two younger brothers, Thanh, age 6, and Tam, age 3.

As an officer in the Army of South Vietnam, Senior Major Duy Nguyen was well connected. He was trained in all manner of weapons

and warfare and had worked with the American CIA as a trusted advisor. He was high up in the intelligence community, necessitating a high degree of extra caution and security. He had served in the army for 19 years and had been assigned to high level security positions, based upon his skills. He was also fluent in French and English. He was trusted by the high echelons of the Army of South Vietnam, and the US CIA representatives. He knew this put him on a list of those wanted by the Army of north Vietnam.

He was married to the daughter of a wealthy plantation owner. He had chosen a military life. By 1975, they had four children. They had a very nice house on the Mekong River, in a town called My Tho, in South Vietnam.

Due to the unstable political climate, a sandbag shelter had been built behind the house to protect the young family in case of gunfire. Over the past year, random episodes of violence had been steadily increasing, leading to the need for greater security. Major Nguyen knew he was a marked man, and continually warned his family to be constantly aware of their surroundings, and not accept anything from strangers. He cautioned them all to stick together whenever possible.

A new maid was observed pacing the distance between the house and the nearby Mekong River. A few days later an artillery barrage fired at their house caused the family to retreat into the sandbag shelter. Damage was slight, but the warnings could not be ignored. The new maid never returned.

Trang was called into the school office in the fall of 1974. A young woman, identified as a messenger from her mother Diem, had been instructed to take Trang home early. Trang had never seen the woman before. She had been carefully instructed by her mother to never go anywhere with a stranger. Trang looked the strange woman over and noted she was barefoot. All their house workers wore shoes, so Trang refused to leave with the woman. That woman had not been sent by Diem. Trang dodged a kidnapping. It made the entire family more aware of the hazards.

Major Nguyen could tell, based upon his regular interactions with both the Vietnamese intelligence officers and the U.S. Central Intelligence Agency, that South Vietnamese governmental and civil stability was waning by early 1975. The borders had become porous and episodes of violence more frequent and scattered both in rural and metropolitan areas. The nature of the violence was increasing. Military and civilian populations were being targeted. The ability of the South Vietnamese Police and military police to prevent or control these episodes of violence was waning, and threats became more serious and frequent. Rumors of the US military planning to depart South Vietnam were also becoming more prominent.

When Major Nguyen questioned his superiors and CIA officials, he got more questions, not answers. By early 1975, Major Duy Nguyen became convinced the South Vietnamese government would soon collapse. He knew that if he stayed in-country, he would be caught and executed, and his family kicked out of their home to become street dwellers. The thought was intolerable. It was time to act.

There were only a few avenues of escape. Traveling into North Vietnam was unthinkable That left travelling west into Cambodia or Thailand. These were not as bad, but Cambodia, which bordered South Vietnam, was infested with Communist sympathizers and military personnel. Departing Vietnamese military officers and their families would likely be captured and imprisoned, to be returned to Vietnam for execution. The US military would be unlikely to assist all six family members before governmental collapse. After the collapse riots would ensue, making escape through the US military risky and unreliable.

He knew it was time to plan for the collapse of the South Vietnamese government, and escape.

This left only a few choices. Vietnam was bordered on the west by Cambodia, but to the east and South was a vast ocean, named the South China Sea. It was a wide open but perilous option. But it seemed the only viable option available to this group.

Major Nguyen had formed many friendships over his military career. These partnerships included many high-ranking South Vietnamese officers, as well as CIA officers. One who was high ranking in the CIA will be referred to as "Mr. Williams." That was not his real name, but it was the only name Major Nguyen knew. Mr. Williams was a trusted colleague. He affirmed Major Nguyen's concerns over the impending collapse of the South Vietnamese government.

There were only a few people who could be trusted with such an escape discussion, let alone the actual plan. As he looked at the map, he realized the best route to consider was the South China Sea. As the family lived adjacent to the Mekong Delta, an oceanic route made the most sense. If a boat large enough to safely carry their precious cargo could be found, a seagoing exit seemed to be the best route. Yet it was still perilous.

It was late March 1975. The stability of the South Vietnamese government remained unknown, but it was apparent that a collapse was imminent. It appeared that even "Mr. Williams," the CIA operative, was searching for escape plans. The CIA operatives had been made aware of a large fleet of US Naval vessels, including aircraft carriers, remaining off the eastern coat of Vietnam. While these ships would be safe, the means of reaching those ships were limited. Helicopters would be a good route but acquiring passage on one would not be easy. After consideration of his options, he realized that a solid naval vessel would be the most reliable means of transportation. When viewing possible escape routes, he determined that departure from My Tho down to the Mekong delta, and southwest across the South China Sea would be the best route. The risks would be high, but a delay in departure would surely be deadly.

Major Nguyen approached a few of his trusted military colleagues with his thoughts. All agreed the time was getting close. South Vietnamese money was traded for small gold tablets which could be used to secure safety, shelter, and food. Such purchases were quietly made.

A boat large enough to hold the immediate family and a few trusted colleagues was secured nearby. Very small bags of necessary personal items were prepared and kept in a secure site in their home. Back-up plans were also made, in case of unforeseen hazards. He realized that he could not possibly plan for every hazard. Guns and ammunition were quietly acquired and safely stored.

Those hazards rapidly began to surface.

As April 30, 1975, dawned, the radio announced the surrender of South Vietnam to the military forces of North Vietnam. The military was officially disbanded. It was time. Rapid action was important.

The Major collected his family and headed down to the dock area. The word had gotten out and the small group organized by the major had swelled to unbelievable proportions. There were close to 100 people desiring to escape from the communist regime. Most were military officers and their families. They were armed.

The small boat arranged by Major Nguyen would no longer do. He searched for a larger boat and found one probably large enough, but its' seaworthiness was not clear. Nevertheless, time was of the essence and the group had to leave. As the day progressed, rumors of impending hazards surfaced. Isolated gunshots could be heard and were getting closer.

They realized that, if captured, all their possessions would be seized. Lam, aged 10, was unlikely to be searched. The few small gold bars which had been quietly purchased over several months were given to Lam for safe keeping. He put them in his pocket with his handkerchief. As the small band left the port, they realized their selected boat was unsatisfactory for the trip. Another larger boat in the harbor was selected and taken for their emergency exit. By then, the "small band" was now about 100 men, women, and children.

Shortly after departing by boat from the Mekong Delta, they were approached by a large South Vietnamese Naval patrol boat, travelling into port. They were hailed and questions raised about their identity and destination. Both groups approached this interaction with caution. The sailors were South Vietnamese Naval sailors and were armed. The pilgrims were also armed South Vietnamese but carried their families with them.

The group now included more than 100 families and crew from the Naval gun boat. There was no extra space.

By that time, the official word from Saigon, now re-named Ho Chi Minh City, was that the South Vietnamese Army had surrendered. This meant that all military personnel were no longer under direct control of the government. The communist North Vietnamese Army was in full and official control. All who resisted risked death. More importantly, former South Vietnamese soldiers and sailors could be rounded up, imprisoned, and shot. Or simply shot on sight.

Rumors of such actions preceded the appearance of the North Vietnamese army forces.

The Nayy Boat with the pilgrims had little choice. If they returned to port, they could be arrested and shot. The original crew believed the risk of returning to port was too great. An agreement was made between the ship personnel and the refugees. They would work together and agree to avoid violence. They would travel away from Vietnam. They would continue to operate their patrol boat, but Major Nguyen would navigate. All armed personnel would keep their arms. Violence was agreed to be avoided.

The level of trust, however, was very limited. All military personnel controlled their own weapons. Major Nguyen informed them that the trip to Malaysia would take five days over open sea, headed southwest.

Still, this was a restless peace. Trust was agreed, but an air of distrust was always present. By now, they were in open water. The navigator was former Vietnamese Army Senior Major Duy Nguyen. He stayed at or near the helm with his family always in sight. His loyal soldiers stayed together, armed, and back-to back throughout the ship. This was a day and night watch. The Major later reported he did not sleep for five days.

While out at sea, the atmosphere became a bit more relaxed. In retrospect, Major Nguyen stayed constantly at the helm, with the four children all at arm's length from Ms. Diem. Lam kept one hand in his pocket, aware of the value of the gold tablets. Trang helped control Thanh and Tam. Food was scarce and consisted of scraps of food, crackers and a few military rations. The presence of fear had a significant effect on their appetites.

The trip was frightening. Lam later reported the waves to be the size of a five-story building, with the little ship riding atop those waves. The Major kept a constant eye on his compass, with his hand on the helm, and his service pistol within quick reach. Sleep was not an option. After four days of steady travel, the sailors became progressively agitated. They were tired and afraid, as there had been no land sighted since departing the Mekong Delta and the South Vietnamese coast. Residual food and water were getting short. All around them were armed men, some they knew and trusted, others .... not so much. The sailors approached Major Nguyen. They threatened him as they had still not reached land. He reassured them. "Tomorrow."

They threatened him with death if he was wrong.

As the sun rose the following morning there were seagulls. Harbingers of land. Soon there was a coastline. A Naval boat approached their large fishing boat and announced they had entered Malaysian waters. The Malaysian Navy demanded to know their purpose.

Major Nguyen announced they were refugees seeking asylum. They were instructed to halt progress and be prepared to be boarded. The sailors huddled in one part of the ship; the refugees moved to another. As the refugees boarded the Naval vessel, Major Nguyen warned the Malaysian ship commander that the sailors may not be trustworthy. He warned the Malaysian Naval officers of ammunition on board the ship. As the last of the crew boarded the Malaysian vessel, they opened fire on the now abandoned fishing boat. It exploded and sunk, along with any questionable ambition of the remaining South Vietnamese sailors.

The Nguyen family was taken to the Malaysian beach, where they were to stay in a small tent for over two months. Food was scarce, and their belongings became threadbare. Food was purchased with the gold carried by Lam. They remained in Malaysia for about 4 months.

Major Nguyen heard of the plight of the Vietnamese who remained in country. He realized their entire home country had been overrun, and communism had been established as the rule of the land. He had an idea for a possible rescue for him and his family. He did not know the real name of his former CIA contact, Mr. Williams, only that he worked with the CIA. So, he wrote a letter addressed only to "Mr. Williams, former CIA agent Saigon, Vietnam." The letter was addressed to CIA Headquarters, Washington, DC. He explained their escape from South Vietnam, and that they currently were living in a tent on the beach in Malaysia. He placed the letter in the mailbox, with little hope of a response. This was his only shot.

Several weeks later, Mr. Williams and another CIA agent arrived at their tent, with food and clothing, and an offer to find them a new home in the US. Mr. Williams expressed his gratitude for all the Major had done to help in Vietnam. They were then taken to Guam, where they stayed several weeks, and finally to San Francisco.

As they arrived in San Francisco, they were provided new clothing and blankets, food, and multiple vaccinations. They were offered several areas of the country for permanent residency. Due to their tropical lives up to that time, they chose the American southeast. They found a place in Texarkana. The climate there, while milder, was closer to that of South Vietnam.

Several of their relatives had also escaped from the Vietcong. Their immediate relatives included brothers, sisters, first and second cousins, aunts and uncles and their families ... all safely escaped.

They were all transported to a new home in Texarkana. This was a very large, old, abandoned house which they named "The Haunted House," as the previous residents had died violently, and the house had been vacant for several years. They were to stay there for about a year. Jobs were found for those old enough to work. The children were enrolled in a local school. Trang was sent to the third grade, Lam to the 5th. Neither could speak English. But they learned quickly out of necessity. Family discussions remained in Vietnamese. The crowded house, with all twenty occupants from the same family and all immigrants from their war-torn South Vietnam, consisted of twenty Nguyens, from different branches.

Job opportunities in Texarkana were limited. In 1975, the gulf coast was thriving. There were many job opportunities for those willing to work. The family heard of a small town in Louisiana called Lafayette. There were jobs opening where employers were willing to train willing candidates. The Nguyens left for Lafayette.

Mr. Duy was hired by a company which manufactured and serviced helicopters transporting people to and from oil rigs on the Gulf Coast. As a former military man, he had no mechanical training, but he was willing to learn. He began as a janitor but worked overtime helping the mechanics. Soon, his mechanical skills were recognized, and formal training ensued. He worked as much overtime as he could. He had six mouths to feed.

His work efforts were not enough to feed the growing family. Ms. Diem took a job at a convenience store. Trang saw to it the house was maintained, with the help of her brothers. Everyone had jobs to do, and they all worked together to get those things done.

Lam had been placed first in the 4th grade but was quickly determined to be advanced beyond that level. He was transferred to the 6th grade, after winning a statewide Math contest. The following year he placed third in a similar statewide challenge. He later stated that the math was easier than English.

Trang also progressed quickly. Their language skills rapidly exceeded those of their parents.

Their progress attracted the attention of the local Lafayette business community, who assisted them in obtaining full scholarships and monetary assistance at the University of Louisiana, Lafayette. They continued to live at home, only a few minutes bus ride from the University campus.

They both advanced quickly in school. Their grades remained

well above average. As high school ended for Lam, college scholarships appeared to aid in his advancement. Trang also advanced rapidly with similar scholarship offers. They both completed undergraduate studies at the University of Louisiana, Lafayette. Both excelled and were accepted to Medical School at the LSU School of Medicine in Shreveport, Louisiana.

Lam completed training in Internal Medicine and practiced for several years near Lafayette, in a small town called Jennings, LA. He later returned to complete fellowships in Cardiology at Tulane, and Interventional Cardiology at Duke. On completion, he returned to Jennings where he remains in active practice as the only Cardiologist in a 50-mile radius.

Trang pursued several avenues of advanced training in Houston, Texas, in Internal Medicine, Anesthesiology and Family Medicine. She then practiced on the Faculty at the University of Texas, Southwestern Medical School in Dallas. She was there five years, then transferred to the University of Cincinnati where she completed a PhD in Epidemiology. Her dissertation, dealing with the failure of the popular spine fusion surgery to relieve pain and improve function was published in *The Spine Journal* and cited on the front page of the *Wall Street Journal* on 12/20/2010. She remains active in Medicine, including clinical research and Epidemiology.

Thanh completed training as an accountant and helps to manage the medical practices of both Lam and Trang. The youngest brother Tam works as an executive for a pharmaceutical company in Baton Rouge, La.

This becomes a fine example of an American success story. It is more than "rags to riches." It represents the success of a family, close knit by life threatening changes, surviving a military invasion of an entire country and escaping over the open sea into a series of foreign countries, and finally arriving in America with little more than the shirts on their backs. Through grit, hard work and dedication, they survived and thrived. They are now returning some of the kindness through their continued personal and professional efforts.

Whenever possible, April 30 is celebrated by all family members who can make it to Lafayette. The clan has gotten much larger now, with Cousins, Aunts, Uncles, children, and Grand Children.

But the lessons learned from their struggles were never forgotten.

David Randolph MD, PhD, MPH is a Cincinnati native who graduated from Indian Hill High School in 1968, Southern Methodist University in 1971, and Ohio State College of Medicine in 1975, as a Junior AOA honorary selectee. He completed a PhD in Epidemiology (Causation Analysis) in 2016, through the University of Cincinnati and remains in active practice in Occupational Medicine, Epidemiology and Toxicology. He remans active in Epidemiologic research projects the study of medieval European history.

22 | *Hatchet Face*

JAMES SAMMARCO

SOMETIMES a moniker best describes a person's appearance, and this is one of the times. I never learned his real name but Hatchet Face was Sicilian; he came to America as a bachelor and remained here the rest of his life, never returning to his native land. His face was unusual, some would say "ugly", deeply lined from the sun, long and narrow, with a forehead slanting backward, with broad cheek bones inclining toward a narrow bridge and long, tapered nose. His hair was cropped short, salt and pepper and slicked to stand up on his head. He was of medium build, muscular, neat in appearance and dressed in a white shirt and black tie like a waiter in a Palermo trattoria. Some would say his temperament matched his face, but this was to prove otherwise.

In western Sicily, he wore old shirt and trousers with holes, his only clothes. He was a contadino, an ignorant, illiterate peasant born in the Barracco latifundium system, a vast array of vineyards near Marsala, that produced and exported marsala wine by the family, Barracco. The workers were poor uneducated families, housed on the estates for generations. They spoke a dialect, Trapanese, one of multiple subdialects spoken in the island's provinces, the result of multiple invasions and occupations over centuries. Families represented descendants confined by necessity to protect themselves from war and occupiers and the dialect often was not understood by other Sicilians.

He was recruited by a padrone, a man contracted by an American company seeking laborers to fill the rapidly expanding need in industry and farming in northeastern United States. The promise of a good job and wages along with freedom, was attractive to him. He did not even know what or where America was and it took some talking by the padrone to convince him that this would be a better life. Despite his acceptance, however, it was not easy to leave his home. This would be a change and Sicilians hated change. After hundreds of years of occupation, rape of their land and de facto enslavement, they trusted no one. This lack of trust was so strong that they resisted education of their children and learning foreign languages, even Italian. Their customs and superstitions dated back twenty-five hundred years to the Ancient Greeks and Carthaginians.

Following the WWI armistice in 1918, Hatchet Face traveled in steerage to New York City. He debarked from the ship on a wharf in Manhattan with only the clothes he was wearing. He walked to the Italian district on Elizabeth Street bordering the Bowery to an address on a piece of paper that was pressed into his hand by the padrone as he boarded the ship in Palermo. He found the tenement and climbed to a tiny apartment on the sixth floor. There he found a small room with a sink and a toilet where he stayed, along with eight other men, for one week, waiting for a train to take them to upstate New York. There, he picked fruit during the summer and fall for the Contadina food company. Afterward, he moved to a factory town, in Lodi, New Jersey, loading trucks for a tool manufacturing company with slightly higher wages, working five and a half days a week. In one short year, he had left an impoverished existence in the Mediterranean, crossed the Atlantic, traveled by train to Buffalo, New York, picked apples for weeks, moved to a factory town in New Jersey and finally was ensconced in a tiny apartment earning double the wages. He could the pay the rent, feed himself and even buy a new suit. Was this not heaven?

He was punctual, polite, anxious to be in America and strived to learn English. He wore a suit with vest, trousers, coat with a starched white shirt and tie to work daily, washing his shirt every other day. His peasant origins made him solitary and passive in his contact with strangers, pointing to vegetables when shopping rather than pronouncing them incorrectly in English for fear of embarrassing himself before a clerk. Passing children laughed at his face, but this did not seem to bother him. He had been ridiculed to some extent all his life and his muscular appearance and willingness to work anywhere and look anyone in the eye, sent a clear message that he was not one to trifle with.

My father introduced me to him, on a hot summer day, as we were returning home after picking up packages from his friend, Ori, a bookkeeper. He took a different route through Lodi on Main Street and stopped at a corner ice-cream shop. He had my attention. We walked in and there behind a marble counter and six red cushioned stools, dressed in black trousers, white shirt and black bowtie, sat a short swarthy faced, some would ugly, man reading the morning paper. When he saw my father, he laid down the paper and stood, dropping his head slightly showing "respecto" to the man who helped him buy the shop. He had purchased it two years earlier, in part with money, my father as "cambiuvalutu", moneylender loaned him, on a handshake. My father put his hand on my shoulder and introduced him to me as Hatchet Face. "He owns this candy store. Do you want an ice cream soda?"

I was eight years old. I shook his hand and sat on a red padded stool, watching him make it. His face looked very strange, but to an eight-year-old boy sitting next to his father and waiting for an ice cream soda, that meant nothing. I ate the cherry first.

For several years Hatchet Face walked past the shop, morning and afternoon, going to and from work. There was a Catholic girl's school nearby and the students passed the shop every day, a surefire way to have a steady stream of customers. A passion grew in him to be an "American businessman" and he worked and scrimped and saved until he had enough money to buy half of the shop in cash. He told my father about his dream and asked him for a loan. The sign on a large brown sheet of paper taped to the front window announced, "OPEN FOR BUSINESS!," UNDER NEW MANAGEMENT". Some children were startled when they first came in, some giggling or whispering comments about scarry and ugly. But Hatchet Face didn't mind as he declared that he was now "...gonna be a real American". When he did become a citizen, he drove to my father's business dressed in his suit, at three in the afternoon. Standing like a soldier in my father's office, he saluted and proudly announced "Tudaya, oma maka a citizen! You no canna call mi, 'God Dam Forena,' no mor."

My father stood and smiled as he walked around his desk and hugged him. Hatchet Face was crying.

When school started in September business picked up. Students formed in lines on the sidewalk to buy ice cream and Cokes on their way home from school. They loved the little Italian man with the strange face who spoke broken English and worked feverishly to fill their orders. He made needed repairs in the store and even installed a ceiling fan for the comfort of customers on a hot day. The shop was not in a busy part of town but he could pay expenses and even pay back some of the money my father loaned him. He bought a small round marble-topped ice cream table with two wire chairs and put them on the sidewalk outside the shop. The weather was still warm and young mothers pushing a carriage or giggling schoolgirls, walking home, stopped to sit, eating ice cream or enjoying a soda. The work in the factory during his early days, was becoming a memory, and he was content.

He was a quiet man of clean habits, and each evening after closing the shop, he made his dinner and was accustomed to finishing a glass or two of wine that he made in the basement. In the fall, when grapes were harvested in California, he asked the landlord if he could make wine by the coal bin. It was prohibition but the law permitted 200 gallons of wine to be made per household. He purchased enough Alicante grapes with sugar and water in "brick boxes" to make two barrels of wine a year. The grapes made drinkable wine which he used to pay some of his debts during the year. Alicante grapes were preferred because they made a lot of wine, dark in color, could be packed in bricks, sold legally and the wine was passably drinkable.

Another year rolled by and although successful, he sensed he was missing something in his life. Now, he felt lonely. He asked his friend, Mimmi, with whom he played poker once a month, why he "felt so down". Mimmi understood immediately and told him that he needed a girlfriend, maybe even a wife, who would take care of him and solve all his problems. Mimmi was well dressed, owned his own business, traveled extensively and was married. As a young man, Hatchet Face would hear comments or laughter from girls and boys and guessed that they were laughing at his appearance. People can be cruel if one attracts them for the wrong reason, and now in his forties, he had no desire to face more ridicule.

"Really?" Mimmi asked, and convinced him that such companionship would complete his life. Mimmi's wife would have no part of this. Hatchet Face had few social skills, so Mimmi convinced him he would find a "rufiana" (matchmaker or "troublemaker" in Sicilian parlance) who knew all about such things. Sure enough, a woman fifty-three years old, a widow, Mariuccia Sparafucile was from the Piedmont in northern Italy. Her husband, a bit singer in a City Opera Company had suffered a fatal heart attack during a performance where they both were working two years previously. She worked there as the head wardrobe mistress and was now available. Hatchet Face was cautious when they met, afraid that she would be revolted by his face. But after their meeting, Mimmi convinced her that he was healthy, slim and muscular, and that everything was in working order. She did not seem to mind how his face looked. Her late husband was no Adonis and she would take Hatchet Face as he was, successful, polite and clean. She told her current boyfriend that she was now engaged to another man and it was time for him to go. Their wedding was a simple ceremony before a Justice of the Peace. Mimmi and his wife acted as witnesses.

All went well for three months. Then the "ruffiana" had a visit from Mariuccia. She was upset. "What could be the problem, you two seemed so compatible?" the matchmaker asked.

"Signora." She said, in English or Italian, when it mattered, "I was a married woman before and I know the duties of a wife. But this man is insatiable. "Every night after dinner, he goes downstairs to the basement where he keeps a barrel of wine. He drinks wine and then comes upstairs and 'vuole portarmi a letto e fare sesso. Ogni notte!' (he wants to take me to bed and have sex. Every night!). Signora, I am a mature woman and this is too much. I don't want him anymore, he's an animal."

The ruffiana called on Hatchet Face and told him of his wife's demands. He was impassive. He said nothing for some time. Then, avoiding the issue and the rolling of his hand over, as Sicilians do, he answered, "What can I say? After work, I come home, have dinner and a glass of wine, then I want to enjoy my marriage. C'è qualcosa di sbagliato in questo?" (Is there something wrong with that?) Ultimately, the matchmaker saw that Hatchet Face was a peasant and like one, ignorant and uneducated. And so, the marriage was dissolved. Mariuccia went back to the opera and Hatchet Face, returned to his soda fountain but no longer felt lonely.

Over the next three years the foot traffic from the school and neighborhood decreased. With only a few customers each day, he sat by the door reading the paper, waiting for a customer to walk in for an ice cream or candy bar. Sales of root-beer sodas and sundaes dropped. Chocolate sauce, strawberries and cherry topping condiments sat in stainless steel containers under the marble counter, becoming thick and gooey. Half-opened ice cream containers formed frost on top giving them a stale taste. The ice cream sodas had no fizz, and the high school students stopped coming. Dust collected everywhere. He seldom noticed these things and ignored them. Eventually, the inevitable happened. The bills and overhead were far more than the cash flow and he went bankrupt.

Hatchet Face did what he did when he first came to Lodi. He put on his starched shirt, pressed suit, slicked back his salt and pepper hair and walked into the employment office of the manufacturing company where he began years ago. There, he sat in the waiting room, for four hours until a passing secretary recognized his unusual face. For two weeks he worked loading trucks. During this time, the factory bookkeeper died, and he was recognized as an old employee, who had recently owned a business. His skill set was needed.

He spent the next twenty years bringing his company from the brink of bankruptcy to become a successful manager of Personnel and Public Relations. He never became fully literate in Italian or English. His thick broken English became his hallmark and his insight of a person's character and potential, earned him the lasting appreciation of management, until his retirement.

He was not affluent or educated, but quiet, and in his old age reclusive. He enjoyed being alone. After Mimmi died, he seldom left his apartment, preferring to listen to the radio station broadcasting in Italian, from Manhattan. He read little and in the age of television and ethnic sitcoms, he avoided both.

Years later when my father and I were reminiscing about the people that I met in my childhood, he told me that he had a call from Hatchet

Face a week before he died, thanking him in making him "American". "You have no idea," he said in dialect, "how much you helped me."

Few people attended his funeral. My father was there and gave me his thoughts. He said, "If, when you die, you have enough friends for a game of poker," and raising his hand he said, "that's five, then you are rich man."

Hatchet Face had paid off his debts including the one owed to my father. Poverty, the will to survive and personal integrity, were great drivers of his ultimate success. And he took the chance. There is a perception that a peasant from an unknown place, with generations of oppression and no education, cannot achieve anything worthwhile. Yet given the opportunity, even a peasant, was able to achieve the things that matter. And for Hatchet Face, that mattered, and he was pleased.

Thank You.

Giacomo J. Sammarco as a child and teenager sang professionally in opera, and as a soloist with Columbus Boychoir. He attended Dartmouth College, Tulane University School of Medicine, Case Western Reserve University School of Medicine, served in the US Public Health Service, published numerous articles in orthopaedic journals, chapters in orthopaedic texts, and edited four books. He and his wife, Ruthann, (nee Busse), spend much of their time at their vacation home in Chautauqua, NY, where they participate in educational and entertainment presentations and enjoy their extended family throughout the seasons.

23 | *Poems*

PAUL SHORTT

This Terrible Weight

I can't breathe
Oh Mama, don't leave
This terrible weight
Of being Black
Is on my back
I can't take it no more They done me for sure
They stole my life
They stopped my heart
They want us all
Kept far apart
Do you believe me?
Do you believe me?

Do you believe
When I say
We *All* can't breathe?

A Last Mother's Day

I saw them near

St. Margaret's Hall,
Three generations

Comprised them all. In the lead

The beaming child
Looked up at me,
A joyous smile.
Close behind
Two parents clung,
Their arms around
The three as one.
Close behind,
Listing left,

Shuffled the fourth, Whole life had run,

Staring down

Somewhere in time, Of Her that now

Was left behind
In a bed
Seen just before –
His Dear other

Whom they all adored. Whose Final Day

Was soon
To come.
The Arc of Life,
Still joined as One.

Paul Shortt, Professor Emeritus of Theater Design and Production, UC-CCM, continues to work as a designer and consultant of theater, architecture, interiors, and landscape projects. Paul also indulges in short story, poetry and playwriting. Most of all, he loves being a father, grandfather, and husband to Marcia since 1970"

24 The Comfort Crisis

PETE STRANGE

The author as a young'un.

IN this age of scientific wonders, of continuous communication, of endless bombardment of information, we are getting far too much of our experience second hand. Artificial intelligence is the close cousin of artificial experience. Kids enter the house or car with their devices active, never looking at the world around them — even communicating with their neighbor, two feet away, by text. They seek comfort and experience from a screen. Here is just a little of what they are missing.

The roar of the diesel engine when the tractor starts up, the clank of the blades when the bush-hog is activated; and the mixed smells of diesel exhaust and fresh-mown fields as the work progresses. There was that day when the noise of the tractor upset a family of voles who scampered across the field in front of the mowing; and a Bald Eagle swooped down and snatched one of the voles into the air, clutched in its talons. A bad day for the vole, but a magnificent reward for the worker driving the tractor. Watching videos of eagles hunting is no substitute for witnessing the event.

Learning about the honeybees. Google tells us that they are really smart animals, living in a structured society ruled by a queen, and that they create the only food found in the pyramids that was still edible after a millennium. Good information, but nothing like swatting at the honeybees' "scout" who was sent out to see what you were doing cutting weeds around their hives. Grandpa told you about the scout and told you if you left it alone, it would simply go back and report. That bee scared you, so you swatted at it; and almost instantly there were a dozen bees swarming around your head. There is nothing quite comparable to a bee sting to focus your attention on the lesson.

Having to make your way from the house on a cold winter night to use the outhouse could cause a high level of bladder control before making the trip, and a high level of bladder shyness within that cold wooden structure. There was no time or interest in playing on a phone while doing your business. If you were able to hold it until the morning, you were often jumping from one foot to the other behind the line at the one-holer.

First you rubbed sulfur or kerosene on your wrists and ankles to keep the biters away while you picked the blackberries; then after the picking you rubbed alcohol or ammonia on the bites to keep them from itching — often after you had scratched them raw. That was all part of the preparation that led to a much higher level of appreciation for the berry cobblers to come.

Trying to soap up and rinse fast so that the cistern pump could produce a strong enough stream to wet you down and rinse you off. And, watching out for the Wiggle Tails that often came out with the water, if you didn't remember to turn the first rain out on the ground in the hot summer. Those mosquito eggs were just lying in the wet gutters waiting to become part of the water supply.

Getting warmed up four times by the firewood: once when you cut it, once when you split it and piled it, once when you hauled it up to the house and once when it went into the Warm Morning stove or Heatilater fireplace. The warmth of the cutting was only partially from the effort. Much of the sweat came from the wild fury of the chainsaws and the awful whirring of the twenty-four-inch blade on the cradle saw. That cradle saw was especially scary if you had read Frost's "Out, Out."

Getting the tractor stuck in the creek, while showing off for the girl down the road, and having to beg your uncle to bring his big truck to pull it out. Then going right back and working all day with house jacks to lift the big, flat rock onto the rock sled and haul it up to the house. That piece of shelf rock — two feet wide by six feet long and eight inches thick — still resides as part of the sidewalk behind the house. And the friend who helped — who became a heart doctor — still talks about that day in the creek as one of the best days of his life.

Nothing big here. No breakthrough. No unicorn returns. Just the kinds of experiences that create a resilient attitude – and a certain amount of earned appreciation for automation and comfort. Without the doing, the thinking lacks context and the creativity lacks connection to the real world. It seems appropriate to steal and modify a line from Oliver Wendell Holmes, "I would not give a fig for comfort on this side of effort; but I would give the world for comfort on the far side of effort."

Kipling's poem "Tomlinson" makes the clear case for engagement and action, when St. Peter says,

> *"Ye have read, ye have heard, ye have thought; and the tale is yet to run:*
> *By the worth of the body that once ye had, give answer – what have ye done?"*

And then Satan sends Tomlinson back to earth with the words,

> *"Go back to Earth with lip unsealed — go back with an open eye*
> *. . .*
> *And: the God that you took from a printed book be with you Tomlinson!"*

Of course, if you can get the attention of the young, and you share those experiences of a time gone by, you will get the usual response, “Daddy: aren’t you lucky you came to live with us.”

Pete Strange was born into construction, working at building houses and churches from a young age, along with his family members in Kentucky. Out of fear of his mother, Pete attended the University of Cincinnati, graduating with a degree in Civil Engineering. He spent the next fifty years working for his co-op employer, Messer Construction. Starting with a call from Sister Jean Patrice Harrington, Pete embarked on a journey in serving the community that included service on more than forty non-profit boards. Pete’s proudest accomplishments have been guided by his wife Ginger. They include three children and eight grandchildren: all data points proving that Pete married into a stronger gene pool.

25 | *Oh Democracy*

JOSEPH TOMAIN

Introduction

THERE were four of us. Two law teachers, Bert and I from Cincinnati, and two practicing lawyers, Bill and Peter from New York. We met in Atlanta for the last leg of our trip. Twenty hours later, our plane touched down. Outside the airport, things felt familiar. Moderate dry temperature, palm trees, red sandy soil. It seemed like the Southwest or Southern California.

From the airport to the hotel to rest and recover. On the next morning's walk, within 100 yards or so of the hotel, I found myself in a residential neighborhood. Looking through fences and gates, I saw comfortable single-family homes, trimmed lawns, neat arrangements of hibiscus, birds of paradise, and lilies, among others. Then I noticed that all the homes were surrounded by either fences or walls taller than I was, and on top of those fences and walls were coils of razor wire. No Toto, we're not in SoCal anymore; we're in Joburg — Johannesburg, South Africa.

History of Apartheid

The events that brought us to South Africa began decades before and held a particular resonance with us. In 1913, after South Africa gained its independence from Britain, legislation was passed forcing Black Africans to live on reserves and limited available jobs. In 1948, as the

Black Africans line up to cast historic votes in their country's first democratic election.

world was moving away from imperialism, colonialism, and antisemitism, and moving towards civil rights, the ruling Afrikaner National Party formalized apartheid in law. Racially segregated residential areas were continued but now forced separation was backed up by state police power. South African citizenship was stripped away, intermarriage was illegal, having a friend of another race was suspicious, and travel between white and non-white areas was restricted and patrolled. Passes, for Blacks, were mandatory.

In the 1950s, legislation required registration by race and separation was enforced as the police aggressively removed Blacks from the cities and moved them into their "townships," "homelands," or "Bantustans." In a transparent effort to ameliorate the harshness of the separation laws, the Bantustans were granted a veneer of self-government, and state-run primary and secondary schools were established in the homelands. However, rather than offering a curriculum leading to higher education and a path to the professions, these schools were training grounds for manual labor ending in menial jobs and perpetual second-class status. Black South Africans, as intended, remained economically dependent on White South Africa.

Apartheid laws became increasingly brutal. Whites were 13% of the population, Black South Africans 76%, and the remainder was comprised of mixed, Indian, and Asian peoples. If the Whites were to keep control, force was necessary, and the Indemnity Act of 1961 made it legal for police officers to either torture or kill non-whites "in the pursuit of their official duties." Carte blanche brutality was legalized.

Radical racialism could not but lead to opposition and effective opposition needed to be organized rather than random. The African National Congress (ANC) was formed in 1912 but remined largely ineffective against consolidated power. New organizations were needed. The Pan-Africanist Congress (PAC) (1959), the Inkatha Freedom Party (IFP) (1975), the Black Consciousness Movement (mid-1960s), and the United Democratic Front (1983) were liberation movements that became more militant as apartheid intensified.

Repression will meet with resistance just as violent repression will meet with violent resistance. Liberationist political groups organized a countrywide demonstration in March 1960 to abolish South Africa's pass laws. As 20,000 protesters gathered near a police station at Sharpsville outside of Johannesburg, the police demanded that the protesters surrender their passbooks or be arrested. According to official reports, the police were stoned by the protesters and in retaliation the police opened fire with machine guns killing 69 and wounding nearly 200 others including women and children. A state of emergency was declared, more than 11,000 people were detained, and both the PAC and ANC were outlawed.

Fast forward a decade and a half. In June 1976, Black school children opposing the Afrikaner set curriculum led to a series of demonstrations and protests. Reminiscent of the Children's Crusade in Birmingham, Alabama over a decade prior, it was estimated that 20,000 students took part and they were met with police violence ending with an estimated 700 fatalities.

Our Training

In 1994, our delegation of four was sent to South Africa on behalf of the International Commission of Jurists to serve as foreign election observers in South Africa's first democratic election. The first order of business took us to the University of Witwatersrand where we joined over 300 others in a large auditorium to learn about our roles. After a brief welcome and introductions, we were given instructions about how to register and obtain our badges and other credentials.

After we were issued our election regalia, our instructions could not be clearer. We were observers. We were not to play any other role. We were to watch, keep our hands off, and, if we were to receive a complaint during the voting process, we were to take that complaint to an election official. In short, we were to do nothing but sit and watch and later report. After the formalities, we were assigned to precincts outside of Pretoria.

A Joburg native, George Baloyi, offered to guide us. Before we left the Capital, George took us to one of the townships on the outskirts of the city that consisted of dirt roads and cramped together shacks made of corrugated metal, random pieces of wood, tar paper, and cardboard. These were not the materials of choice; they were the materials of availability. George was familiar with the area, and he strongly advised us not to visit after dark. Then, on the way from Joburg to Pretoria he pointed out monuments and battlefields of the Boar War and memorials to the "achievements" of the Afrikaners.

Once in Pretoria, we checked into a Holiday Inn and arranged to meet George the next day. He gave us a tour of the area and took us to a local village. "Village" is far too grandiose a word for the area we visited. We drove to a very small hilltop with a dozen or so shacks more barren than those that we had seen in the Johannesburg townships. When we arrived, we only saw children under 5 and women over 60. No adults. They were either away at school or working.

As our translator, George asked the women if they knew about the election. Indeed, they did. He then asked them if they were going to vote. Indeed, they were. They assured him that they fully intended to vote, and they knew that there was a voting precinct a short way from the village. They emphasized, though, that they were not going to vote at that near precinct, instead they would walk 11 miles to the next one. In response to the question "Why?" they told us that the men of the village worked on that plantation, and they were worried that the owner might try to influence their vote so they would travel to where they felt safer.

The primitive utter poverty of those huts stood in stark contrast with the cooling towers of a nuclear power plant that could be seen just behind the hill on which the village sat. The contrast between prehistory and modern technology was palpable.

After this visit, George took us to the central Independent Electoral Commission (IEC) office in Pretoria. At first glance, the scene was chaotic. Dozens of people were literally running around training monitors, putting up voting booths, distributing credentials, and mediating complaints. The chaos was an illusion, things ran smoothly. Perhaps because the outcome was foreordained.

Nelson Mandela and the Elections

Nelson Mandela was always a political man. He was also a man of opposition, sometimes peaceful, sometimes not.

Born in 1918, he began his political life with Gandhian opposition to apartheid through peaceful protests and demonstrations. In 1952, he was jailed for violating curfew laws. Then in 1956 he was tried for treason but acquitted. After that, he questioned nonviolent resistance and left South Africa to receive military training. When he tried to reenter, he was arrested for leaving the country without a permit and, while he was in prison, documents were discovered about his plans for guerrilla warfare. He was then tried with others for sabotage. Expectations were that he would be convicted and executed.

He was convicted but not executed and in 1964 he was condemned to life in prison. At his sentencing he said that "In its proper meaning equality before the law means the right to participate in the making of the laws by which one is governed . . . ." He added "all the rights and privileges to which I have referred are monopolized by whites, and we enjoy none of them." Thirty-two years later, he took the oath of office as the president of South Africa including a pledge to "uphold and maintain the constitution and all other laws of the Republic." His political journey took him from peaceful protest to criminal violence to the presidency and to a world historic transition of power.

At the end of the 1980s, South African president P.W. Botha began meeting with Mandela. After Botha's retirement, Mandela continued to meet with President F.W. de Klerk to assess the changing political climate. On February 11, 1990, de Klerk released Mandela after 27 years in prison. Then, bans were lifted against political parties such as the ANC and the PAC.

As Black South Africans gained their political voice, tensions rose not only between the races but also between Black political parties. Most troublesome, the militant right-wing Inkatha Freedom Party, located in the province of KwaZulu-Natal, had violently attacked the ANC and posed a threat to the any peaceful resolution of apartheid.

The discussions between De Klerk and Mandela broadened to include other political parties and the decision was made to hold a constitutional convention. In December 1993, an Interim Constitution was passed and a Transitional Executive Council (TEC) was instituted. The world realized that power would shift from White South Africa to Black. Additional legislation established the Independent Electoral Commission (IEC) and on February 2, 1994, de Klerk announced that elections would be held 10 weeks later on April 26, 27, and 28.

Ten weeks was a remarkably short time for such a dramatic political moment. The TEC was charged with the responsibility of insuring that the legislative initiatives passed by the constitutional convention would go into effect without substantial changes. Then the IEC had to organize elections that involved hiring, training, and staffing 9,000 polling places as well as hiring, training, and the credentialling of over 10,000 domestic and 3, 000 foreign election monitors.

The IEC also established election tribunals, investigation procedures, and mediation processes to address election complaints. The IEC had the additional responsibility of educating voters about their rights and duties and about the political issues that were on the ballot. The success of voter education was evident when we visited the women on that bare hilltop village.

The IEC's final responsibility was to certify within 10 days of the election whether the election was substantially free and fair.

There were 19 different parties on the ballot and voters were required to vote in both national and provincial elections by voting for a party not a candidate. Traditional parties, such as the ANC and the Inkatha Freedom party were on the ballot as was the Afrikaner National Party of the old regime. There were also very specific interest parties including a Woman's Rights Party, a Workers Party, a Muslim Party, and a party called Sports Organization for Collective Contributions and Equal Rights or SOCCER. The agendas of those parties are self-described.

Our Observations

The logistics of a first election seemed insurmountable, complaints about election rule violations were multiplying, and there was continued worry about violence especially from right-wing Afrikaners wanting to hold on to power and privilege, and from the militant IFP believing that Mandela and his moderate ANC were moving too slowly and were too accommodating. As the election approached, the number of alleged campaign violations grew. George brought a typical complaint to us. He asked what we thought about one party posting derogatory remarks about another. Is that a campaign violation? Our response was "No, it wasn't a violation; it was the ordinary stuff of political campaigns." Most complaints were no more serious.

As announced, the elections were to take place for three days from April 26 through April 28th. April 26 was designated as a special Election Day to cover prisons, hospitals, and other places where it was difficult to vote such as old age homes and drug rehabilitation centers.

In the middle of the elections, a fourth day was added because some provinces ran out of ballots and the turnout was greater than expected.

It was estimated that over 20 million people would vote and although there was no formal voter registration, voters were asked to present some form of identification. Many had pass books that satisfied the requirement, many were given temporary papers, nevertheless millions lacked the suggested forms, but officials accepted travel documents, and other forms of identification. Elections officials also accepted the testimony of a friend or relative who could confirm that when someone said: "I am Imka Nkosi" than all that her companion needed to say was that "Yes, I can identify her as Imka Nkosi" and then Imka could vote. Apparently South African election officials are more trusting than some in the US. Double voting was easily circumscribed. After voting, each voter's hand was stamped with an invisible ink that appeared under ultraviolet light.

On the first day of elections, Bill and Peter were sent to observe voting at prisons. All prisoners were allowed to vote except those who were convicted of rape, robbery, murder, or attempts to do so. In the three prisons that they observed, more than 3,000 prisoners voted without a complaint.

Bert and I were assigned to Kalafong Hospital in a township outside of Pretoria. Kalafong was an extraordinarily ramshackle affair for Black patients. The first patients to vote were those on stretchers, followed by those in wheelchairs, and then on crutches. Memorable was the sight of voters ambulatory enough to walk balancing IV bags on their heads and waiting to vote.

We arrived at the hospital just before the voting began and I noticed a nurse standing behind a gurney. She signaled me and asked me to come over and help her patient. In clear and brazen defiance of our instructions to only observe and not participate in any way, I could not do anything other than assist. The nurse introduced me to a very frail woman lying prone on her stretcher and we had an immediate connection. She looked exactly like my favorite aunt. The woman was named BTomane (pronounced Bee-**Toe-Main**) exactly how I pronounce my last name. More surprisingly, her name was exactly my mother's name.

My mother's first name was Bernice, but everyone called her Bea (thus pronounced **Bee-Toe-Main**.) How could I not respond?

The nurse told me that her patient wanted me to go into the booth and vote for her. I leaned down and asked her who she wanted me to choose. Her answer, clear and strong, was one word "Mandela."

At the end of the day, we returned to our hotel. Before dinner, I turned on the television and saw a familiar sight. Apparently, the US format for the evening news is ubiquitous. On the TV, were two newscasters both 30-ish, both telegenic, and both could have sat on any news set in our country. As they were recounting the day's events, the male newscaster turned to his colleague. As he broke from the script, he looked at her and then looked at the camera and said: "This is the most peaceful day I can remember." There was a break in his voice, and I am sure if he continued much longer, the viewing audience would have seen tears.

The newscaster was correct. During the elections there was almost no violence. There was a bomb threat at the airport, there was a bloody encounter in KwaZulu/Natal home of the Inkatha Freedom Party, and minor skirmishes here and there but not much else. At last count, over 250,000 people were involved in preparing, training, observing, and carrying out the elections, more than 50 million ballots were printed and distributed, and after waiting in lines for three, four, and more hours, millions voted.

Our Report

Our last responsibility was to report on each polling place that we had visited. In each case we found: (1) no illegal activity; (2) all voting procedures were followed; and (3) no voting irregularities.

We concluded our report "The South African elections of April 1994 were substantially free and fair and reflect the political will of the South African people." The 1994 elections witnessed a remarkably peaceful transition of power from White to Black, widespread participation in the franchise, and democracy in action. I know it to be true. I saw it. I was a witness.

Coda

Ten years late, I was working on a project in Phnom Penh, Cambodia and staying at the lovely Sunway Hotel two blocks from the Mekong River and reminiscent of the Spartan ambience of the Holiday Inn in Pretoria.

One morning I noticed a bulletin about a conference of East Asia election officials being held in the hotel and was given permission to attend. During a coffee break, I was standing with a small group. After we introduced ourselves, an election official from the Philippines, asked me how the 2004 US election was coming along. I said fine. He responded that he was concerned. I took the bait and asked him why. His said that he was worried that the Philippines would have to send election observers to the United States.

I understood this gentle poke at American arrogance and his sly reference to *Bush v. Gore*. The group caught the joke. After all, this was 2004, why would the world's longest running democracy, known especially for its tradition of peaceful transitions of power from one president to the next, just as I witnessed in South Africa a decade before, need elections observers?

If I only knew then what I know now, outside election observers do not sound so fanciful.

The author as foreign election observer.

26 | Julius Dexter: Our First Citizen

ROBERT VITZ

HANGING on the wall in one corner of our club's library is a very fine lithograph of the three-story Dexter mansion which once stood on the corner of Fourth Street and Broadway, directly across from the University Club. In 1914 the structure was razed to make way for the imposing Western & Southern Life Insurance building. Perhaps of greater familiarity to many of you is the Dexter mausoleum, the iconic image of Spring Grove Cemetery. Edmund Dexter, Sr., the man who owned the house and the first occupant of the mausoleum, was born in England in 1801 and came to Cincinnati in the 1820s. Here, taking advantage of the bad water and the large number of adult single males, he amassed a considerable fortune in whiskey production, "Old Dexter" being his most celebrated brand.

Edmund Dexter joined the Literary Club in 1858, just four years before his death at the age of sixty-one. While there is little information in our early records about his participation, three of his five sons also joined our club: Charles, Edmund, Jr., and Julius. Of these three Dexter siblings only Julius left a significant mark on the club, as he did for so many other local institutions.

Born in Cincinnati in 1840, Julius Dexter grew up in the house at Fourth and Broadway along with his four brothers. After attending Brooks' Classical School, located nearby on East 4th Street, he entered Harvard College where he rowed crew before graduating in 1860. Then it was on

The Dexter mausoleum in Spring Grove Cemetery

to the Cincinnati College of Law, then housed in the College Building on Walnut Street. Following a short stint in an army regiment during the Civil War, he returned to the city and resided in the family home. After several years he abandoned law when his father's death left him with the wealth that allowed him to devote his life to various civic organizations. During the early 1870s the city directory lists him as librarian of the Ohio Historical and Philosophical Society, an early name for the Cincinnati Historical Society. He held this position for several years without accepting any remuneration. This was a practice he continued for the rest of his life.

Music was an early passion of Dexter's. In the years after the Civil War, he joined the Harmonic Society, performed with the Carl Barus Orchestra, and sang in the early May Festivals. His close friendship with George and Maria Longworth Nichols no doubt helped him become an early member of the May Festival Association, Music Hall Association, and the College of Music boards. Indeed, as chairman of the of the Music Hall Association building committee in 1877, he walked almost daily from his East Fifth Street home, where he now lived with close friend Eugene Bliss, to the building site in order to oversee construction progress. As many of you will recall, Corbett Tower in Music Hall was originally named Dexter Hall.

Julius Dexter's unselfish approach to board obligations may be seen in a letter written to Bliss by a mutual friend. "I think Julius needs your care and supervision—he acts like a demented person, and all [because of] the Music Hall. If I tell you how he passes his day you will believe me when I say he is angry. First, he refuses to stay in the country with the Nichols people [George and Maria Longworth Nichols whose home was on Joseph Longworth's Grandin Road estate] because they do not have breakfast early enough to enable him to be on the Music Hall grounds at 8 o'clock. So he takes an early breakfast at the St. Nicholas [Hotel] and rushes up to the corner of Elm and Twelfth Sts. There he stays till 10, then comes to his office and reports to me the quarrels he has with Mr. Blair, the brick contractor."

Contemporaries recognized his selfless contributions. At the opening ceremony of Music Hall in 1878, George Ward Nichols pointed out that "his singular integrity of purpose and act, his patience and determination, his large knowledge and excellent judgment made the building what it is." Others may have contributed more money, but no one gave more of his energy and abilities than Julius Dexter.

Dexter's management skills invariably led to his being selected either secretary or treasurer of his numerous board memberships, and, as we know from our own club, these are the two most important and time-consuming positions in any organization. Nor were his interests limited to music. He served on the boards of the Historical and Philosophical Society, the Cincinnati Public Library, the Cincinnati Astronomical Society, the Society of Natural History, the Cincinnati Art Museum, the Zoological Gardens, the Queen City Club, The Optimists Club, the Archaeological Society, as well as the short-lived Cincinnati Academy of Fine Arts. There was also the little-known Theology and Religious Library which maintained a collection of printed works for the use of clergy and teachers of religion. And during the decade of the 1880s, he also headed the Fidelity Safe Deposit and Trust Co., as well as serving as president of the Cincinnati, Hamilton and Dayton Railroad. This was a busy man.

In 1873, following the departure of William F. Poole, the Cincinnati Public Library opened a search for his replacement as head librarian. Supported by such strong civic leaders as Edmund Pendleton, William Procter, Judges Manning Force and Stanley Matthews, John Herron, Learner B. Harrison, Nicholas Longworth II and Rufus King, Dexter's candidacy looked promising. However, it was not to be. The Rev. Thomas Vickers, a Unitarian minister who later became a somewhat controversial president of the University of Cincinnati, stepped into the turbulent waters of nineteenth-century library politics.

In his spare time, Julius Dexter dipped his own toe into political waters. He served one term as a Republican in the Ohio State Senate. Later, he switched his allegiance to the Democratic Party, both because of Grover Cleveland's strong endorsement of the gold standard and his own dislike of the Republican presidential candidate, James G. Blaine. In 1886 Dexter had the honor of hand-delivering to President Cleveland an invitation to the dedication of the new Cincinnati Art Museum. In a letter, Dexter wryly summed up the disinterested president's reaction: the invitation "took in preparation 149 minutes, and in realization 1 ¼ minutes." Ten years later he even ran for the Ohio governorship as a gold Democrat. But neither national politics nor political office was really much to his liking. However, with the rise of Boss George B. Cox and his political machine in the mid-1880s, Dexter turned his considerable energy to local political reform.

In 1885 he joined the Committee of 100, soon becoming its treasurer. The Committee of 100, a sort of bi-partisan forerunner to the Charter Committee, was made up of local business and civic leaders who sought honest and efficient government. Its membership reads like a Who's Who of Cincinnati: Larz Anderson, D. H. Baldwin, Andrew Erkenbrecker, Charles Fleischman, David Gamble, Melville Ingalls,

Henry Probasco, Harley Procter, Stewart Shillito, Lewis Seasongood, Alexander McGuffey, etc., etc., etc. Initially, the Committee investigated the recent local election, and it actually succeeded in convicting nine men for fraud and discovering evidence of widespread malfeasance in the city's government. But long term results proved more elusive. Boss Cox remained in control of the city's government for the next 25 years.

About that same time, Dexter took on the challenges of Cincinnati's finances when he became president of the Sinking Fund. The Sinking Fund served as a watchdog over the city's finances and indebtedness and certified the annual taxation rate. In the era of Boss Cox, this was a challenging task, but Dexter's moral compass made him a highly effective leader. As one newspaper editor wrote at his death, "He was a public servant without a single ulterior, selfish motive, and could neither be bought nor hoaxed nor bulldozed. Even the most corrupt of scoundrels who have in late years infested our civic life respected and feared Julius Dexter." So important was Dexter to Cincinnati that many thought of him as the city's first citizen, and during an era of corrupt politics and increasing urban discord, he shines like a beacon of rectitude and fiscal responsibility.

But what was Dexter like when he gathered with fellow Literarians at 8:00 on Saturday evenings. He had joined the Club in 1864, the year of re-birth following the hiatus brought on by the Civil War. Three years later he became the club treasurer, and in 1875 he served the first of his two terms as president. Although never easy to capture a person's character from club records, the memorial written shortly after his death in 1898 singles out his conversational powers, his unfailing courtesy, his appreciation of humor and love of witty stories. In essence then, he fit in very well. While his attendance declined during the very busy last ten years of his life, he continued to present papers.

As you might expect, the topics of many of his Club papers reflect his public concerns. He wrote about monetary issues, the importance of public education, the role of the University of Cincinnati, and the economic impact of the Cincinnati and Southern Railroad. Unfortunately, club records do not include papers from the 1860s and 1870s, and his last two papers, written in 1894 and 1897, failed to be included in our bound volumes. Consequently, we have no way to appreciate his writing. On one Friday evening in October, 1898, as Dexter traveled to his friend Edmund Kittridge's house for dinner, he felt ill. However, after resting for a while, he joined his host for dinner, but only a few minutes later he suffered a massive heart attack and died. On the day of his funeral at Christ Church Cathedral, city flags were lowered to half-staff. Pallbearers included fellow Literarians Thornton Hinkle, William W. Taylor, Herman Goepper, Reuben Warder, and Stuart Shillito, and every major newspaper in the city featured a long obituary outlining his public service and strength of character. Of course, interment took place in the Dexter Mausoleum where he joined his father and two older brothers.

Yet, today, Julius Dexter is scarcely remembered. The mausoleum represents the family and Dexter Place in East Walnut Hills takes its name from his brother's home. Dexter Hall in Music Hall had its name changed to recognize the Corbetts. The scholarship in his name at Harvard no longer exists. So, would it not be possible to find a way to memorialize this man who gave so much to this city? Although Thea Tjepkema of the Friends of Music Hall is creating a digital history of Music Hall that will include Dexter's role, this seems insufficient to this old school historian. Perhaps a another space in Music Hall could carry his name? A gallery at the art museum? Perhaps a bronze plaque could be placed in his memory at the Cincinnati Museum Center, or at the Observatory, or the public library? Could City Hall not find an appropriate way to memorialize this "first citizen," and surely some local distillery might want to revive the Old Dexter label, with an appropriate picture. Unfortunately, for a man who gave so much for the betterment of Cincinnati, we have shamefully neglected Julius Dexter.

Robert Vitz is a native of Minneapolis who grew up in Cincinnati and graduated from Walnut Hills High School and DePauw University before obtaining a Ph.D. at the University of North Carolina, Chapel Hill. He taught U.S. history at Northern Kentucky University until retirement in 2008 and is author of The Queen and the Arts: Cultural Life in Nineteenth Century Cincinnati and At the Center: 175 Years at Cincinnati's Mercantile Library. He has been a member of the Literary Club since 1987.

27 Witness: The Calling of St. Matthew

JAMES WESNER

SAN Luigi dei Francesi is architecturally undistinguished as Roman churches go, but a magnificent vision awaits the few tourists who venture inside. Passing from the bright exterior into the dim nave and proceeding to the fifth chapel on the left aisle, the visitor encounters a device common to Italy's ill-lit churches. He produces and deposits the necessary coin, a floodlight goes on, and there it is: one of Caravaggio's great masterpieces, on the left wall of the Canterelli Chapel: The Calling of St. Matthew.

The sudden illumination is a fitting introduction to the canvas, which shows a beam of light from an open door flowing diagonally across a small room and falling on the faces of four figures, three of whom look up in astonishment at two figures who have just entered. The fourth figure, an old man wearing spectacles, looks down at a table where the group has been counting money, while a fifth figure remains hunched over coins on the table. The Scriptures tell us that one of them is Levi, a tax collector whose Christian name will become Matthew, and that this is the customs house at Capernaum.

The entering Christ, seen in profile, points directly at the group; his companion, St. Peter, facing away, also points in a parallel movement. A red-bearded man in the center of the five, points either to himself

The Caravaggio masterpiece

or to the hunched over man, in a gesture that matches the planes occupied by the hands of the other two. Is he Matthew, acknowledging his identity by pointing to himself, or is he denying it by pointing to the fifth man? The ambiguity seems intentional, but the red-bearded man's errant hand may be more simply explained as reflecting the artist's desire to produce symmetry in the parallelism of the three gestures. Is the fifth man Matthew hiding his face to avoid the Call? Or is his position merely another artistic device to suggest motion, as explained below? Our doubts are resolved in favor of the red-bearded man when we realize that two other paintings in the chapel use the same man as the model for the saint.

There is no ambiguity in Christ's gesture. It is a direct quotation from Michealangelo's Creation, an image that dominates the ceiling of the Sistine Chapel, showing Adam's hand as it receives life from the hand of God. All Italians were familiar with this powerful image and knew it as an expression of the doctrine of Christ as the Second Adam, one who would redeem the world from the sin brought into it by the first Adam's fall. The power of Caravaggio's symbolism is overwhelming. A door opens, a beam of light illuminates the faces of the men about the table, and the Second Adam calls one of them to Redemption: "And he saith unto him, Follow me." Matthew 9:9 (KJV). Words are unnecessary here. The beckoning gesture is enough.

And who are Levi's companions? The three on the left are old and ill dressed and look the part of tax collectors. As a group, they form a triangle that balances the two figures of Christ and St. Peter on the right of the frame. The two in the center form a pivot between the other shapes, but they seem out of place. Both are dressed in high style, with plumes in their fashionable hats. The older of the two is armed; the younger is barely an adolescent. A soldier and his page, perhaps? The boy's face is fully lit, and he appears almost frightened by the sudden appearance of the two strangers who have just opened the door. His right arm is awkwardly raised as he pulls back from the table. The soldier is looking up, gripping the table and the bench on which he is sitting as if to rise. But we know the tension will subside as the one who is Matthew will soon leave the room to follow Jesus.

It is curious that the two figures most distant from Jesus have not looked up from the table despite the dramatic entry. We can expect that they will do so almost immediately. Caravaggio has given us a sequence of actions that adds fluidity to the composition by suggesting movement that is not there. It is like a cartoon which shows the characters acting through time in a static picture. And it works. There is movement on the picture. Jesus and St. Peter enter and point; the soldier, page, and St. Matthew look up; St. Matthew points, and we know the spectacled man and hunched up man will look up almost immediately after.

I find this dynamism as remarkable as Caravaggio's use of chiaroscuro and color to suggest a depth that is not there. The beam of light is a light yellow-brown that contrasts with the darker brown of the window shutters above and the near-black of the shadow below. The beam and shadow are on the same plane as the wall, but the contrasting color makes the shutters stand out. St. Peter's lighter yellow cloak and Jesus's red sleeve appear in the shadow as if separated in space from the wall behind. That red is matched by the sleeve of the slouched-over man and by the slightly lighter sleeve of St. Matthew and the red piping of the youth's waistcoat. The beam falls fully on the faces of the startled group, highlighting them in the darker background, while the soldier's black and white costume contrasts sharply with the dark shadow of the door.

A compelling picture, to be sure, but is there a dark note here as well? The painting on the opposite wall, called The Martyrdom of St. Matthew, shows the fate awaiting some who accept the Call. It is a brutally ugly depiction of St. Matthew's crucifixion that was initially rejected because it showed the saint as an old man with dirty feet who was unworthy of veneration. Not shown are the worse fates of the four other subjects who did not respond to the Call. What did the hunched man see when he did look up? Did the spectacled man cease his fascination with the coins on the table? Did the soldier and page realize they were in the presence of the Second Adam? In the Gospel account, the Call was directed only to St. Matthew. The other four were not called and could only be astonished by what they witnessed. What fate awaited them in this life and the next we will never know.

There are more facts to recite about the painting, if you want to hear them, and more coins to be dropped into the slot to keep the illumination going, if you want to stay further. But the point of this short essay is that on that first visit to San Luigi dei Francesi in Rome I had witnessed a miracle in color and contrasting light and darkness that has remained in my memory for over 50 years.

Jim Wesner is a recovering redneck who was born north of Shreveport, Louisiana, but grew up in New Orleans and hopes you will forget the Shreveport part. Long retired from his last job as General Counsel of the University of Cincinnati, Jim amuses himself with reading and writing about history, art and literature.